Praise for *Teach What You Know*

"Mr. Trautman is a highly regarded expert in peer mentoring. It is impossible NOT to learn from him. This book completely captures both the passion for mentoring and the infectious, enthusiastic teaching style that Mr. Trautman projects in his workshop. The value proposition for this book is quite simple—significantly better mentoring, significantly reduced frustration for mentor and apprentice, and more knowledgeable and effective employees. If you struggle at mentoring, then you must read this book."
James J. Huntzicker, associate dean for Industry Relations, Oregon Health & Science University

"Steve's book is a great resource for both new and experienced mentors. It will help you figure out your approach to mentoring, understand your unique role, and avoid the pitfalls of not being pragmatic enough in something as intuitive as mentoring. The book is full of helpful tools, precise to-the-point lists, and recommendations for a successful and rewarding mentoring relationship. This is a must read for a first-time mentor."
Irada Sadykhova, manager of Learning Strategies, Engineering Excellence, Microsoft

"Trautman knows more about being a new employee than your new employees know. He knows the business of knowledge transfer, and the philosophies in this book are perfect for today's labor market challenges."
Paul Boman, CIH manager, Health and Safety

"Do you find yourself reading books that just 'make sense,' so you end up reading the entire book but not doing any of it? Don't let that happen with this book. The 'tools' Steve presents in this book work great. We've been using them for more than a year at EA Canada with dramatic improvements in onboarding time and knowledge transfer. Here's the key: when you find a tool in the book that sounds perfect for your situation, stop reading and actually use the tool at least once before you resume reading."
Jerry Bowerman, vice president, chief operating officer, Electronic Arts Canada

"If we were all better at sharing what we know and helping our co-workers improve their performance...how much waste could we take out of today's organizations and our daily activities? This book offers useful tools and approaches for doing just that...learn how to better manage your time while improving the support you provide those associates who rely on your expertise and knowledge."
M. Tamra Chandler, managing vice president of Global Solutions and People, Hitachi Consulting

"Steve's book is the most practical and useful book I've read about mentoring. He's done an excellent job capturing the essentials of his workshop and the tools he teaches. I've been able to apply his tools to real world scenarios and found them to be extremely effective. Bravo!"
Bill Fishburn, program manager, Intel

"If you want to end the dangerous practice of letting people fend for themselves in a new job and calling it "On the Job Training" (OJT), Steve Trautman has authored a common sense process and very readable approach to peer mentoring that offers real OJT, while quickly producing the results you need."
Jim Blaylock, PMP, senior consultant, SummitQwest

"With this book, Trautman provides great tools and techniques for peer mentoring and excellent advice on leveraging on-the-job training in the modern organization. Very organized and readable, this is a beneficial "how-to" guide for managing the apprentice relationship."
Lockwood Lyon, project manager

"We all play different roles throughout our careers. This book is an excellent tool for defining the steps for success in each role. Learn faster, teach better, and create success."
Sara L. Thompson, project manager, senior professional in Human Resources, Washington Mutual

"Steve offers common sense, practical solutions to the challenges we all face daily—both in his fast-paced workshops and in this concise manual. Any one of his suggestions could change your life and make you want to try another. They are all here in this book."
Nicholas K. Fowler, director, Aerospace

TEACH WHAT YOU KNOW

TEACH WHAT YOU KNOW
A Practical Leader's Guide to
Knowledge Transfer Using Peer Mentoring

Steve Trautman

www.practicalleader.com

PRENTICE
HALL

Upper Saddle River, NJ • Boston • Indianapolis
San Francisco • New York • Toronto • Montreal
London • Munich • Paris • Madrid • Cape Town
Sydney • Tokyo • Singapore • Mexico City

Many of the designations used by manufacturers and sellers to distinguish their products are claimed as trademarks. Where those designations appear in this book, and the publisher was aware of a trademark claim, the designations have been printed with initial capital letters or in all capitals. The author and publisher have taken care in the preparation of this book, but make no expressed or implied warranty of any kind and assume no responsibility for errors or omissions. No liability is assumed for incidental or consequential damages in connection with or arising out of the use of the information or programs contained herein.

The publisher offers excellent discounts on this book when ordered in quantity for bulk purchases or special sales, which may include electronic versions and/or custom covers and content particular to your business, training goals, marketing focus, and branding interests. For more information, please contact:

U.S. Corporate and Government Sales
(800) 382-3419
corpsales@pearsontechgroup.com
For sales outside the United States, please contact:
International Sales
international@pearsoned.com

 This Book Is Safari Enabled

The Safari® Enabled icon on the cover of your favorite technology book means the book is available through Safari Bookshelf. When you buy this book, you get free access to the online edition for 45 days. Safari Bookshelf is an electronic reference library that lets you easily search thousands of technical books, find code samples, download chapters, and access technical information whenever and wherever you need it.

To gain 45-day Safari Enabled access to this book:

- Go to http://www.prenhallprofessional.com/safarienabled
- Complete the brief registration form
- Enter the coupon code 82EA-FEGD-KTXY-NADY-HHCC

If you have difficulty registering on Safari Bookshelf or accessing the online edition, please e-mail customer-service@safaribooksonline.com.

Visit us on the Web: www.informit.com/ph

Library of Congress Cataloging-in-Publication Data

Trautman, Steve.
Teach what you know : a practical leader's guide to knowledge transfer using peer mentoring / Steve Trautman.
    p. cm.
  ISBN 0-321-41951-0 (hardback : alk. paper) 1. Mentoring in business. 2. Leadership—Study and teaching. I. Title.
  HF5385.T73 2006
  658.3'124—dc22

2006010825

ISBN 0-137-14368-0
This product is printed digitally on demand.

This book is dedicated to all the peer mentors who spend part of their day teaching others what they know. What would we do without you?

CONTENTS

ABOUT THE AUTHOR

Steve Trautman is the author of the Practical Leader Series, including the Peer Mentoring Workshop. These programs have helped thousands of business leaders, managers, and employees upgrade how they communicate, improving performance and quality while managing change more effectively.

Steve's expertise in rapid knowledge transfer was born from his years at Microsoft in the early 1990s. He developed Peer Mentoring there, as a solution to the intense on-the-job learning needed to manage the software development process. It became the model for the program that Steve and his colleagues have since delivered for companies that span the full spectrum of business.

While a program and group manager at Microsoft, and later as a general manager at Expedia.com, Steve walked in his clients' shoes. As a result, he understands first-hand the everyday realities of leading, teaching, and learning on the job. His subsequent consulting work in a variety of industries has allowed Steve to see and understand the challenges faced by employees from the front lines and factory floor on up to the chief executive's office.

Steve lives in Seattle with his family. Between his speaking and consulting engagements, you can find him in his garden or on adventure travels that, in the past, have taken him from the North Pole to the Equator, and from the jungles and forests of Central America to those of Asia and the Pacific Northwest.

PREFACE

This book is the first comprehensive how-to manual for knowledge transfer. It gives subject matter experts a set of practical tools to organize their experience into manageable chunks, teach that material, and then make sure that the information was received as intended. The content stems from my experiences delivering a workshop I developed more than 15 years ago to help engineers at Microsoft communicate with and teach each other in a fast paced, no-nonsense business environment. That means there is no fluff, just straightforward, get-it-done advice that has been tested and refined in the real world.

The ideas have been further customized for many major organizations including Microsoft, Intel, Nike, Nordstrom, Hewlett-Packard, Boeing, Standard Insurance, U.S. Army, U.S. Air Force and U.S. Coast Guard, Food Services of America, Electronic Arts, Phelps Dodge, Southern Company, and others. The concepts have been honed in a variety of industries, roles, and work environments, including software development, IT, government/military, call centers, manufacturing, engineering, research, biotech, sales organizations, social services, mining, project management, unions, and many small businesses. In each situation the issues are basically the same; people with experience need to teach their co-workers how to get things done.

The degree to which this transfer of knowledge goes smoothly can have a tremendous impact on the transitions that employees face every day. Whether orienting a new employee, recovering from a reorganization, rolling out new technology, merging with another company, or preparing to retire, people run into situations where they're either teaching what they know or learning from their co-workers. Everyone benefits from clear, concise, and productive communication. This book sets a standard that anyone can follow.

ACKNOWLEDGMENTS

I have to start by thanking Steve McConnell for suggesting that I write a book of this sort. I wasn't sure I could do it, but he thought I could, and said as much. It made me start to believe it, too. I also want to acknowledge the important contributions of my two long-time friends and colleagues Stacey Dickinson and Sherryl Christie Bierschenk. Both Stacey and Sherryl have brought their experience, ideas, and energy to our practice. The work we do is much the better for it.

My wife Sonja Gustafson and our kids, Lucas and Grace Trautman, have offered their strong support for me during this project. Dad's "homework" assignment took a long time, but they've kept their senses of humor and loved me through it.

Finally, I want to thank David Pritchard, my last boss at Microsoft, who encouraged me to continue thinking about and working with the Peer Mentoring Workshop after I left to set up my own practice. He was my first client, and the early work I did with him launched this (albeit meandering) career path for me. There are few things in my professional life that I've enjoyed as much. I appreciated having a chance to start out among familiar faces.

INTRODUCTION

*If you have ever responded to anyone who stopped by
to ask a question, you're transferring knowledge and
that makes you a peer mentor.*

ABOUT THIS BOOK

This book stems from my experience joining Microsoft in 1990 as a localization program manager. I arrived in time to help ship Microsoft Word 1.0 in German, French, Italian, Spanish, and Portuguese. I was singularly unqualified for the technical requirements of the job, barely knowing how to double-click, let alone having any experience in a software development environment. I was what they called a "talent" hire—someone who was reasonably bright, and a good project and people manager. Because the industry was so young, there weren't a lot of people with experience available. I appeared trainable, so they gave me a shot.

Advice about getting up to speed as a new employee at Microsoft, in those days, amounted to this: "If you're smart enough to get a job here, you're probably smart enough to figure out what your job is. Find something that needs to be done and do it!" As a result, I did what everyone does when they start a new position with no real training: I banged on doors and wandered into meetings, and I asked a lot of questions as I tried to figure out my new job. The people on my team were really terrific and made a lot of effort to help me, but there was one big problem: When they talked I couldn't understand anything they said. It was as if they were speaking a secret language. I just couldn't follow them. After a few weeks I was so stressed out that I was seeing bugs in my sleep, my hair was falling out, and I had developed a tic under my right eye. I thought I would never survive. At the same time, I also was hiring people from around the world to come to Redmond, Washington, and work in their native languages on the software. They were having an even more difficult time getting up to speed than I was. Something had to be done.

In a fit of insomnia and frustration I decided to make a deal with my co-workers. I would teach them how to be teachers—so they could teach me (and my team) how to do our jobs. I helped them think about what they needed to teach and how they could break it down into manageable chunks, teach it, and ensure we learned—all backed by a semblance of a plan. They quickly agreed because they needed us all to be productive and take on our share of the work as quickly as possible. With all of us working together to try to solve the problem, the Peer Mentoring Workshop was born as a handful of Microsoft PowerPoint slides.

We knew the plan was working when we realized we'd cut the typical ramp-up time for a new employee in half. Instead of spending three to four months wandering around trying to figure out how to do their jobs, new employees were working independently and productively in less than two.

That was the beginning of trying to figure out what good peer mentoring was all about. During much of the past 15 years, my colleagues and I have been developing the ideas put forth in this book by teaching the workshop we now call "Peer Mentoring: A Practical Approach to Knowledge Transfer." We consult with organizations in software, manufacturing, health care, mining, social services, retail, consumer products, military, utilities, IT, sales, call centers, and more. As my colleagues and I have customized the program for each different organization, our thinking about knowledge transfer has evolved. Still, we've found that the problems and the solutions are nearly universal.

The common theme of our work is that the need for knowledge transfer stems from the *transitions* most of us experience every day. For me, the big transition that spawned this work was both being a new employee and managing new employees. This book definitely addresses the orientation of new employees, but because many other transitions also call for improved peer mentoring skills, this book is intended to support them as well.

TRANSITIONS CREATE NEED FOR KNOWLEDGE TRANSFER

At the heart of every transition are people, people who *know* (I call them peer mentors) and people who *need to know* (the apprentices). Everyone falls into one of these categories, and depending on the moment, they might even go back and forth from one to the other. For example, I might teach you something I know in the morning and then turn around and ask you to teach me what you know in the afternoon. Much of this is never really spelled out; it just happens during the course of working together.

Sometimes people are clear about their role as expert and peer mentor, but often they're not. Sometimes they know that they should teach but don't know how. Sometimes they know how, but don't want to. Sometimes they're the apprentice and need to learn, but aren't even aware of it. You get the idea. The opportunity for confusion is real.

How organizations understand the need for predictable knowledge transfer in the trenches as well as from the top down has a profound impact on how smoothly the transition goes. The following list includes some examples of common transitions. As you read through the list, check off how many of them you're facing today:

- New technology (such as introducing a new knowledge base or a new customer relations management system) in which some people get more training and have to bring their new skills back to the larger organization

- Reorganizations in which new teams are forming and people are transitioning from one part of the company to another, so employees have to get up to speed, as well as hand off their old responsibilities
- Recent hires of employees, contractors, vendors, partner companies, or interns
- Mergers and acquisitions, with two or more companies needing to integrate systems, staff, cultures, technology, and so on
- New process launches to improve productivity or respond to changing government regulations
- New customers requiring newly formed project teams to focus on meeting new objectives
- Recent layoffs, during which remaining employees have to pick up the work of those who left
- Recent retirements, during which workers leave before they can fully train others about the knowledge they've gained through their years of experience
- Business changes that require cross training to improve flexibility
- Outsourcing that requires having to partner offshore
- New physical space for offices or production
- New markets, products, and customers

Do any of these sound familiar to you? When I lecture, I ask this question of live audiences, and I ask how many organizations face five or more of these challenges at any given time. At least half of every group waves a hand. Transition and change are around you all the time. The question is, how are you dealing with them?

Throughout any transition much information must be known. Think of all the skills, processes, standards, tools, templates, policies, success metrics, and requirements that must be known in your department or organization, whether big or small. These tangible elements are actually the easy ones to transition from person-to-person, because they can be seen and accomplished within tight parameters. But what about all of the other information that must be known, such as history, tribal knowledge, collaborative team issues, customer issues, culture, and communication strategies? These are all much more amorphous and loose. So, how do people get to know them?

From *other people*, that's how. They learn all of this information from the people sitting right next to them. Formal training is still important and cost effective in situations where many people need to learn one skill, but even with the best formal training, most of us will still learn the bulk of our job skills from a co-worker.

IDENTIFY THE PEER MENTORS AND APPRENTICES

I'll bet that for every transition above, you could easily make a list of the peer mentors (subject matter experts) and the specific apprentices in your organization. They're the people who know what is going on, and how to get the work done; and the people who need to know, but don't. Now imagine how well things would go if those peer mentors were really good at explaining themselves and ensuring a transfer of knowledge and understanding to the apprentices, and the apprentices could develop and demonstrate their new knowledge consistently. It is likely that you have some of that happening already, because some people are naturally good at this. Imagine what would happen if nearly *everyone* had a baseline of skills to replicate themselves in a predictable way.

This isn't some far off utopia. It is happening already in many forward-thinking organizations. This book tells their stories.

My colleagues and I have studied and are replicating the behaviors of those great masters who are naturally good at knowledge transfer; that is, the people who already excel at teaching what they know. We've found that each time *they* face a new question, they instinctively assess the situation and respond with an eloquent repartee seamlessly expounding on only the most salient information in exactly the right format to aid their befuddled apprentice.

Then there are the rest of us mere mortals. When faced with a question, we do one of many things:

- Jump up, slap on a red cape, and leap out of the cube with a hearty "I'll save you!" That's easier than taking the time to teach anything. Right?
- Talk until we say something—starting in the middle, looping around through 12 years of experience, and landing with a hopeful, "Did you get all that?"
- Jump to the white board and carefully diagram the schematic of the bowels of the ACME 2000 Turbo Jumpracer, when all you asked was how to find the "on" switch.
- Grunt some unintelligible instructions and hope the apprentice will go away.

Wouldn't it be great if a peer mentor would, when faced with an opportunity to transfer knowledge, whether it be formal or informal, be able to take this approach:

- Recognize that they have something to teach and define it in terms of a measurable learning goal.
- Quickly assess what the apprentice already knows and wants or needs to know.
- Ensure that the apprentice has the minimum required setup (vocabulary, workstation, access, etc.) to be successful.
- Organize the topic into a brief lesson plan.
- Teach from the lesson plan that matches the apprentice's learning style, and assess progress along the way to make sure the apprentice isn't lost.
- Send the apprentice off with specific instructions on what to do next.
- Follow up with peer-appropriate feedback.

While that process sounds great, it probably also sounds like a lot of work. After all, we're all busy people. Who has the time to be this rigorous? Having enough time is universally the biggest concern that I hear when I talk about Peer Mentoring. I promise, up front, that the individual tools or ideas that I present in this book will typically take you no more than 5–10 minutes to use on your first try. They're designed with the busiest of people in mind—people who need to teach others on the job every day, while carrying a very full workload themselves. I also promise that the results will be immediate. You can read about the tool, put the idea to work immediately, and see improvements in real time.

WHO SHOULD READ THIS BOOK

At the heart of this book is the person I call a *peer mentor*, because most of the time this person doesn't have any authority (they're literally peers), but they do have plenty of often undefined responsibility to help their colleagues learn how to do the work at hand. While many of the ideas in this book translate very well to the more traditional notion of mentoring, sometimes called *career mentoring*, this book doesn't try to address all of the nuances of those relationships. I see that as a topic for another book.

Every organization has peer mentors who already tackle the role with a variety of approaches, and an equally varied success rate. If you're a peer mentor already, this book was written for you. It'll help you better define your role and manage the expectations of your manager, as well as your apprentices.

The other two players in the knowledge-transfer triangle are the manager and the apprentice. This book supports the people playing both of those roles as well, partly by helping managers and apprentices better understand the peer mentors, and partly by giving direct advice to help guide the relationship from all three perspectives.

Here are some of the forms these three roles take:

Primary Peer Mentors are people who are regularly called upon to teach what they know in either formally or informally structured relationships, typically with new team members. They provide an "umbrella" of support for the apprentice that includes developing their skills, but also includes looking after their adjustment to the organization, answering random questions, and helping them get their feet on the ground. In this book, primary peer mentors will find a substantial menu of tools, advice, and a clear process that they can apply to this role.

Silo Peer Mentors are people who are subject matter experts and have a deep "silo" of knowledge. They usually don't look after new hires or take on broad relationships, often because they don't want to or aren't good at it, but they do teach others about their specialty. If they're good at transferring their subject knowledge, the organization experiences greater consistency in that area, and they reduce the organizational reliance on themselves as the only one who knows a particular skill or piece of information. Acknowledging that silo mentors exist is a good practice, but it is equally important that their skills be replicated in others to reduce risk. Silo mentors can use this book to clarify what is expected of them and then put a plan in place to make the knowledge transfer process more productive and less painful for everyone.

Retiring Employee Peer Mentors are people who are in their last few years before retirement and have been identified by their organizations as having "singular knowledge." This means that when they leave, there will be a problem if they aren't carefully replaced. Many organizations, especially union or government organizations, have 30 percent or more of their population at or within five years of retirement age at any given time. Those close to retirement can use this book to develop a plan for downloading some of their experience and skills to others before they retire.

Apprentices are the people who are learning from the peer mentors. There is a section at the end of every chapter for them called "When You're the Apprentice." In some instances the apprentice will be a really obvious person, like a new employee. Often, though, the apprentice is someone less obvious, like a current co-worker who is cross training on a new specialty, or a client, a contractor, or even the boss. There are many ways that an apprentice can take responsibility for his own training and improve the quality of the time spent with peer mentors. Apprentices are motivated to learn so they can stop making mistakes and feeling awkward. They can use the ideas in this book to expedite their own training and development.

Managers and Executives should look for answers to their organizational questions at the end of every chapter in the "From a Manager's View" section. Every company relies heavily on peer mentors to keep information moving and to develop consistent skills and competencies across the organization. Managers will learn to recognize this incredibly valuable resource and begin to support it so they can maximize the potential of their peer mentors. They'll also find some very specific advice on how to implement Peer Mentoring programs in their companies.

As a side benefit, it turns out that peer mentoring skills are a foundation to any good manager's toolkit. When I deliver the Practical Leader Management Series, we always start with the Peer Mentoring Workshop as a prerequisite for everyone attending. If attendees haven't already mastered peer mentoring skills, we want to start by developing those skills before moving on to more complex management topics. Even very experienced managers are receptive to the ideas we present.

Project Managers (responsibility without authority) and **Team Leads** (responsibility with authority) can use peer mentoring tools and ideas to improve the overall communication and management of the people on their teams. They'll want to ensure that all of the silo mentors are identified and have been asked to transfer their knowledge to others on the project team. They'll also want to ensure that every new project or team member is assigned a primary mentor to ease their introduction to the team and reduce the sort of thrash that comes with new help. It is also common for leads and managers to choose several of the tools from this book to implement across their whole teams. They see this as a way to improve general communication and manage expectations.

Aspiring Leaders can read the book to develop their own leadership skills and style. When interviewing for their first management position, candidates can show their potential by explaining how they've demonstrated great knowledge transfer and communication skills through mentoring their peers. Having some specific stories to tell will help them stand out when they're competing for a promotion.

Human Resource Managers and **Training Managers** should use this book to boost their new employee orientations and to ensure that a training plan like the one described in Chapter 4, "Developing a Training Plan," is developed for every new or experienced employee. We want them to see peer mentoring as a way of creating an "army of trainers" that will stretch their training budget further than ever before. It will greatly improve the impact of their existing training and development programs if they can have ongoing support from trained peer mentors

Small Business Owners can use the book to ensure that they've cross trained their limited staff to stay as nimble as possible and get the most out of everyone. By implementing these ideas, small business owners can ensure knowledge is distributed effectively among their employees without formal training sessions that may be impractical in a small business setting.

HOW THIS BOOK IS ORGANIZED

Each chapter in this book is centered on one of the common problems peer mentors, apprentices, and managers face every day in trying to get their jobs done.

For those of you who learn best by seeing the "big picture" before diving into the details, I recommend you read Chapter 10, "Peer Mentoring in Practice," first, as a way of seeing the whole process in summary, including a case study, before reading the rest of the book.

If your primary concern is knowledge transfer to remote outsource partners or a distributed team, I recommend you read Chapter 9, "Peer Mentoring from a Distance," first, as a way of orienting yourself to how the tools will work for you. Then, read the rest of the book for the details.

If you have new employees as your apprentices, you should read the book from cover to cover to learn a complete approach to knowledge transfer. You'll see a path that starts with setting expectations and developing a training plan on the apprentice's first day on the job, and goes all the way through teaching, assessing learning, and giving the kind of feedback an apprentice will want to hear as they start to develop in their role.

For those of you who aren't mentoring new employees, you can pick up the book and browse for challenges that you're facing at any given moment. You can read one chapter at a time and implement the ideas in that chapter, returning to the book once you're ready to move on to a new problem.

If you're an apprentice, I recommend that you read the entire book just like the peer mentors do. Why? Because you won't be an apprentice long, and you'll want to be good at teaching others as soon as you're called on to share your knowledge. I have written some specific advice for you in the "When You're the Apprentice" section at the end of each chapter. If you follow that advice, you'll find yourself moving quickly from novice to strong contributor in no time.

CONVENTIONS USED

In order to make this book more useful I've incorporated three conventions into the design.

PEER MENTORING PROCESS

At the beginning of each chapter, you'll find a variation of the graphic shown here that presents the entire flow of a successful peer mentoring relationship and helps you see how that chapter's tools fit into the big picture.

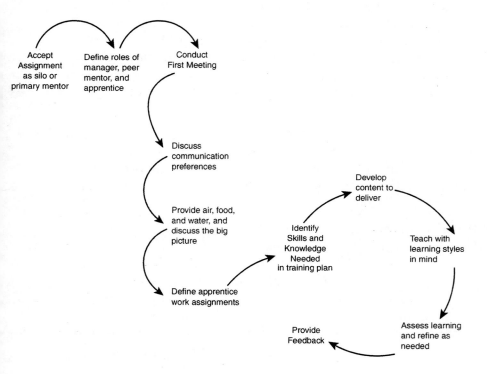

Accept Assignment as silo or primary mentor

Define roles of manager, peer mentor, and apprentice

Conduct First Meeting

Discuss communication preferences

Provide air, food, and water, and discuss the big picture

Define apprentice work assignments

Identify Skills and Knowledge Needed in training plan

Develop content to deliver

Teach with learning styles in mind

Assess learning and refine as needed

Provide Feedback

TOOLS

I use the word "tool" to describe the checklists, templates, worksheets, and standards that you can use to improve communication and knowledge transfer. Each chapter has one or more tools. You can easily identify them by looking for this icon:

APPRENTICE AND MANAGER SIDEBARS

Each chapter ends with two sidebars. "From a Manager's View" is directed to managers, so that they can support these ideas in their teams. "When You're the Apprentice" is directed specifically to apprentices to help them drive their own training.

WHAT'S IN THE BOOK

As I mentioned earlier, each chapter in this book is centered on one of the common problems peer mentors, apprentices, and managers face every day in trying to get their jobs done. It is modular in approach, so even if you're only interested in facing one of the issues today, you can read the related chapter and put those ideas to work before returning to read the rest. As you read through this brief introduction to each chapter, think about how it relates to your current job and how you'd benefit from using the tools provided to improve your situation.

CHAPTER 1: ROLES IN PEER MENTORING

Who is responsible for what?

Because peer mentoring is usually very informal, participants' roles and responsibilities are often vague. This chapter provides a common language that can be used to define the expectations of the manager, the peer mentor, and the apprentice so there is less frustration and greater efficiency. Learn how a manager and a peer mentor can tell the apprentice, "We've been thinking about you and we have a plan to help you get up to speed. Let's talk about what you can expect from us and the best approach you can take for your own development." In a matter of minutes this sets everyone's expectations and sets the stage for success.

CHAPTER 2: MANAGING TIME AND COMMUNICATION

How do I stay in touch with my apprentice and still get my day job done?

For most peer mentors, transferring knowledge isn't explicitly on their task list. It comes under *other duties as assigned*. There is no doubt that it is harder to keep up with your own work when you're a peer mentor. This chapter offers practical tips for keeping daily interactions useful, while still getting your regular work done. Specific topics include improving e-mail communication, controlling interruptions, improving one-on-one time, providing quick status reports, and guiding better problem-solving questions. You can pick one or more of the tips and put them to use immediately.

CHAPTER 3: FOCUSING ON THE MOST IMPORTANT INFORMATION

Where do I start?

Too often a peer mentor's vast knowledge overwhelms the apprentice. This chapter helps mentors figure out where to begin, what doesn't need to be said, and how to organize needed information into manageable, useful chunks. The worksheets in this chapter will spark some interesting conversations about how you introduce your apprentice to the content and its relationship to the "big picture." By using these tools, you can quickly build the foundation of understanding, or deal with an apprentice who takes far too long to stabilize in the new role.

CHAPTER 4: DEVELOPING A TRAINING PLAN

What are the skills, measures, and resources needed to do the job?

This is the most important chapter of the entire book, because it provides a way for peer mentors to "deconstruct" their jobs into a list of specific skills (things you know how to do), measures of understanding (test questions you'd have to pass to prove you learned those skills), and resources that can be used to pass the test (such as classes, peer mentors, web sites, documentation, etc.). Having a plan to use as a point of reference means your apprentice will be able to drive far more of his own development, which will keep you from bouncing all over the place.

CHAPTER 5: TELLING WHAT YOU KNOW

How much should I cover and how do I deliver it?

In order to cover information effectively, you'll need to develop basic lesson plan and delivery techniques. This chapter explains how to identify the least amount of information necessary to make your point. It also offers tools for content development, including the 5-Minute Meeting Plan and the keys to giving effective demonstrations.

CHAPTER 6: LEVERAGING LEARNING STYLES

What if we aren't on the same page?

Not everyone learns the same way, so peer mentors shouldn't teach every apprentice the same way. This discussion outlines some key learning styles and helps you recognize how to teach to an apprentice who might have a different learning style than you do. Armed with this understanding, you can adjust your teaching and make the knowledge transfer process more successful.

CHAPTER 7: ASSESSING KNOWLEDGE TRANSFER

How do I know if they are learning anything?

Ensuring that an apprentice is really learning requires more than just asking, "Are you with me?" You have to determine your apprentice's prior experience and knowledge before beginning your mentoring session and use direct assessment questions to track their progress while you're teaching. This chapter helps peer mentors formulate simple questions that they can ask in any situation to make sure they're not wasting time rambling on when little is sinking in.

CHAPTER 8: GIVING AND GETTING PEER-APPROPRIATE FEEDBACK

When and how should I say what I am thinking?

What does it take to create an environment where a peer can quickly and safely give feedback to a colleague? The secret is to focus on the goals that were set and to talk about whether those goals were exceeded, met, or not met. This chapter offers some simple language that a peer mentor and an apprentice can use to help each other perform at their best, using guidance received from the people who see their work most closely, their peers.

CHAPTER 9: PEER MENTORING FROM A DISTANCE

What if I rarely or never see my apprentice?

Many teams have members spread all over the globe. The key to making long-distance mentoring work is a disciplined approach to managing the relationship. This chapter discusses how you can use each Peer Mentoring tool described in the other chapters to improve communication and knowledge transfer when distance is a factor.

CHAPTER 10: PEER MENTORING IN PRACTICE

What am I going to do with what I've learned?

None of these ideas would be worth much if they didn't change the behavior of the reader. In this chapter you'll learn to notice the "triggers" that remind you to use the skills and tools presented. You'll also learn to identify and avoid obstacles to success. Worksheets are included to guide the planning. Finally, you'll find an extensive case study that tells how one company successfully put peer mentors to work.

APPENDIX A: PEER MENTORING TOOLS AT A GLANCE

This appendix is a compilation of all of the Peer Mentoring tools offered throughout the book. They're shown here in the order in which they appear in the text.

APPENDIX B: SAMPLE TRAINING PLANS

This appendix includes six sample training plans for different jobs. They provide you with additional perspective on the ways others have deconstructed a portion of their role.

ONWARD

As you read through this book, I hope you'll find a common-sense approach to knowledge transfer and peer mentoring that you can imagine using for yourself, as well as sharing with your co-workers. There are many reasons to improve your ability to teach what you know. I hope this book will make you more successful at it right away.

1

Roles in Peer Mentoring

Who is responsible for what?

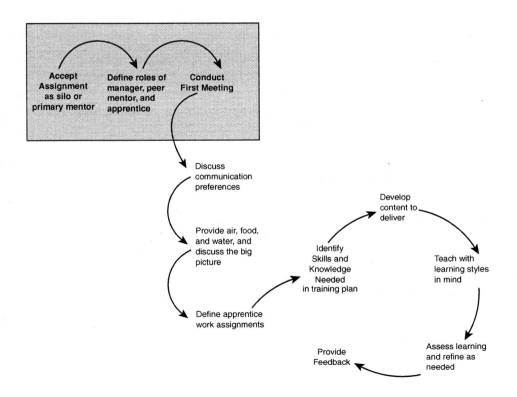

Accept Assignment as silo or primary mentor

Define roles of manager, peer mentor, and apprentice

Conduct First Meeting

Discuss communication preferences

Provide air, food, and water, and discuss the big picture

Define apprentice work assignments

Identify Skills and Knowledge Needed in training plan

Develop content to deliver

Teach with learning styles in mind

Assess learning and refine as needed

Provide Feedback

Are *you* a peer mentor? How do you know? If you think you are a peer mentor, how do you know what is expected? What if you're overdoing it or missing the boat entirely?

Peers helping peers learn how to do their work isn't a new idea— it's how nearly everyone learns their job. But how do you, as the peer mentor, the teacher, fulfill this role? Are you actively ensuring that your co-workers learn how to do the work in a specific way; or are you just sitting back, taking questions as they come? Should you monitor quality and give feedback, or just help clean up messes? Are you setting the standard for your specialty, or just setting a "good example" and hoping for the best? Do you develop a training plan, or let them figure it out on their own?

That's a lot to think about. If you're like most people in this situation, you have tried a few approaches and have a rough idea of the role you can play. You're making the best of it. This book should help you do much better than that. It starts by helping you figure out what you've signed up to do. By the end of this chapter, you should have some very specific language you can use to help answer all of the questions above and better define your role— whether it is as a peer mentor, a manager, or an apprentice.

HOW ARE ROLES DEFINED NOW?

In reality, the peer mentor's job description usually falls under "other duties as assigned," and transferring knowledge is taken for granted if you're a team player. It makes sense that when anyone on the team needs to get help, they should be able wander to the next workstation and ask questions of someone who is doing a version of the same thing. It also makes sense that the person in the next workstation is also busy doing other things. They just fit answering co-worker's questions in between the daily tasks of their job. Sometimes this works just fine; subject matter experts teach, their co-workers learn, and everyone gets up to a similar level of productivity in short order.

How well does that work in your organization? The reality you experience is probably far less predictable than you'd like. Usually you get assigned the role of peer mentor like this: Your boss is sitting at his desk reading email on Friday night and sees a reminder that that there is a new hire starting on Monday. He smacks himself on the forehead, because he knows that this newbie is going to need some help getting started, and because he also knows he hasn't taken any time to think about it. Just then he looks up and you walk by on your way home for the weekend. He sees you and hollers out the door, "Hey, there is a new guy starting on Monday, can you 'look after' him and help him get up to speed?" Your defenses are down because it's late and you're really tired. You stammer a bit but can't think fast enough to avoid taking on the new responsibility, so you just agree.

With that, a peer mentor is born.

Often it isn't even as clear as "Hey, can you look after the new guy"—you just sort of stumble into the role. During the course of your career, you have come to be known as the "guru" for your specialty. You're the one your manager expects to set the standard. Everyone knows it, so you get the questions, do the training, and troubleshoot whenever something goes wrong.

The trouble is that in both situations you don't really know what you've agreed to. You probably have some ideas in your head from your past experiences, and your manager may have some too; but how do you know that you both see the job the same way? How will your apprentices know what to expect? Too many questions can lead to unmet expectations—the heart of many frustrating problems.

PLOTTING A MENTOR SPECTRUM: WHERE DO YOU FIT?

The first step in making peer mentoring work is clarifying three roles: the manager, the peer mentor, and the apprentice. There is a broad spectrum of acceptable possibilities here. The trick is to work with your manager to clarify where you land. You should know what your boss means when he asks you to "look after the new guy," or "set the standard" for your specialty.

An example of how this continuum might look is described here and shown in Figure 1-1.

- **Active Mentoring.** At one end of the continuum, the role of peer mentor could include meeting and escorting the apprentice to a desk; helping him or her set up a workstation; providing introductions to co-workers; assigning some work; providing a primer on the first tasks; writing up some documentation for him to follow; scheduling regular check-in meetings; having lunch together; and offering a ride home after work.

- **Passive Mentoring.** At the other end of the spectrum, the role of peer mentor could mean simply answering questions if the apprentice happens to be able to find you at your desk.

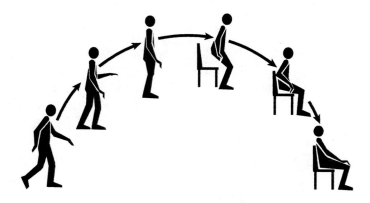

Figure 1-1   Be sure your role is defined as active, passive, or somewhere in between.

In my experience, a role falling anywhere on this spectrum is fine, as long as everyone (manager, peer mentor, and later, the apprentice) talks it over and agrees on it. What happens in the absence of this conversation? Well, both you and your boss point at each other saying, "I'm sure he's doing it!" or you trip over each other, trying to do the same things at the same time.

CAST OF CHARACTERS IN PEER MENTORING

I'm going to introduce you to four different players who have a big role in this book.

PEER MENTORS

One way to help clarify the job is to separate out two different ways people transfer knowledge:

- **Primary Peer Mentors.** Regularly called upon to transfer knowledge, primary peer mentors often orient new hires or take on other long-term relationships, such as cross training a person to a new position after reorganization. Primary peer mentors have an "umbrella" of knowledge and responsibilities. They look after their apprentices' big-picture needs, answer general questions, and teach specific skills. They're on deck for everything, from soup to nuts.

- **Silo Peer Mentors.** Subject matter experts with a deep "silo" of knowledge, the silo peer mentors are generally better suited to teaching their specialty and not as well suited to worrying about apprentices beyond that. Some silo mentors are people who are expected to establish, teach, and monitor a standard practice among existing employees. Others are responsible for keeping an eye on quality, especially when the manager isn't a subject matter expert.

It is common for managers to be concerned about the silos of information that exist in their organizations, because there are many problems that arise when information or skills are too narrowly held. One solution is to identify the silo mentors and then redefine their roles to include outreach and training of others. Including such sharing of knowledge in their roles means they are no longer the only ones who know a specific concept or skill. If you think your organization would benefit from mining the knowledge of silo mentors, you should bring it up with your manager.

MANAGER

Managers include supervisors, project managers, team leads, and others who use peer mentoring tools and ideas to improve the overall communication and management of their human resources. They want to ensure that all of the silo mentors are identified and have been asked to transfer their knowledge to others on the project team. They also want to ensure that every new project or team member is assigned a primary mentor to ease their introduction to the team and reduce the sort of fumbling around that comes with new help.

APPRENTICES

Apprentices can come from anywhere, and may or may not be formally assigned to you as their peer mentor. The most obvious source of apprentices is new employees, but that is not the only place to look. They may already be in your company, but may be new to your group. They may be new to your kind of technology. They may be older than you. They may know more or less than you about other topics. They could be an intern, a temporary employee, a customer, or even your boss. They might come from a team that you collaborate with. They could be the person who covers for you while you're on vacation. You might have a long-term relationship with the apprentice that is clearly defined, or you might just answer random questions from them as they come up.

PEER MENTORING IN PRACTICE: THE IMPORTANCE OF ROLES

One of my manufacturing clients had traditionally taken each new employee, contractor, or cross-trainee (their apprentices) through safety training and then quickly moved them out to the assembly line to shadow another employee as a way of learning the work. The employee being shadowed (the peer mentor) was simply whoever was working on that workstation that day. The peer mentor would usually find out about this new assignment when their shift started with a supervisor making introductions. The roles of the manager, the peer mentor, and the apprentice were never clarified. This is a very common way to bring people up to speed, but it wasn't working very well in this situation.

For starters, despite the fact that virtually any employee could be shadowed, not all employees were well suited to the task. For example, even though the employee produces a satisfactory product, their approach may not always be the one to be replicated. Efficiency and quality are keys in manufacturing, and not all employees are equally committed to these goals.

We also found that some of the peer mentors would take an *active* role in teaching what they knew about the workstation (giving an overview of the documentation, explaining a few of the nuances of the process, offering some advice on how to reduce scrap and maintain quality, providing the most common steps for troubleshooting), whereas others would simply do their job and let the apprentice watch, fielding questions only if the apprentice asked. Virtually none of the peer mentors made any effort to connect with the new employee after their shift ended. It didn't occur to them to follow up.

As the new apprentices observed the workstation, the supervisors also played different roles. Some stopped by the workstation regularly to bring documentation, check quality, and answer questions. Others left most of that up to the peer mentor who had equal access to the information. Once again, with none of this being consistent, some of the new hires were well supported, and others missed out.

Finally, the apprentices were often at a loss for knowing what to do. Should they just watch or jump in and help? What if they wanted to read the procedure manual before watching the demonstration? When was it appropriate to ask questions? Were they watching this workstation because they would be working there tomorrow, or was the purpose just to give them an overview of the plant? Did they need to perform exactly as their peer mentor did, or how much leeway did they have to develop their own style?

As I said, this isn't an uncommon scenario at all, so it shouldn't be surprising that sometimes this "jump in and go for it" approach actually works! When the stars are aligned and the right combination of assumptions, personalities, experience, and timing hit, the apprentice can get up to speed quickly and all can go well. Unfortunately, this "magic" experience is not predictable. When it doesn't go well, the costs in terms of quality, scrap, and reduced output can be devastating. That is the problem we need to solve.

CLARIFYING ROLES

A closer look at the orientation experience on the shop floor shows that there were too many unclear roles and expectations to ever achieve consistent results. A few quick changes could fix that. Here's what you can do:

- Identify a handful of experienced employees on every shift to serve as primary peer mentors. (Their role is to build a relationship with the apprentice, answer general questions, and ensure that he feels a connection to the team.)

- Handpick silo mentors from the workstation specialists for each shift. These individuals should work in a way that the manufacturer wants replicated (we want more employees just like that). We can actively work around those who aren't suited to either of the primary or silo mentoring roles.

- Involve the supervisors in defining what is expected of the silo mentors in terms of their active or passive participation, and provide written instructions to explain how they are expected to do this job.

- Hold a 10-minute First Meeting (explained later in this chapter) between the apprentice, the supervisor, and the peer mentor(s) at the beginning of each shift to clarify roles, set goals for the shift, and decide how and when they will all stay in touch.

- Provide the chosen peer mentors with training on how to transfer knowledge and a toolset to help them do that consistently.

Once the peer mentor and manager roles and expectations were established in our manufacturing example, the results were positive and immediate. Apprentices reached productivity faster and performance was improved. Some of the peer mentors genuinely enjoyed teaching others, and once they really understood the level at which they were expected to contribute, they could relax and just do it. The supervisors and the apprentices also had a better understanding of what was expected of them, and could do their part to make the knowledge transfer process work.

LANGUAGE TO SEPARATE MANAGER FROM PEER MENTOR

Role definition includes figuring out the difference between the manager role and your role as peer mentor. In a perfect world, your manager would drive this discussion and you'd simply get a clear idea of what is expected, negotiate the details, and head off to work. Unfortunately, most of us don't live in that perfect world. Throughout this book, I will suggest many times that managing your manager may be necessary. Why? Because your boss is probably not an "A+" boss (but hopefully not an "F" boss, either). Most of us work for a well-intentioned "B" or "B–" boss. That means your boss probably doesn't know how to define the roles effectively, so you have to do it—and why not? You have plenty to gain from defining the roles each of you will play.

Take a moment to read through the Role Definition Worksheet provided in Tool 1-1 and think about each task outlined and who is responsible for it. Are you responsible, is another peer handling that task, or is your manager on top of it? If there are tasks specific to your organization that are missing from the list, just add them at the bottom of the worksheet. You can use the list to guide the role-definition discussion with your manager and work out the details for your specific peer mentoring situation.

Notice that none of the items in this worksheet are *characteristics*, such as patience, kindness, or thoughtfulness. They're all *actions* you can take to get your apprentice up to speed; and, that is where I want to focus this effort—defining what you are going to *do*.

You also have to think of the worksheet as a list of the differences between a peer mentor and a manager. For example, who will assign project work? What about responding to apprentice requests to take time off for a doctor's appointment? What about giving feedback? Are those types of decisions to be a part of your role, or do they belong solely to your manager?

Be sure not to say that you *both* own a specific task. It is far better to agree that the primary ownership of a task is held by either the manager or the peer mentor, with support from the other. If you just define the owner of the task as both the manager and the peer mentor, you are not making the situation any clearer.

Tool 1-1 Role Definition Worksheet

Task	Owner	Comments
Get a workstation set up.		
Provide updated "Air, Food, and Water" checklist (see Tool 3-1).		
Introduce apprentice to the rest of the team.		
Set up First Meeting to clarify expectations.		
Assess what the apprentice already knows.		
Write work goals for the apprentice.		
Write a Training Plan (see Chapter 4).		
Request and respond to status reports.		
Teach specific topics from the plan (silos).		
Request help from other silo mentors.		
Monitor the quality of the apprentice's work.		
Provide big-picture context around the project.		
Discover and teach to the apprentice's learning style.		
Give consistent, timely feedback.		
Ask for feedback from the apprentice.		

Deciding on the primary ownership of the tasks on the worksheet is a question about boundaries. It is much easier to move forward when you clarify everyone's position.

PUT INTO PRACTICE: MANAGING THE MANAGERS

I was teaching Peer Mentoring for the State of Washington a few years ago. The attendees were all from the same department (representing several teams). None of the managers were present. The group had been through a huge reorganization, and everyone was in the midst of cross training and adjusting to their new roles. When I taught the section on role definitions, there was quite a buzz in the room. The attendees really connected to the fact that they were all working under a set of assumptions that had never been discussed. With so many different ways to interpret their own roles in transferring knowledge, it was no wonder the transition wasn't going very well. Many of them had more than 10 years of service with the state, and could have been set up as the expert on any number of areas. In some cases more than one person was working to shape the same area and train everyone else. In other cases, no one had taken responsibility. The conversation on role definitions seemed to hit a nerve.

THEY FIGURED IT OUT

Using their definition of a silo mentor, I asked them to list the topics that would form the silos of knowledge for their newly formed department. They quickly drafted a list of tools, processes, standards, technology, and relationships that defined their organization's role in supporting state government employees. They also agreed quickly on a list of their silo mentors, and divided the roles among them. Next, I asked who might need a primary mentor. The group quickly identified the handful of employees hired in the last year, as well as some temporary contractor employees and a couple of vendors who normally work off-site. The primary mentors were easy to identify, because they were people who had already popped into that role naturally.

Then I asked them to develop what they believed to be the list of expectations for themselves in the roles (silo and/or primary) that they'd picked up. For most, this was a matter of going through Tool 1-1 and marking it up. In addition to editing the table, nearly everyone found a couple of things missing from the list that were specific to their situation.

The final step was to send them back to their managers with their list and a few questions to clarify roles. Here is some language I suggested to aid in the conversation with their managers:

> When I look at the work of our team, it seems as if you need me to help out in supporting the "Widget" silo (or the newly hired employee). I'd like to better understand what you're hoping I'll take on. I've made a list of the things I think you'd like me to do and the things that I think you or someone else is handling. Could we sit down for a few minutes to go over my list and make sure we're on the same page?

The employees who took the workshop went back, en masse, to their managers, armed with their best assumptions of roles, and laid the list down in the middle of a brief conversation. The results were just what you'd expect. Sometimes the list was spot on. Often it needed only a few tweaks, and sometimes there were big changes. The discussion almost always caused the managers to notice work that they'd taken for granted, or never even thought about. At the end of these brief conversations, everyone's expectations were clearer.

THE MANAGERS RESPONDED

I heard about the role-defining conversations from the managers a month or so later, when I was asked back to teach Peer Mentoring to them. They said it was a little startling, at first, to have their employees drop by with such direct questions. But the results were so helpful in reducing the noise from the reorganization, they quickly adjusted, and wanted to know more about what they could do to improve knowledge transfer in their teams.

I want to point out that these state employees had the benefit of critical mass (many people from one team taking the class together) in moving the managers to think about things differently. That dynamic isn't a requirement. I often teach people who are the only person from their whole organization attending the workshop. I still send them back to "manage" their managers in the same way. When you think about it, what manager wouldn't appreciate an employee working to clarify the situation and offering to help out in a very specific way?

WHAT IF I'M A SILO MENTOR?

As I said earlier, there are two kinds of peer mentors: primary and silo. Silo peer mentors teach a very narrow topic—not how to navigate the larger role. The need for narrow knowledge transfer is common after reorganizations in which people take on new roles. It also happens when a team is looking for greater consistency in the way they deliver their product or service, or when a team has members with deep specialties that they want to replicate in others.

Remember, the silo peer mentor has deep subject matter expertise and is generally better suited to teaching his or her specialty and not worrying about the apprentice's needs beyond that. Figure 1-2 shows the relationship between primary and silo peer mentor. Some silo peer mentors are people who could define a standard practice among existing employees. Others are responsible for keeping an eye on quality, especially when the manager isn't a subject matter expert.

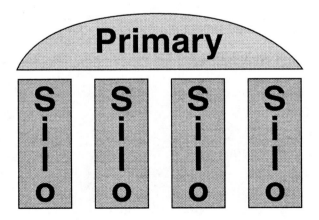

Figure 1-2　Primary mentors have an umbrella role; silo mentors focus on a subject.

Sometimes a primary peer mentor and a team of silos will be called on to help one person get up to speed. This works really well, because it shares the training load, and ensures that the silos can deliver their content consistently from one person to the next.

If you recognize yourself as more of a silo mentor than a primary mentor, you should still sit down with your manager to clarify your role. Ask yourself if you are *actively* driving your expertise into your team by defining a skill set to teach, setting up a plan to teach it, and then working until your co-workers get the information, or if you are just *passively* answering questions as they come up. There is a big difference between these approaches in how you'll serve in your role as a mentor.

PUT INTO PRACTICE: MANAGING SILO MENTORS

A few years back, I had a client who was the vice president of procurement for a major retailer. He didn't have any new employees; everyone had at least two years with the company. His problem wasn't orientation, but rather getting all of his people to work more consistently. He had some employees who were terrific at writing contracts and others who negotiated the best deals. One employee was really great at identifying the best vendors, while another excelled at managing the internal customers. As I conducted the needs assessment, I remember thinking that collectively, they had one good brain. Unfortunately, the pieces of that good brain were all in silos. I needed to help them even out the skill set of each of the specialists—in effect creating more silo experts. Here is what we did:

- Defined all of the silo topics and created a list that included, among other items, contract writing, contract negotiation, needs assessment, legal, vendor selection, performance management.

- Selected one or two people from the existing team who were considered the best at this particular role, and declared them the silo mentor(s) for that topic. In this way the silos were spread across the team.

- Inventoried the skills that each of the silo peer mentors had to share (see the training plan in Chapter 4, "Developing a Training Plan").

- Conducted a gap analysis for each of the employees relative to the silo peer mentor for that topic. We needed to quantify the difference between the best silo we had and everyone else.

- Asked everyone who was a silo peer mentor to meet with those who needed help in their specialty and conduct a First Meeting (covered later in this chapter) to discuss how they'd work together to bridge the skill gap.

- Trained them on peer mentoring skills and rotated each of them through the emerging system. In this case everyone was both a silo peer mentor and an apprentice at one time or another.

After about a year, the entire team was cross trained and had a consistent skill set. We knew this because we could compare each person's skills to the skills listed on the training plans that the silo mentors had established. The team had methodically removed the silos that had been such a concern in the beginning by having each silo mentor replicate his skill set within his peer group.

WHAT MAKES A GREAT APPRENTICE?

The apprentice has a very real job in learning from you. Because nearly all of us are in learning mode at one time or another (and some find themselves there at least as often as they are teaching), you undoubtedly have experience being an apprentice. Remember, and draw upon those experiences, as you think about the expectations you have of your apprentices.

Don't forget that apprentices can come from anywhere. They may already be in your company, but new to your group. They may be new to your kind of technology. They may be older than you. They may know more or less than you about other topics. They could be an intern, a temporary employee, a customer, or even your boss. You might have a long-term relationship with them that is clearly defined or you might just answer random questions from them as they arise.

I think of someone as my apprentice if I hear from them in one form or another more than once a day. You don't have to overly formalize the role just because you're getting regular questions; but if you're spending time training or supporting someone, it is good to consider ways to help them use your time well.

Whatever their circumstances coming in, all apprentices want two things: to get the information they need to be successful, and to do it as painlessly as possible.

WHAT DO YOU SUGGEST?

Think about ways you can help your apprentice along. You know your organization and its culture, what it values in its employees, and how things get done. What can you offer as suggestions for being successful and working with you?

One way to develop the advice you might give to your apprentice is to think about what they sometimes do that makes you crazy. Do any of these problems frustrate you?

- Not listening when you explain things
- Interrupting you too frequently, or in an annoying way
- Asking too many questions
- Not asking enough questions, because the apprentice just does things his own way
- Asking the same question over and over
- Failing to understand the first time you explain something
- Making poor decisions because the apprentice doesn't get the "big picture"
- Making mistakes even though you just told the apprentice what to do
- Failing to take ownership
- Coming to you with a problem, but without a suggested solution

Does that list sound about right? Keep going; I'm sure you have a few additional pet peeves, too.

Once you make your own list of what *doesn't* work for you (that is the easy part), make a list of what you actually *want* (this is a little harder).

Let's take the first problem as an example. Don't you hate it when your apprentice doesn't listen? They glaze over, fidget, or appear disinterested. Well, what are the behaviors of someone who appears to *really* be listening? It turns out they all do at least three things:

- **Take notes.** Did you know it is OK to tell your apprentice to take notes? Here's how you might say it:

  Hey, I'm going to be covering some information now that isn't well documented. You'll want to take notes so that you can get the details down exactly. One missed keystroke will be a problem. Do you have some place to write this down?

- **Paraphrase.** There is only one way to know for sure that the information you've been communicating is making it into your apprentice's head. You have to ask them to explain it back to you. We'll work on this in detail in Chapter 7, "Assessing Knowledge Transfer," but here's a really quick way to ask the apprentice to paraphrase what you've been teaching:

  Hey, I just covered a lot of detailed information. Why don't you read your notes back to me to make sure I've been clear? That way, I can help you make sure your notes are complete before you have to use them.

- **Ask well-thought-out questions.** We typically say, "Stop by any time, there are no dumb questions." That statement is actually two lies in a row. There are lots of times when you don't want to be interrupted, and there are plenty of dumb questions. We'll talk about how to reduce dumb questions in the next chapter, but I do like to be clear with my apprentices. Here's what I say:

The information that you need to do your job can't be figured out entirely on your own. If you don't get good at coming after the information by asking questions, you're going to fail. The folks who get up to speed the fastest are the ones who think about their questions and then ask them without worrying that they're going to look stupid. Asking well-thought-out questions is your key to success.

Think about how many of your frustrations would be reduced if your apprentice did these three things consistently. What else might you say to give good advice on how to be your apprentice? For example, we hate it when our apprentices refuse to cut the apron strings and take on the work without us. What are the *behaviors* of someone who does a good job of taking ownership?

- **Seek clarity on tasks.** You should be very clear in defining what you want them to do so they don't take off and do their own thing, or conversely, rely too heavily on you. Here's what I suggest:

  Hey, when you're assigned a task, it would really help me if you could take a quick minute to tell me what you understand the assignment to be (the deliverable), the timing for getting it done, and how you'll know it is good enough (success metric). Then, you can talk me through your plan for getting the job done. I'll give you any advice or guidance I can to make sure you're on track.

  The subtext is, "...then I expect you to do exactly what you outlined without much more of my help." In some situations, you may want or need to say that part out loud. Use your good judgment to decide when you need to be explicit.

- **Say what you already know.** It is common to teach people who have some experience in the subject you're covering. Let your apprentice know that you expect him to remind you about that experience whenever you're either over or under the mark. I'd say something like this:

I know you've had some background in this area. Please don't let me tell you things you already know, and speak up if I'm going over your head. That sort of feedback will help us use our time well. It is important that you don't hold back and just let me go in the wrong direction.

■ **Track what you've tried.** You can help your apprentice a lot better if he brings problems to you and tells you what he's already tried. By asking him to bring his attempted solutions, you're making it clear that you expect him to have tried something before coming to you and dumping it back in your lap. I might say this:

I'm glad to help you problem-solve. When you come to me with a problem, you need to have thought through a solution to the best of your abilities. Come prepared to say what you think. If you've already tried to solve the problem, you should track the options you have tried. Explaining what you have already done will help me check out the way you think. It will also help me offer new approaches.

Giving advice to your apprentice shouldn't sound like a lecture. Even though you're peers, you often have the upper hand simply because you have more experience. Don't forget that you're building a relationship as much as you're training your apprentice. It is a relationship that you'll invest in now, and over time, draw upon—often far more than you imagined. Your communication comes off best when you're clearly looking out for his best interest and the tone is one of support.

Once I've figured out the advice I want to give my apprentice (tailored for their experience and the demands of the job), I usually start off the conversation this way:

I've worked with a lot of people over the years in helping them get up to speed. I've noticed that some of them seem to get up to speed faster than others. There are some common ways they go after it. Would you like to hear about what I've seen work?

No apprentice would ever turn down an offer of help like that!

CONDUCT A FIRST MEETING

Now that you've thought through the roles and expectations of the three players, the manager, peer mentor, and apprentice, you'll want to put it together and get everyone on the same page. Organize a brief meeting very early on in the relationship (during the first day or two for a new employee) for the three of you to talk this over. If you're mentoring a new hire, you're going to say something like this:

> Hi, welcome. We're glad you're here. We've been thinking about you and have a plan to help you get up to speed. I'm going to be your mentor and you and I will work together in this way.... This is your manager. Here's how your relationship with him or her is going to work.... Because you are a new hire, we wanted to give you a training plan and some advice on how to get you started on the right foot around here. We also wanted to talk about the kinds of projects you'll be taking on and how we're going to stay in touch as you get up to speed.

That is basically the speech you got on your first day, wasn't it? I seriously doubt it. You probably got one more like this:

> Oh. Hey. I thought you weren't starting until next week. I'm sorry, what was your first name again? Right. Well, (yelling over his shoulder) Sarah! Do we have a place for.... I'm sorry, what was your name again? Right, Sarah! Do we have a place for Steve to sit? Listen, I think she's in her office down there. Go track her down and she'll get you set up. I have a meeting and then a plane to catch. We'll talk when I get back in a couple of days. Sorry we're so unorganized around here. OK, then, I've got to go!

Now, which scenario do you think would result in a more productive apprentice during the first week on the job and going forward?

Conduct a First Meeting very early on to set expectations and put together a few ground rules. Above all, let the apprentice know that joining your team is a great choice and that productivity and success are right around the corner. Tool 1-2 provides a checklist of items to discuss in your First Meeting.

Tool 1-2 First Meeting Worksheet

Purpose:

- Welcome the apprentice to the team, and/or to the new role.
- Establish clear roles and responsibilities for the manager, peer mentor, and apprentice (see the Manager and Peer Mentor Worksheet).
- Discuss the high-level team objectives (what the team is working on).
- Establish a role and general work goals for the apprentice (their piece of the team's work).
- Introduce the customized Training Plan.
- Discuss the peer mentor's and the manager's priorities in relation to project work and the plan for contingencies.
- Discuss a plan for ongoing communication.

In addition to the roles and responsibilities, what other topics should you cover in your first meeting?

1.

2.

3.

FIRST MEETING FOR SILO MENTORS

Should you have a First Meeting if you're not mentoring a new hire? Absolutely. The conversation won't start with the welcome speech but it will still have all of the other elements. This might even be more important when you're mentoring a co-worker that you've known for years. In that scenario, the First Meeting clarifies the manager's expectations of your role and "deputizes" you to teach what you know. This can help manage egos and ensure that you can focus on the work.

You can also have a First Meeting for someone who started six months ago. It starts out with, "We just read this really great book, and realized that we missed an important step in your orientation process. We'd like to rectify that now by clarifying a few things...."

Working off of the lists in Tool 1-2, here's a checklist for the silo mentor's First Meeting:

Tool 1-3 Silo Mentor's First Meeting Worksheet

- Establish roles and clarify whether the silo mentor is going to be actively pursuing his apprentices, or simply waiting for them to set up meetings and work through their training plan. Decide who is responsible for driving this relationship. Include any notes on the role of the manager (might be very limited).

- Establish learning goals for the apprentices so they know which specific skills they'll be learning from the silo mentor.

- Plan for regular communication with each other.

- Decide when you'll be done with this mentoring relationship. This usually comes when the apprentices can explain the key concepts from the specialty and take on the work associated with it. The expectation should be discussed in this meeting.

SUMMARY: PUTTING IT INTO PRACTICE

The good news is that you can get all of this done in not much more time than it took to read this chapter. Here's how the ideas would lay out in a workflow:

1. A new hire accepts offer, or the decision is made to train someone on a skill.

2. The manager asks someone to be a peer mentor.

3. The peer mentor (including silo mentors) and manager define their roles (20 minutes).

4. The peer mentor develops a customized training plan (20 minutes).

5. The manager, peer mentor, and apprentice have a first meeting (30 minutes).

6. The apprentice makes great progress and actually gets work done right away! (Saves hours in the first week alone.)

In Chapter 10, "Peer Mentoring in Practice," I'll put together all of the ideas in the book and show you how they work together.

FROM A MANAGER'S VIEW

Most of this book is written for peer mentors but managers may wonder what to look for in selecting effective peer mentors. Here are a few thoughts on that subject.

What are the characteristics of good peer mentors? How does a manager select the best person? Can anyone be a peer mentor? The short answer is that not everyone can or should be a peer mentor. Peer mentors need to meet two criteria:

They have to be competent and someone whose skills and attitude you want to replicate. You'd like more employees just like this one. How many people do you have teaching in your organization who may not be the best person to teach others, they just happen to be the one doing it? This is something for you to watch carefully. One of the benefits of being clear about asking specific people to be peer mentors is that you may also exclude some less desirable employees from filling that role.

They have to want to. Some people just dont want to be a mentor, either because they're afraid to help others for fear of losing their own job, they're antisocial, or they just don't feel like making the effort. People who aren't interested in being a mentor cannot be made into good mentors. You just need to find someone else.

Picking a peer mentor is a very individual decision. You won't find an all-purpose mentor test in this book. That said, here are several suggestions that can help you discover who may be a good mentor:

Try not to select by default. People who have done mentoring in the past, or are good at multiple projects, may have the right skills. They may also have very full plates. Or they may be burned out on mentoring.

Pick peer mentors who want to help others—preferably people who have some selfish motivation, such as an interest in being a manager some day or in shaping the future of their specialty. They might be anxious to take a vacation without a beeper, or interested in taking on a new role without bringing their old job along. Pick people who have a real motivation. They'll be more interested in taking the role seriously, and therefore better at it.

Plan to reward mentors for their efforts. Can you write it into their performance review, acknowledge the work in a team meeting, offer a small gift to show your appreciation, or at least say, "thank you?"

Divide up the job. As a manager, you can create a group of primary and a group of silo mentors. In some cases, you might decide you could be a silo mentor because you have the best grasp of particular skills.

Whatever guidelines you use to find a mentor, realize a manager's involvement needs to extend beyond choosing someone. Ideally, a manager will set the high-level goals of the training, be available as a support person for the mentor, regularly check in on the progress being made, and offer constructive feedback throughout the mentoring process.

WHEN YOU'RE THE APPRENTICE

You'll have a much better experience getting up to speed on your new role if you start with clear expectations. Ideally, your manager would make sure that everything in this chapter happens for you but if it doesn't, don't hesitate to go after the information yourself.

Ask for a First Meeting (see the "First Meeting" section earlier in this chapter) as soon as possible, even if you started your new role some time ago. Ask questions so that by the end of that meeting you are able to explain the following:

- The differences between the roles of your manager, your primary peer mentor, and any silo mentors

- The ways in which each of them can serve as a resource in helping you get up to speed, plus any constraints on their availability

- What they expect of you and any advice they can give you on how to get up to speed quickly

- Your mentor's expectation of the assigned goals' deliverables or the level of skill you will be able to demonstrate

- The typical timeline during which most people are apprenticed to their primary peer mentor (How long does it usually take to get up to speed?)

2

Managing Time and Communication

How do I stay in touch with my apprentice and still get my day job done?

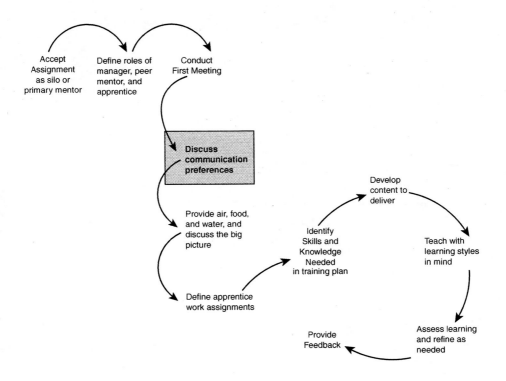

One of the greatest frustrations for peer mentors is that they just wish they had more time in the day to be available to their team-mates and still get through the stack of work in their inboxes. The constant drumbeat of e-mail, drive-by problem-solving, 30-minute quick questions, and general interruptions makes it a stretch to get anything else done. The answer is often just to work longer hours; daytime is for the team, and overtime is needed to stay current with your own work.

We perpetuate this drain on available work time by saying, "Stop by any time, there are no dumb questions." Yet, there are plenty of times that you don't want to be interrupted. This chapter has some tricks you can use to create some communication guidelines.

Making time for yourself starts with developing some awareness of your own preferences. You have to

1. Figure out what you do and do not want in the way of communication with your apprentices.
2. Then, ask for what you want.

That advice may sound simplistic, but it requires some thought, some attention to your own way of working, and some action on your part. You don't have to be at the mercy of your apprentices to be a great peer mentor. It would be better for everyone if you were clear about what works best and moved your encounters in that direction. By the end of this chapter you'll have the language and tools to help you set a few rules of engagement with your apprentices.

NOTICE WHAT'S HAPPENING NOW

Ever hear of the "boiling frog?" The story goes something like this: If you drop a frog in hot water, it will jump right out of the pan, but if you put a frog in cold water and gradually heat the water to boiling, the frog will stay in the pan and cook.

You're the frog. Somehow the water got really hot without you noticing. You're just about cooked.

When pressed, if you are like most of us, you have a hard time explaining where the time goes in a day. You're busy. You feel pressure to get through all of the work in front of you, but many times you will never actually get caught up. You'll go home every day with work undone. That makes taking time for your apprentices even more of a challenge.

There are many books and courses on time management, so I'm not going to try to work through all of the ways you could be more efficient. I do, however, want you to think about all of the *people* who take your time, and begin to manage them differently.

The first step to changing the way you manage your interactions is to start noticing how you currently spend your time and with whom. The Pay Attention exercise is a simple self-awareness exercise you can use to get a grip on your current situation. The idea is that until you can identify your current habits and the ways you already interact with your apprentices, it will be hard to move toward a better approach.

The following exercise will help you develop greater awareness of how your time is being used up. After working through this exercise, one of my clients, who is a vice president of sales for a software company, noticed nearly three hours every day simply evaporated. While he knew he was very busy with people lined up outside his door and was working long hours, he really couldn't account for his time. That worried him. Was he using his time to the best advantage of his team, or was he simply busy? This exercise helped him to be sure.

PAY ATTENTION EXERCISE

Start by printing your calendar every day and carrying it around with you. The calendar already includes your scheduled meetings. For all the time you have between meetings, note what you were doing. Don't worry about how you felt, or including too many details. Just try to document what was happening. Your notes will include the following types of information:

- Whom you interacted with
- The type of interaction (meeting, stopping by, calling, or sending an e-mail)
- A couple of words describing the topic of the interaction
- The amount of time you spent on the interaction
- Solid blocks of time working on your own tasks

ANALYZE THE DATA

You should be able to gather all of this information in a few minutes per day. Mark up your daily calendars for at least a week. Then go back and spend 10–15 minutes to analyze your findings.

1. Put a "+" next to all the items that were expected, valuable, *and* planned for.

2. Put a "–" next to all the items that were anything else. This is the step in which you will notice all of the times you are interrupted by others, had to spend time fighting fires, taking calls, answering questions, and so on.

3. Count the number of interruptions and add up the amount of time devoted to any one person or one topic. Note how many of those have a minus sign next to them. Those minus signs highlight the areas of concern.

4. Note the blocks of time where you were (mostly) uninterrupted or spent more of your time on planned activities. See what you can do to expand on those.

Now you have a picture of why you do or do not get your job done and have identified your apprentices (if that wasn't already clear). You also have a snapshot of your interaction problem and can think about it further.

- Who is interrupting you most?
- Who is not on the list and should be (ever clean up a mess made by an apprentice who didn't ask for help)?
- What kinds of information do you have that bring people to you? Are you a silo mentor without realizing it?

■ How much of your time is spent in the same unplanned activities every day? If the same activities appear on your list often, you should plan time to take on those challenges.

This exercise always provides my clients with a snapshot that is neither biased nor emotional. It simply provides the facts. With those facts in hand, the individuals can begin taking action to improve both their own productivity and the value they can add to their teams. If you haven't ever done this sort of exercise before, make an appointment with yourself for first thing next Monday. Print out your calendar and get started. Make the morning appointment a reoccurring one for the next one to two weeks to keep you on track with your data collection. Then do the analysis. You'll be glad you did.

IDENTIFYING YOUR PREFERENCES

Once you take a hard look at your current situation, you can start to make some changes that will improve your productivity. The first thing to consider is the communication guidelines you want to put into place. They will help you improve the consistency of information flow and reduce the thrashing around that takes so much time.

Look back at the calendar from your Pay Attention Exercise and make a list of the people who use you as a resource most often. How do they contact you? How many of them just stop by? How many e-mail you? How many call you? How often do you see each person? Are they bringing you information, or are they asking you to solve problems? How many are peers? How many are managers or people outside your team?

Now look at this list and think about those who are the biggest pains in the neck and those who are the easiest to work with or bring you important, timely information. Your gut feelings here tell you a lot. I'll bet it isn't difficult at all to put people into one camp or the other. Now, try to think about the differences in the way people from each of the groups interact with you. Think about when and how they contact you; how they interrupt you; what kind of preparation they do before arriving, and so on. Do you see some differences?

Thinking about these differences will give you some insight into your own preferences. Knowing those preferences is crucial to improving your situation. Understanding your preferences is what I meant by developing your self-awareness. You need to be able to articulate your preferences as a first step in getting more of what works for you. After all, you're the finite resource stepping up to help others. You should be able to set some ground rules to make your time with them work for you.

TELLING ABOUT YOURSELF

The Pay Attention exercise will help you sort out what works for you and what doesn't work for you. From there, you have to start to articulate some specific behaviors that you'd like to see from your apprentices. Here's how the conversation is going to sound:

> Hey, I've enjoyed (or, I'm looking forward to) spending time helping you get up to speed. Because we (will) spend time together every day, I thought I'd give you some ideas about the best way to get the most information from me as quickly as possible. For starters, I get a ton of e-mail every day and I'd like to let you in on the secret to getting a quicker response from me (see the "Handshake E-mail" section). I'd also like to tell you how to best interrupt me so that you have my full attention (see below for guidance). Finally, I want to tell you about how my day flows, so you'll know the best times to stop by and the times to avoid unless it is an emergency (see more ideas below).

A word of warning, please don't use this or any other exercise in this book to make life *more* difficult for your apprentices. The advice you're giving is truly about helping them get what they're after faster, not putting the apprentices in an unnecessary box. Notice that the tone in this language is all about helping your apprentice understand you and the combination to your lock. Right now they may come at you with a sledgehammer, or never even attempt to open the lock. Because they should be accessing you regularly, why not just give them the combination?

PERSONAL PREFERENCES

I've been thinking about this for years so I have a pretty long list of personal preferences that I'll share with you. When I'm the mentor, I will choose a handful of thoughts from this mental list. The preferences I choose depend on the length and purpose of the relationship. I share my selections with my apprentice early in the relationship. A more extensive list makes sense for a longer term, more formally assigned relationship. For those who ask for my help sporadically, I might only pick one preference to share. For me, that would be my preference on being interrupted.

Here are some of my preferences:

- E-mail is better than voice-mail, unless I'm traveling.

- While I have several voice mailboxes (home, mobile, office) I prefer to have all of my voice-mails on my cell phone when I'm traveling. If I am not traveling, please use e-mail. Please don't leave the same voice-mail on all three of my numbers.

- I get up very early and do most of my big picture planning, writing, and thinking between 6 and 10 A.M. It is my most productive and concentrated work time. Please don't stop by between those hours, unless it is an emergency (and that definitely means don't loiter in my cube and tell me about your weekend).

- After 10 A.M., I'm available to help you the rest of the day.

- If you need to interrupt me, the best way to do it is simply to stand in my doorway. Don't cough, pace, talk to my office mate, flop in my chair, wave your finger and ask if I have a second, or in any other way try to make your presence known. I'll already know you're there, because I have good peripheral vision. Just stand there and give me a few seconds to look up at you and invite you in. I promise I will acknowledge you in less than 30 seconds, but I have to finish what I'm doing first, so I don't lose my thought.

- You'll know it is a bad time to interrupt me if I put the crime scene tape over my cube door. If you see that, please send me an e-mail and don't interrupt me unless (describe an appropriate emergency worthy of an interruption at that time). I'm already concentrating on something else.

- If you think you might need more than 15 minutes of my time for a quick question, I'd really appreciate you send me an e-mail or set up an appointment, rather than just stop by.

- By 4 P.M., I've been working 11 hours or so and I'm starting to fall apart. With that in mind, please don't bring me a hard problem late on a Friday. I might end up crying and running away. Late in the day is a good time to talk to me socially or do light brainstorming—not diving deep on a crisis.

- If I am here working after 6 P.M. or on a weekend, I am trying to get caught up on my own work. I'm not available to you unless we've scheduled time in advance. It's nothing personal, but it would be best if you didn't even say hello.

- NOTE: Because we're peers, I can't really make you do any of these things, but I will say that if you do, you're going to get a much faster and more satisfactory response from me.

HANDSHAKE E-MAIL

My most important preference has to do with the biggest time sink of my day: e-mail. We use e-mail in the place of human interaction, because it is so much easier to fire off a message than it would be to track a colleague down and have a conversation. With some caveats, this works as designed. One of the big problems with e-mail is that in using it to pass work back and forth, we lose the clarity that comes from the connection people make in person.

In person, you might find yourself handing over a document to be edited, and the editor making a commitment to getting it done by saying, "I'll have this to you by Tuesday." You'd shake hands on the agreement and both of you would expect the work to be done and back in your hands by Tuesday. In e-mail, it doesn't work the same way. When you want something done, you send a note into cyberspace and then many times just sit around and hope what you asked for gets done. The approach shown in Tool 2-1, is designed to put the handshake into the e-mails between you and your apprentice.

Tool 2-1   Handshake E-mail Worksheet

 Answer these questions when you give your apprentice advice on how to improve the quality and responsiveness of your replies.

- Is there a difference between your interpretation when a recipient is on the "To:" line versus the "CC:" line?
- What would you like to see in the "Subject:" line to help you sort through your e-mail?
- What suggestions do you have for developing the body of the e-mail?
    - Do you prefer anything specific in the first part of the body (such as a clear statement of what you want)?
    - Do you prefer bullets or paragraphs? Detailed content or quick synopses?
    - How long is too long for an e-mail?
    - Is there anything you'd like to see in the closing statements (such as timing, alternative resources/references, etc.)?
- If someone sends an e-mail to you, what is your usual response time, and how will they know if they should resend the message?
- Is there anything else you can offer in the way of suggestions for sending you e-mails that will help you to be as responsive as possible?

Many of you get more than 100 e-mails every day. You might spend upwards of 20 percent of your time wading through them. Have you ever thought about the differences between a well-written e-mail and one that is difficult or impossible to get through? Here is one way to explain e-mail preferences to your apprentice. You might say the following:

I get a ton of e-mail. When you send me an e-mail, I want you to know that I'll be a lot faster in responding and getting you what you need, if you follow this format:

- Only put me on the "To:" line if you absolutely need me to read the whole email.

  If I am included on the "To:" line too often, and the message isn't that important to me, I begin to ignore messages from the senders.

- If I am on the "CC:" line, it means the choice of whether to skim the e-mail or read it thoroughly is up to me.

- Please put something specific about the content of the mail on the subject line. For example, say, "Weekly status report for the ACME project," not "Please read!"

- If you need me to do something specific for you, put my name on the "To:" line and the word "ACTION" in the subject line (followed by the specific content noted above).

- In the body of the e-mail, write what you want from me and when it is due to you in the first three lines so that I can see them in Microsoft Outlook preview mode. Don't make me wade through the whole message to figure out what you want.

- Use the rest of the body of the e-mail to provide information that will give me context and help me to help you. Please use bullets wherever possible, because they're easier for me to read.

- I hate "e-novels." I'm going to warn you that I have a habit of deleting e-mails that are more than one screen long. Sometimes I don't even read them. Often the messages are too long because the topic is either too complicated for e-mail, or you just haven't cleaned up your thinking enough to be ready to share it with me. Please make an effort to tighten up your thinking and edit your message before hitting "Send!"

- If you send me an action item, I will always plan to reply within one business day and tell you one of three things (here's where the "handshake" comes in):

  - Yes, you can count on me to do it.

  - No, sorry, I want to warn you that because I have other higher priorities, I am not going to be able to do this. You should make another plan. I know this may sound harsh but it is much better than making you wait to see that I never really had a prayer of getting to it!

  - Yes, I'll do it but it will be later than you asked. Here is what I can offer....

- As my peer, you never get to use the "!" or the flag in Outlook!

- If I don't reply within one business day, it is because, for some reason, I didn't get to your e-mail. This is rare, but possible, so when you don't get a reply, please resend your message. Don't wait two weeks and then get mad at me because I didn't reply. Also, don't resend the message every hour. Resending your message on the second day always does the trick.

Now, remember that these are *my* preferences. I've thought a lot about them over the years and I know that these work for me. Your list may be identical to mine, or you may have very different ideas. There is no right answer. As long as you're within the bounds of professionalism and good taste, you can edit the following list of preferences as you see fit (subject to feedback from your team):

- You're not a morning person at all and the thought of having a perky colleague pop into your office at 9 A.M. (unless a triple latte for you is involved) makes you want to puke. Your best time for solving hard problems might be 5 P.M. when I'm headed for the showers.

- You'd rather that no one stop by because you really have trouble with interruptions. It is much easier and often faster if you get an e-mail first. You're on e-mail all the time so this works great.

- You have a specific definition of an emergency (such as, when a system is down or the building is on fire) and when that happens, all of your preferences are void.

- You have specific ways the "!" and the flag in Outlook should be used.

- You wear headphones to say that you're off limits (or, the headphones don't mean anything but you'd rather not be tapped on the shoulder when you're wearing them).

- When your office door is closed, you're on the phone with your spouse or taking a nap and don't want to be interrupted (or, it doesn't mean anything at all, just knock and come in).

- You have times when you prefer others to use or not use your cell phone, Instant Messenger, radio phone, pager, home phone, smoke signals, carrier pigeon, and so on.

- You'd really like to be able to take your coat off and get your first cup of coffee before anyone tries to ask you a question.

- Mondays (or the first day of the quarter, or full moon, or Tuesdays) are really bad for you because of some rolling commitment. On those days you'd really appreciate being left alone.

- You have to leave to pick up your kids or catch a bus at a certain time every evening. You'd really appreciate not being caught for a quick question one minute before that time.

- You prefer a lot of written material because you like to think about things in depth. Long e-mails are better than long conversations for you.

- I have one client whose workstation is permanently set to face away from the door, and he hates being sneaked up on. He has put a rear view mirror on his cube wall and tells his apprentices to make sure they stand in the path of the mirror to get his attention.

SAYING WHAT WORKS FOR YOU

Do any of these situations and preferences sound familiar? I'm sure you could add to the list. It may be helpful to start with what drives you nuts, and then work backward to figure out what you want. Whatever it takes, the point is that in thinking about your preferences and sharing them with others on your team, you are much more likely to get interactions that work for you.

Some people worry, though, that listing their preferences is too prescriptive. I've heard it said like this: "It is pretty presumptuous of me to tell others precisely how to communicate with me. They're going to think I'm a little full of myself, aren't they?" That kind of response isn't my experience at all. Instead, apprentices are grateful to have a roadmap to follow. Wouldn't you be? If you don't tell people the best way to communicate with you, how do they figure it out? Trial and error, that's how, and the error part is hard on everyone. In a perfect world, both you and your apprentices would just know how to interact effectively, but they clearly don't or you wouldn't be frustrated.

You may have never thought about how you want the interactions with your apprentice to flow. Just thinking about what you want and what you don't want is a big step forward. Then, you have to tell your apprentice and get him or her on board. If you don't, some will figure out your preferences over time. Some will never figure them out. This can make interaction with you as troubling for your apprentice as it is for you. Why not just be clear up front?

If you find the list too long, or it feels to nit-picky, choose the top three things that would help your apprentice to communicate with you most effectively. Bring your apprentices and co-workers in on your secrets, and you'll make life easier on everyone.

ASK YOUR APPRENTICE

After you discuss your communication preferences, it makes perfect sense to ask your apprentice what works best for him (see Tool 2-2). It will be important for you to go first, however. Just as these may be new thoughts for you, your apprentice will not likely be able to express preferences without first hearing some examples. This is all information you and your apprentice would likely discover over time, but in the interest of efficiency, it pays to clear up your preferences from the very beginning. Because your apprentice is likely to be a mentor some day soon, you'll have done the apprentice and your organization a favor by showing that it is acceptable to think about preferences and ask for communication along specific lines.

Tool 2-2 Telling About Yourself Worksheet

Note
Discuss this during your first one-on-one meeting with your apprentice.

How do you want the apprentice to interact with you? Write down your preferences even if they seem minor. The more information you give your apprentice, the better the result you can expect, for both of you. Also include any advice for interacting with others on the team. After you have expressed your preferences, ask your apprentice to identify how he or she would like to interact with you.

1.

2.

3.

4.

5.

SETTING UP "MENTORING TIME"

Another way to manage your interactions and communication with your apprentice is to set aside a brief, but regular, chunk of time for the two of you to get together. This reserved time is especially important for primary mentors, but is useful for silo mentors, as well. For a new hire, you might agree to meet for 15 minutes twice a day, just to check in. For an experienced employee who is learning a new skill from you, 20 minutes once a week might be sufficient. You pick the time that works for you. Encourage your apprentice to be prepared with questions that have come up since you last met.

This regular one-on-one is an opportunity for you to go over assigned work, check on quality, troubleshoot any issues that have arisen, discuss future projects, and answer any questions that have piled up. While it creates a time for regular communication that is beneficial for any employee, it is especially important if your apprentice is "extreme" in interacting with you. For example, you might have an apprentice who could be described as chatty, meaning that you see and hear from him too often. When this apprentice runs into a problem or has a question, there seems to be a spring in his chair shooting him into the air toward your cube. It is rare that you go an hour without some interaction with this type of apprentice.

Or, you could have an apprentice who acts more like a mole. This type of apprentice *never* comes to get you. He believes that asking questions is an imposition or a show of weakness and that if he just churns on the problem long enough, he is bound to find the solution on his own. He doesn't even seem to mind being stuck. It's all part of a day's work.

Both types of apprentices are a problem, in their own way. Setting up a regular time to meet will help them level out their interactions to something between the two extremes. In other words, you'll see them at regular intervals that are somewhat within your control. Still, there are times when they will need you between meetings. You don't want them to stay away because they don't have an appointment. What do you do then?

WHAT TO DO BETWEEN MEETINGS?

For both the chatty apprentice and the mole, you need to clarify how and when to check in with you between meetings. For example, if you're talking to the chatty apprentice, you could suggest holding all questions until the next meeting, *unless he gets stuck and can't go on.* If stuck, the apprentice should spend at least 30 minutes (more or less, as you see fit) trying to solve the problem before coming to you. When he arrives at your desk, the first question you should ask is, "What did you do to try to solve the problem on your own?" Listen for the logic employed in trying to solve the problem, and give feedback or additional ideas based on what he says. If he is *slowed down but still productive*, you might ask him to do an hour of problem-solving before coming to get you, depending on your own availability or the importance of the project. If he is *just wondering* what you think about something, or has general questions, you can make it clear that those items should wait for your next scheduled meeting.

For the mole, you have to use the same techniques, but with a twist. If the mole is *stuck and can't go on*, you have to say, "You're only *allowed* to be stuck for one hour (again, more or less, at your discretion) before you *have* to come and get help." You normally can't afford to have your apprentice stalled for an indefinite amount of time before returning to productivity, and should say so. If the mole is *slowed down but still productive*, you might allow two hours or a half day for him to figure out how to improve efficiency. After that, tell him that you expect a knock on your door, not more churning. A mole will never *just wonder*.

You can also use a system like this to explain when problems must be brought to you immediately. You might say, "Please don't stop by before 9 A.M. unless...," and then give the most common emergency situations in which your apprentice will likely need your help. As with everything else, don't overdo the controls on this idea. You definitely do not want to communicate that you're too unavailable. Your apprentice needs backup, and you don't want to hear about real problems too late to be able to take care of them. With a little discussion, you can strike that balance.

WRITING QUICK STATUS REPORTS

People generally say that they hate status reports for two main reasons: Writing them takes too long and no one reads them anyway. True? One of my clients said that she wrote her status report in Spanish for six months to see if anyone would notice—and no one did! No wonder people hate them. If those are the main problems, they are worth fixing because status reports provide a vital link between mentor and apprentice. They also provide a record of the relationship that can be used to keep a manager up to speed and document the successes of your efforts.

TEN MINUTES TO WRITE ONE SCREEN IN E-MAIL

You and your apprentice can start by developing a plan for the week's training and tasks every Monday morning. Then, after working all week, ask your apprentice to write a status report before heading home on Friday. This is where we fix the first problem—that it takes too long to write. Tell your apprentice that he is not allowed to spend more than 10 minutes writing the status report, which may not be more than one screen in e-mail. Short and sweet is the only option.

The status report could be requested by you, the manager, or a silo mentor. It could be reviewed by all three, as well. Just agree in advance on how this will work. Everyone has a stake in making sure your apprentice is making progress. Remember, you're not asking him to justify his existence; you're just looking for a snapshot that isn't too painful to produce. Tool 2-3 provides a worksheet your apprentice can use to construct a useful status report.

The first item on the worksheet demonstrates that your apprentice has been working from a plan, rather than just being busy. The second bullet encourages accountability. You want your apprentice to think about specific results and take responsibility for completing them as planned. The third bullet is about teamwork and support. It is the place that peer mentors are most often presented with new information. The apprentice who writes down a concern isn't meekly whispering, "I need help"—he is pulling out the bullhorn and screaming, "I NEED HELP!!" and that gets the attention of a mentor in a surprisingly effective way. The fourth bullet is a future plan that, of course, becomes the first bullet in next week's status report.

Tool 2-3 Status Report Worksheet

- What did you say you would do? (Drives goal setting)

- What did you actually do? (Drives accountability)

- What issues or problems are you having? What do you need help with? (Drives teamwork)

- What are your plans for next week?

REPLY EVERY WEEK

Now we have to solve the second problem I mentioned at the beginning of this section—that no one reads the reports. As the mentor you have to commit to reading and replying to status reports, first thing on Monday morning. It won't be too difficult to do, because the status report is only one screen in e-mail. You'll spend less than two minutes reading it and another two or three minutes making a couple of notes in your reply. Common responses may be

- "Your plan for this week looks good, but I'd do the third thing first because..."

- "I didn't know you were having that problem. I'll make a call on it before noon today."

- "I noticed that you got through everything on last week's list! The 'widget' you built helped Sarah finish her project one day early."

For some of you, writing a status report is already part of your job. Your manager may already ask for one in order to roll up information for his or her boss. If that is the case, you may still choose to use this idea, but be sure that it isn't redundant. Remember, the intent of this tool is to improve the flow of information, not to create another bureaucratic layer.

If you use this template and process, don't forget that your manager would probably love to be copied on the reply to your apprentice's report. Your reply will provide a quick snapshot of the progress. As a side benefit, you'll look very organized and productive yourself.

SAMPLE STATUS REPORT

Here's an example of a corporate trainer's status report, to give you an idea of the level of detail that has worked for others:

What I planned for this week:

- Complete the "Getting to Know Event" assessment and load on the LMS.

- Complete a first draft of the Juniper LRT Trainer Etiquette and Reference Guide.
- Deliver Add BI Web Parts & My Site portal training for the Sales Development Group.
- Conduct my first BI Tool Live Remote training.
- Help in the material development of the "Concepts of Buying" course.
- Define tasks, agenda, and exercises for each day of the Live Remote Training.

What I did:

- Completed the Getting to Know Event Assessment and loaded on LMS.
- Still finishing the first draft of the Juniper LRT training Reference guide. It'll be in by Monday.
- Delivered training on My Site and added BI Web parts to Sales group.
- Delivered BI Tool Live Remote training.
- Created and posted a Live Remote Training schedule on the portal.
- Defined the training user logon profiles and creation requirements.
- Defined refreshing Evant training data and scheduled testing.

Issues/problems I need help with:

- I'm having trouble getting sponsorship for the new customer service program. I've had no reply from Mike, Alex, or Sarah. Could you check in with them?
- I need a contact in the support organization to gather requirements. Who should I call?

Plans for next week:

- Finish the first half of the development of the Evant LRT materials.
- Create and load BI LRT bytes on the portal.
- Test refreshed data and newly created logon profiles.

■ Start the development of the invitation and tracking methods and procedures for Associate's training participation.

STATUS REPORTS ALL AROUND

Now, if you've just read the previous section and are wondering whether this status report template works beyond the mentor/apprentice relationship, the answer is a resounding yes. As an example, I have a client with about 180 employees who took the Peer Mentoring Workshop at roughly the same time. Their founder and CEO decided that the company could stand a little improvement in the way they communicated among teams. He made it a policy that every single employee (from himself all the way to the summer intern) would write a status report every Friday, using the guidelines presented in the workshop: Work on it for no more than 10 minutes, write no more than one screen in e-mail, answer the four questions listed in Tool 2-3.

Every employee could "subscribe" to the status reports of the people they wanted to track. For instance, a project manager might track the status of a person who is scheduled to join his project two weeks out, to see if there is anything that could get in the way. Employees were also encouraged to "unsubscribe" when the need to see a particular person's status report ended. No one was allowed to send their status report to anyone else without that person requesting it, and sending to a group distribution list was not allowed; thus the number of status reports that any one person would read was kept to a handful. This procedure created a regular flow of information that was short enough to be read regularly—something that is rare for any form of status report. This company benefited from an increase in accountability and teamwork, plus far fewer surprises.

HELPING YOUR APPRENTICE ATTEND MEETINGS SUCCESSFULLY

How many times have you told an apprentice, "Hey, you should come to this meeting. *It'll be good for you.*"

It isn't a bad idea to invite apprentices to meetings, but it could be a huge waste of time, unless you also prepare them for the meeting. For example, you probably already tell your apprentice about the purpose of the meeting (why was it scheduled, how often, what kinds of information is shared, what kinds of decisions are made). You probably also give a rundown of the attendees, their roles, their priorities, or top business issues, and so on. These items provide context for the meeting, and are pretty common. I'd also like to suggest you add in a few more details.

PROVIDE SOME LANGUAGE

Vocabulary is a big issue. Every organization has jargon, acronyms, inside jokes, and tribal knowledge that provides the backdrop for these meetings. Learning these bits of information is a significant hurdle to being able to participate fully. You can jump start this process by thinking about the vocabulary that is likely to be used in the meeting and explaining the definition of some of the terms. Even if you can only cover a handful of terms before the meeting starts, and even if you cover them as you are walking to the conference room together, it will help. Understanding at least some of the terminology makes it much more likely that your apprentice will be able to follow the conversation and learn, instead of getting lost immediately.

GIVE THEM A ROLE

Next, think about giving the apprentice a "job" during the meeting. For instance, if my apprentice has industry expertise or just joined us from another part of the company, I might encourage him to ask questions during the meeting and gather enough information to develop and share an opinion on the spot. Or, I might ask him to sit quietly, but still seek to develop an opinion to share with me afterward. In either case, I love to hear what people who are fresh to a situation have to say. As far as I'm concerned, apprentices sitting in on meetings are *not yet part of the problem*. That makes them an interesting addition to the meeting. Sometimes your apprentice will be so green that the only appropriate job he can do is take note of the unfamiliar terms or acronyms used during the meeting. When that is the case, spend a little time after the meeting developing his vocabulary for the next time he sits in.

ANATOMY OF A GOOD PROBLEM-SOLVING QUESTION

You might wonder why there is a section on problem-solving in a chapter that is about communication and time management. In my experience, asking for help in problem-solving is one of the main reasons that apprentices check in with their peer mentors. Helping apprentices to problem-solve is one of the most time-consuming tasks peer mentors face. Have you ever had someone barge into your office and burst into a gush of frustration and confusion that, in the end, was just a simple troubleshooting problem? You have to drag all of the information out of him just to figure out what is going on.

Sometimes an apprentice will bomb in, run through their thinking on the question, and then, after a "light bulb" goes off, they answer their own question—without you ever having to say a word. You mutter under your breath as he turns to leave, "That was neat, but next time could you answer you own question in the hallway? It is kind of distracting...."

Those are two examples of what I call *dumb questions*. I think they're dumb because no thought was put into the question before engaging the mentor. In both instances, the apprentices are doing their thinking on your time, and that is something you shouldn't have to endure. It is unprofessional, really, and yet your apprentice may never have thought about how it affects you. You have an opportunity to guide him in preparing questions before asking them.

Here's an example of a poorly prepared question:

> I've been working forever trying to fix the defect that Joe found on Project X so we can fix it. I can't find anything to help me. No one else is around. I'm going nuts. Can you help me?

Here's an example of a better question:

Do you have 10–15 minutes to help me figure out how to fix the defect Joe submitted on Product X? It is now classified as "urgent." We have a premier customer whose application has been down for two hours because of it. So far, I've looked in the documentation online and searched on these keywords.... I'm able to reproduce the problem, but can't figure out where it is coming from. I asked Bob to help me, and he said he could look at it in an hour but I don't think it can wait. I've also checked in with Joe to see if he has any ideas, but we're stumped. I'm thinking of heading down this path..., unless you have any other ideas. What do you think?

WHAT MAKES A GOOD QUESTION?

Imagine how much faster you can get engaged in the problem if all of the important information is presented quickly and clearly. What are the bits of information you want to hear right away when someone brings you a problem to solve? You could probably rattle off a list of diagnostic questions. If you can capture that list and provide it to your apprentice, he will be much better organized the next time he needs help.

The following are some examples of the kinds of information that you might like your apprentice to prepare in advance. Think about how the information provided by each of the questions will help you get to resolution faster. The question you might want your apprentice to answer is in bold. The reason that question may be helpful to you is in the parentheses.

- **How much time do you think you'll need from me?** (As your mentor, I need to decide whether or not to stop doing what I'm already doing.)
- **Provide a description of the problem in a sentence or two.** (I'd rather not have to listen to you wander around in circles trying to figure out how best to describe the problem.)

- **How big is the crisis?** (I need to know the urgency of the problem and the impact it has on the project or the people involved.)

- **How long has the problem been going on?** (If a process or procedure used to work and doesn't work now, it is different than if it never worked.)

- **What changed that might have caused the problem?** (I need to think about the potential for unexpected consequences of other actions.)

- **What would you like from me?** (Am I giving advice, providing a sounding board, supporting you emotionally, or taking action?)

- **What did you expect to happen?** (I'd like to see where you were going.)

- **What happened?** (I'd like to hear you explain what you saw.)

- **What have you already tried to do to solve the problem?** (I expect you to have tried something and then I want to listen to the logic you employed so I can coach you for the next time a problem arises.)

- **Who else is working on it and what are they doing?** (If any of our best people are already working on the problem, then I need to stay focused on what I'm already doing, rather than jumping in on your issue.)

- **When does the problem need a resolution?** (If there is time, it would be better for me to finish what I'm doing before getting involved.)

Are there any other bits of information that you would like to hear when an apprentice brings a problem to you? Add those to this list. Then, think about the order in which you'd like to have this information presented. For example, do you want to know the level of crisis first? Maybe you don't need to know if anyone else is working on it. The list should reflect the approach you typically take in solving problems. Once you've customized the list, you can start using it to improve your work as a troubleshooter/problem-solver.

Tool 2-4 is a "menu" of pieces of information that you might like
to get from your apprentice. Take a few minutes to select those
you'd like to receive, and put them in the order in which you'd like
to hear them.

Tool 2-4   Anatomy of a Problem-Solving Question Worksheet

___ How much time do you need?

___ Provide a concise description of the problem.

___ Did the process or procedure ever work?

___ What would you like from me (advice, sounding board, support)?

___ What did you expect to happen?

___ What happened?

___ What have you tried to do to solve the problem?

___ Who else is working on the problem?

___ How big is the crisis (urgency, impact)?

___ When does the problem need a resolution?

___ _____

___ _____

___ _____

___ _____

PROBLEM SOLVING: MAKING IT WORK

One of my clients is a manufacturing facility in Beaverton, Oregon. They had a bit of a disconnect between the engineers who design the manufacturing processes (functioning as the silo peer mentors) and the operators who run the equipment on the shop floor (the apprentices who needed their help). The engineers were frustrated because they felt the operators weren't asking for help consistently. When they did ask for help, it would come in a seemingly incoherent fashion. From the operator's perspective, the engineers treated them like they were stupid and weren't helpful when asked.

I asked the engineers to describe the kinds of information that they want to receive when an operator calls for help and they came up with their version of the list in Tool 2-4. It took about five minutes to work through the list and this is what they came up with:

Employees should use a standard format to ask problem-solving questions. Use the format below to ensure the quickest response and the most learning.

1. Estimate how long it may take to answer the question and ask if the peer mentor has that much time available at the moment.

2. Give a clear, brief description of the problem.

3. Say how long the problem has been going on.

4. Help prioritize the issue based on how much scrap it is creating and whether it has stopped production or just slowed it down.

5. Outline what ideas you or anyone else has tried so far.

6. What does the MPI (the manual) say?

7. Explain whether it relates to anything else you know about the situation or equipment (e.g., notes from the machine log, or experiences on other machines).

8. Say whether you have any ideas on what should be done to fix the problem.

When it was done, the operators looked at the list and said, "Is that all I have to do to get a straight answer?" Up to that point, they had felt very unsure about the best way to approach the engineers, and had avoided it, whenever possible, to save themselves embarrassment. They were so excited to finally get this kind of direction that they published small cards with the list on them and taped the cards to the phones on the shop floor. From then on, when they had a problem and needed to call the engineers, they could go to the phone, think through the questions to get their thoughts in order, and then pick up the phone. They said it made them feel smarter because they weren't as intimidated when they had to call an engineer.

Boeing used this idea in a similar way with their 737 assembly line, but instead of posting the list of required information on the phone, they laminated cards and attached them to the security badge lanyards employees wore around their necks. Here's the list that Boeing uses:

Problem-Solving Questions

1. Describe the problem in a sentence or two.
2. Where is the problem located?
3. What may have caused the problem?
4. How long has this been going on?
5. How have you tried to fix it?
6. Who else is working on it and what are they doing?
7. What do you suggest?
8. What do you want me to do?

A Microsoft software development team created this list:

Problem-Solving Questions

1. Tell me how much time you think you'll need from me and what you want me to do.
2. Tell me the severity and the priority of the problem.
3. State the problem in a sentence or two.
4. Say what you think caused the problem.
5. Describe what you thought would happen.
6. Say what have you already tried to do to solve the problem.
7. Say what you think should be done next.

Each of these lists is similar in some ways, and by customizing them to the work environment, they're much more useful to the new apprentice.

Once you have decided what you want in the way of a well-thought-out question, you can plan to introduce it into your world. If you work in a manufacturing setting, you can readily use the ideas described above. If you work in a more traditional office setting, here are a couple of ideas:

- Put your list in a one-page document with a little space between each line item and then post one copy outside your cube at eye level. Maybe, when your apprentice is standing in the hall waiting for you to get off the phone, he will spend a few minutes looking at your list and thinking about the problem. If he wanders away after thinking for a minute, the document may have helped him solve the problem without your help!

- Keep 20 copies of the document in a file on your desk. When someone comes in and starts into a problem-solving question, just pull out two copies of the list, one for each of you. Work your way through the list and ask all of the questions in the order in which they appear on the page. When your apprentice notices that you got to the resolution faster, he will ask for a copy of this neat tool and of course, you'll be glad to oblige because you have plenty more where that came from.

- Come right out and explain that you read a book that had this idea that your apprentice could use to make things go better. No need to keep it a secret.

- During a team meeting, ask your colleagues to help you customize the list I've provided and then talk about how you might use it to improve problem-solving for the whole team.

COMMUNICATING FROM A DISTANCE

Today, it is common to have peer mentors transferring knowledge to people who work on another floor, in another ZIP code, or on another continent. I wish I had a nickel for every time I was asked, "What's the magic bullet for mentoring from a distance?" The answer isn't difficult, but it isn't very popular either. The answer is to do everything in this book, starting with clearly defining the best way to stay in touch. Do it consistently. Do it with the same level of rigor with which you'd manage any other project. In this case the output is a trained, independent, productive, happy apprentice. You're building that happy apprentice, not across the cube wall, but across the world. Taking on that challenge without setting up the relationship in a disciplined way is going to leave you wanting.

The importance of being disciplined in setting up the relationship is especially evident when you are mentoring outsource partners in other countries, because in many cases your business hours don't overlap. One of my clients tells about how he and his colleague in Bangalore, India, manage their relationship. Each of them agrees to a twice-weekly "off hours" phone call to work through content. These calls are typically late at night for one of them, and in the wee hours of the morning for the other. They carefully prepare for those calls to make them as productive as possible. Still, there are inevitably times when they need to reach each other outside of those meetings. They both agreed to share cell phone numbers so that they could be reached outside of business hours. In order to make this work, they talked over the sorts of issues that would warrant a call. They defined an emergency as a problem that would slow or stop the production line for more than 30 minutes. They also agreed to turn their phones off when they weren't available; for example, when they were sleeping. With this agreement, each could comfortably call the other at any hour of the day or night and know that there'd be no negative repercussions. It made it safe to exchange a lot of information, and kept their relationship strong.

A client from Nike's U.S. sales force shared another approach. He works in a different region than his apprentice, so they almost never see each other in person. Both of them travel often and keep very fluid calendars, because they have to respond to their clients' changing needs. He has his apprentice call him every morning at 6 A.M. Central Time, regardless of where either of them happens to be, because he knows that is the only time he is consistently available. He said the call generally wakes him up and there is a little fumbling as a result of that, but at least it is a dependable time for him to talk. An early morning phone call may not sound like your cup of tea, but it works for them and is a great example of the kind of creativity that distant mentors and apprentices need to use.

The issue of mentoring from a distance is addressed in greater depth in Chapter 9, "Peer Mentoring from a Distance."

SUMMARY: PUTTING IT INTO PRACTICE

If you're going to be a peer mentor while still doing your day job, then you're going to benefit from setting up communication guidelines for your apprentice. Setting expectations that are clear and can be acted upon is good for everyone. You'll have to put some thought into what works best for you and then you can use that clarity to get more of what works. Your apprentice won't have to spend a lot of time trying to figuring out your preferences.

Start by clarifying the most common ways your apprentice is going to interact with you. Then, explain what a good e-mail looks like, talk about the best way to interrupt you, give guidance on how to prepare a problem-solving question, and set up regular status reports and one-on-one meetings so that you can stay in touch. Each of these steps will help your apprentice figure out how to work with you and how to learn from you. That is good for everyone.

FROM A MANAGER'S VIEW

As a manager, you should step back and look at the communication styles and personalities of your mentors and apprentices. Sometimes, you'll see a train wreck coming. You might have an energetic newcomer for an apprentice—maybe smarter than average and very verbal. He will be great at some point, but right now just seems to be a bundle of questions and missteps. The peer mentor you're relying on is reserved, a little grumpy sometimes, and definitely not one to sit around chatting. You are already anticipating the conversations: "The new guy talks too much! He's making me crazy," and, "My mentor doesn't seem to want to work with me."

Left alone, this pair is going to have a difficult time working together, but you can help.

Get the mentor to read this chapter and then discuss communication preferences with you. He may need some help sorting his needs out, because many people don't think about their preferences this way. You probably have worked with him long enough to know a few of his preferences that should be listed. Share those as examples. Ask about what would work better, instead of listening to complaints about the "noise" the new guy is making.

Then, send the apprentice in with the questions from the "When You're the Apprentice" section in this chapter. These questions are usually a straightforward way for the apprentice to discover the best way to work with the mentor. But, if you don't encourage it, this conversation may never happen.

For your silo mentors, you should still encourage this line of self-awareness. They often mentor people in troubleshooting situations so the problem-solving question (Tool 2-4) will benefit them. They also do more work in short bursts, with people who are not new hires, so they may take the information in this chapter for granted. Check in with them to ensure the interruptions, e-mails, and questions are coming at them in a way that still allows them to get their regular work done. This is great chapter to help busy silo mentors improve their situations.

Another way managers use this information is in regular team meetings, especially when the team is newly formed or has new members. Your employees could be encouraged to think about their preferences and then share a few of them around the table at a team meeting. Such sharing is a way of getting to know each other and gathering useful information to help enhance your ability to work together. You might even choose to adopt a couple of these ideas for the whole team. The status report, handshake e-mail and problem-solving question are all examples of tools that could be made standard for all.

WHEN YOU'RE THE APPRENTICE

Spend some time discussing the best way to communicate with your mentor so that you get the information you need with as little disruption as possible. By the end of your conversation you should be able to explain the best way to take on the following situations:

- Managing day-to-day communication (e-mail, voice-mail, scheduled meetings, instant messenger, etc.)
- Interrupting with questions
- Providing status reports
- Preparing for and asking problem-solving questions
- Attending meetings and getting the most out of them

As an apprentice, you should also be prepared to explain your preferences—for example, if you are better in the morning or evening; how you like to be interrupted; and any time constraints you'll have, such as bus schedule, child care issues, and so on. You'll want to share them with your peer mentor.

3

Focusing on the Most Important Information

Where do I start?

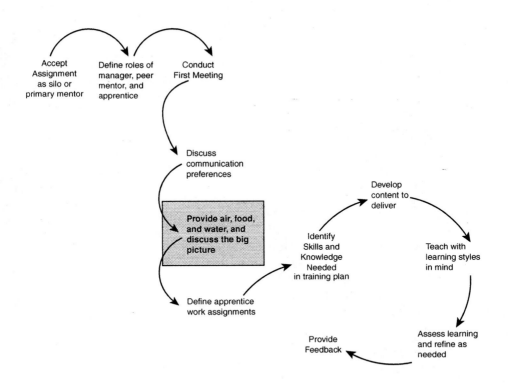

Peer mentors are often plagued by the nagging question of how to take years of experience and put it in context so they can start at the right place and share their knowledge in an orderly fashion. For many, the idea of explaining what they've been doing for years to someone who is just starting out is daunting. Most of us don't even think about what we do. Our work has become habitual, or we've developed an instinct around our specialty that doesn't float into our conscious very much.

Often, when faced with an apprentice eagerly waiting to absorb new knowledge, peer mentors just dive in somewhere, explaining the work at hand, and hoping for the best. The results of this scattered approach are unpredictable. There is a better way.

By the end of this chapter, you should be able to identify the information that must be provided to build a foundation and paint the big picture *before* you deliver information about the details of the job. If you take a little time to give your apprentice a solid footing, everything else you cover will have a much stronger chance of holding up.

ODE TO MASLOW

Did you study Maslow's hierarchy of needs in Psych 101? In case you didn't, it is illustrated in Figure 3-1. I'm going to explain his life's work here in just one paragraph.

Maslow's basic thesis was that people have to worry about things in order. They need to start by making sure that they have air, food, and water, because, well, survival is pretty important. After they take care of their basic needs, they look for a roof over their heads. Then, once they're warm and dry, they can go on to the finer things in life. He called this stage *self-actualization* and I'll equate it to a really nice car, or whatever else makes you happy. In a nutshell, Maslow said that it doesn't matter how nice your car is if you can't breathe.

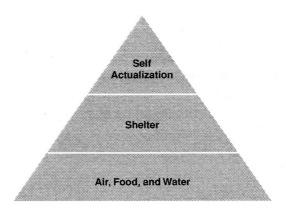

Figure 3-1   Maslow's hierarchy of needs

If you're wondering what I'm talking about, picture your apprentice walking into your office and hearing you say

> Oh good. Your timing is perfect. I'm working on developing the budget for the HVAC on the Walker project. I wanted to explain it to you so you can take on the budget for the Adams project. Have a seat and I'll walk you through the basics...blah, blah, blah.

This doesn't sound too bad at first blush. When you're learning, there are always new bits of information coming your way. This sort of get-ready-here-it-comes setup occurs all the time. To the apprentice, however, being exposed to this method of training is akin to diving in to save a drowning man, but buttoning his coat and combing his hair before you get his face out of the water. The actions are out of order.

Here's what is going on as you start delivering the content. The apprentice is wondering the following:

> Who is Walker?
>
> Who is Adams?
>
> I develop budgets?
>
> How often do I do this?
>
> When will I do it first?

What is HVAC?

Is there a template, or do I just wing it?

Do I have access to that database yet?

Is there any documentation on this process?

Do I use Microsoft Excel for that? I don't have any other software on my computer.

What if I screw it up?

With all of that noise going on in his brain, it is no wonder the apprentice doesn't get the details the first time through. When your apprentice is a new hire, the noise is even louder, because he has a more limited vocabulary, doesn't yet get the "big picture," and is stressed because no office space is available yet.

You can help. Start by conveying foundation information and providing support that the apprentice can't live without. Then build a structure in which he can house new skills. Finally, ensure that prerequisites for any new skills have already been satisfied.

Organize your delivery of content into a logical order and your apprentice's ability to retain the important information will increase dramatically.

START WITH AIR, FOOD, AND WATER

Returning to Maslow's hierarchy, we know that the apprentice needs air to breathe, food to eat, and water to drink. But, what are the equivalents of those needs in a business setting? The first step in applying the hierarchy to working with an apprentice is to think about all the foundational tools, resources, language, access, relationships, and general information your apprentice is going to need to *survive*. It is the stuff he needs to get *before* anyone teaches him any skills. I know first hand what it is like when this basic information isn't provided.

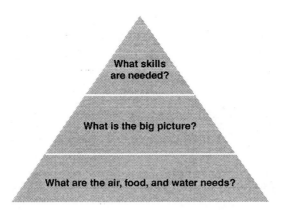

Figure 3-2 How Maslow's hierarchy of needs relates to the peer mentoring process

My first job at Microsoft was working as a localization/translation manager on the international versions of Microsoft Word 1.0. I was what was known as a "talent hire," which means that I wasn't experienced in software project management, but was bright enough to figure it out. The truth of the matter was that I barely knew how to double-click. We were supposed to be shipping the software in a matter of weeks and the Italian subsidiary was screaming about the quality of the translation. The message to me was, "If you're smart enough to get a job here, you're smart enough to figure out what your job is. No one has time to tell you. Go!" There was no computer in my office, no desk, no chair, and no plan.

Oh, and they gave me a thick binder that they said had "all the stuff I would need to get myself set up."

So, I did what you all would have done in that situation: I sorted it out. I found an administrative assistant who would help me get my basic office setup. I found an old computer in the hallway, put it on my desk, and plugged it in. I wandered around asking questions and then tried to use that big book they gave me to set myself up.

The thing I remember most about that big book is that it had very detailed instructions covering all I would need to do to get hooked up to e-mail, download the software I'd need, and get situated in my office. The trouble was that when I followed the instructions, nothing seemed to work. I'd redo it, double-checking each step, and still come up with an error message, or some other problem.

At one point when I was really at my wit's end I remember thinking that my boss was going to walk into my office and say, "Sorry, you'll have to go now. You're far too stupid to work here." I couldn't even follow simple instructions. How could I lead a team and survive this crazy place long enough to ship my product?

Then I noticed something on the spine of the binder: a date. The book was over a year old. Everything I needed was there, but it was all out of date. Of course it was out of date! Portions of it were probably out of date within a week of it being printed. In reality, while I'm sure no harm was meant, handing me the book without a warning about its age was worse than handing me nothing. By being out of date, even if only a little bit, it steered me in the wrong direction.

Once I realized the problem, I got a co-worker to help me get my machine set up. My first order of business was to log into the bug database and see what problems were assigned to my team, so that I could make sure we were on track. After a couple of missteps getting the database software downloaded, I tried to log on. The error message said, "Access denied. Contact your administrator for permission to this database." Well, of course, I didn't know who my administrator was. I had to ask three people before we figured out who I should contact. When I made contact, she was too busy to help me that day, so I had to wait two more days before I could get into the database and start doing my job. I kept experiencing more delays and more frustration.

Some of you might say this was a good learning experience—and it was. But what was I learning? I was learning how to find an administrator and get permissions to a database, a skill I wouldn't need again, perhaps ever.

I did get my office set up and I did survive, but it took me nine days, and more than a few damaged brain cells, to get a place to sit that had working e-mail and a phone. How productive was I during that time? I was actually a net negative on the team, because I had to enlist the help of so many busy people to do such fundamental tasks. With a little thought, you can help your apprentices avoid the frustration I experienced and get to work sooner.

NOT YOUR ORDINARY NEW HIRE CHECKLIST

I want to point out that while the air, food, and water worksheet has much in common with a traditional new hire checklist, it isn't exactly the same. The air, food, and water list provided in Tool 3-1 is usually a subset of the larger checklist. It includes the information and services that are so fundamental that they'll be finished up in a matter of the first day or two on the job. Most new hire checklists cover far more than that. There are good reasons for both. Just put the air, food, and water list on top.

AIR, FOOD, AND WATER CHECKLIST FOR A NEW TEAM MEMBER

When building the Air, Food, and Water checklist, I suggest you start by thinking about it for someone new to the company, because you'll create the most robust list you'll ever need. You can also think about air, food, and water needs for any silos of information that you control and for people who are new to your project team or are transfers from other parts of the company. These types of apprentices will likely need subsets of the list you created for new hires.

OFFICE SETUP

Don't underestimate how disorienting it is to have no place to sit, no e-mail, and no phone; or, to inherit a workspace that is full of historic information that really belongs in the storeroom or the trash. Does your office have a phone system that requires explanation, or a security system that might trip up a new employee? Your new apprentice also needs to know how to get basic office supplies (does he need approval from someone to get paperclips from the supply closet?) and anything that might require special order, such as a lamp. Many companies require completing requisition forms, having them signed, and waiting lengthy periods of time to see the requested item. Anything that can be done to have the proper tools available before your new hire arrives will pay dividends in earlier productivity. My most progressive clients start this process the day the offer letter is signed so that an office setup is ready to go before the new employee's first day.

Tool 3-1 Air, Food, and Water Worksheet

What	Who
Computer setup (correct version of the necessary software tools used and whatever other technology needed)	
Office supplies (basic supplies and understanding your group's process for getting what you need)	
Documentation (current user's guides and white papers, relevant web sites)	
Permissions to the corporate network	
Instructions for joining team e-mail aliases and meetings	
Resources (others who know, examples, history)	
Administrative support	
Introductions to core members of the team	
Building tour	

INTRODUCTIONS

How many people did you meet on your first day on the job, the entire team, everyone on the floor, or the entire company? How many of those people did you remember? If we consider air, food, and water to be only the people you need to meet to survive, how many people does your apprentice really need to meet during his first week? There are probably just four or five key people. In addition to his manager and peer mentor, a new employee probably needs to meet the administrative assistant who has access to things that no one else knows about and one or two other people who can cover for the primary contacts if they're not available. Then, during his second week, you can provide introductions to five more people, and then five more after that, until you've built out a complete contact list.

DOCUMENTATION AND WEB RESOURCES

I already demonstrated the importance of current documentation through my Microsoft story. In my experience, if it is written down, it is out of date. Usually it isn't completely out of date, just a little bit—sometimes only one line on a page. But, how will your apprentice know which line? There is also the problem of volume. If you work for a large company, pointing your apprentice to the corporate network is too much information. I suggest that you specify which parts of the intranet are valuable and which parts are potentially a problem. Think of it as a "warning label" for anything written down. You might explain it like this: "Let me show you the team/company internal web site and tell you which parts are most current and would be most useful for you to look through. I also want to show you which areas are purely historical."

This approach will help you to be sure that you're not using documentation as a babysitter. Have you ever said, "Hey, I'm really busy and I have to run to a half-day meeting offsite. Why don't you read through this web site while I'm away and we'll talk it over when I get back?" It would be far better to have your apprentice go home than to spend hours wandering around in the desert of useless documentation.

SECURITY/PERMISSIONS/PASSWORDS

This one came up in my Microsoft story as well. Imagine learning how to use the team's database and then getting back to your desk, booting it up, and getting an error message. Access denied. Now you have to figure out who administers the database. The path is usually something like this: "It's Sarah, but she's on vacation. Try Michael, he's her backup. But Michael didn't get the brain dump on permissions before Sarah left. After all, that isn't something she does every day." Two days later, you've finally sorted out the permissions issues, but everything you learned about the database is now lost. Start over. Setting up access to all files, labs, tools, databases, and so on is air, food, and water, because you can't do anything without it. While you're at it, don't forget parking passes, cardkey access, and permissions to enter certain areas of the building or campus.

SOFTWARE OR OTHER TOOLS

If you work in an environment with proprietary tools, think about how many versions of those tools exist. What happens when someone uses the 3.04 version and everyone else is using 3.05? The icon on the desktop is the same. The interface appears the same. But if you start to work with the older version, it blows up your system. On Boeing's assembly line, this versioning problem is related to physical tools. What if you drill out for rivets on the leading edge of the wing and you use a drill bit that is one size too big? I'm sure you get the picture.

Make sure that all is in order with the apprentice's workstation and tools before he even begins to learn how to use the tools. The workstation can be fully ready to go, or you can create a step-by-step plan for the apprentice to prepare the work space.

TEAM MEETINGS, TEAM E-MAIL ADDRESSES, AND CORE WORK HOURS

Every team has a way of staying in touch. Air, food, and water includes connecting your apprentice to this network. This part of the checklist typically involves setting up recurring appointments for meetings in his calendar, enrolling him in the team's e-mail distribution lists, signing him up to receive important communications, specifying the hours of the day when everyone tends to be together, and so on. You'll know you've got this list right if you look at your own plans for a month from now and your apprentice is connected to it in every appropriate way.

AIR, FOOD, AND WATER CHECKLIST FOR A SILO MENTOR

Every silo mentor should also have an air, food, and water checklist for his specialty. It is usually a much shorter list, but no less important. Let's go back to the database example I used earlier. Consider a situation in which the silo mentor is working with an apprentice who has been with the company for two years, but hasn't yet learned how to work with a specific database. Before the silo mentor actually teaches the apprentice anything about the database, he's going to ensure that the air, food, and water needs have been handled. Here's how the silo mentor is going to think about this list:

- Office setup? Probably not much to worry about here.

- Introductions? The silo mentor is an administrator on the database. There are two other people who also have administrator roles and levels of expertise, so he is going to make those introductions. Because the silo travels frequently, the apprentice will need to know who else can help with troubleshooting.

- Documentation? Yes, there is a standard for key words, and a standard for the level of detail required for each field. There are also some samples of good and bad entries that could be studied. While others are still using documentation from the prior version of the tools, there are too many inconsistencies to make the documentation useful for the apprentice.

- Permissions? Yes. There is no sense in teaching anything until the apprentice can get into the database. Permissions must be submitted two days in advance to get through the approval process.

- Software? Yes. This database requires a proprietary release of the database that includes some custom components. Using the wrong release would cause data integrity issues.

- E-mail addresses? Yes. Everyone using this database gets regular updates from the administrator through a distribution list.

Look through the list again and notice how much trouble is created if any of these points were not covered in advance. The apprentice could end up using the wrong instructions and enter data with the wrong version of the software, learn everything only to have to wait to use the knowledge, wander around the building looking for help instead of knowing where to go, miss out on the updates, and experience myriad other problems. Each of these problems would affect not only the apprentice's productivity, but also the productivity of co-workers who would be interrupted by his questions and participation in efforts to clean up the messes that would undoubtedly be created.

Think about how long it would take to actually get everything on this list handled before teaching the apprentice anything— probably less than an hour. The tradeoff is well worth the effort.

MAKING A LIST AND CHECKING IT TWICE

This air, food, and water list is one of those things that you can imagine getting lost in the various things that must be done to get a new hire or silo mentor's apprentice on-board. Because of that, I like to put the task into the hands of a person who isn't as busy. I suggest that you have your most recent new apprentice read through this chapter and draft what he thinks would be a useful list. After all, that person probably has the most recent pain from the lack of a complete list, and knows exactly what should be included. Make it a policy that each new apprentice use the list and then update it for the next apprentice. In that way, the list will always be as up to date as the last person hired. Better still, the peer mentors will never have to update it again.

PROVIDE "SHELTER" IN THE BIG PICTURE

After air, food, and water, Maslow said that people worry about finding shelter. I equate this with an understanding of the structure that apprentices need to feel stable and connected and to see how their work relates to everything going on around them.

Just recently, in a class I was teaching, one of the peer mentors said, "I'm really frustrated with my new teammate. He just doesn't seem to get the big picture." Everyone around the table nodded knowingly, so I asked him what he meant by that. He went on to explain that his apprentice couldn't figure out how to prioritize, or problem-solve. He was often confused at meetings, not even understanding the point of the meeting, and his questions weren't well connected to the topic at hand. All of this made him appear to be failing. I asked him to tell me what he'd done to help connect his apprentice to this mysterious "big picture." He went silent.

In a perfect world, managers would take on the role of providing their employees the context of the big picture. In my experience, however, this doesn't happen consistently. Sometimes peer mentors will have to step up. In the case I described earlier, the peer mentor in my class could sense that the apprentice's problem stemmed from not understanding the big picture. The trouble was that he couldn't put his finger on the information he needed to share. I told him about an experience I'd had that I thought would illustrate it.

THE BIG PICTURE IN REAL LIFE

I went to Atlanta a couple of years ago to teach a class. I flew in on a Sunday night and took the train downtown to my hotel. I had the hotel's street address, but no directions. When I got off the train around 10 P.M., and took the escalators up to the sidewalk, the first thing I looked for was some assistance. On my right, at the top of the escalator, was a map as big as a double bed. It had a handsome chrome and glass frame, and clearly detailed all of the city streets in color. It must have been expensive to put it there. Excellent. Finding my hotel was going to be easier than I thought. Standing in front of the map, I did what everyone does when they approach a map. I looked for the *you are here* dot. To my chagrin, while the city of Atlanta had budget for the chrome, the glass, the detailed map, and the labor to get the map placed in exactly the right spot at the metro station, they hadn't managed to get the dot put on this particular map. For me, it was utterly useless.

So, I had to resort to plan B. I felt as if I had no choice but to ask for help in finding my hotel. It was late and I was tired, and I didn't want to lug my suitcase until I figured out how to find the hotel on my own. I turned around and interrupted two shady characters who were standing on the sidewalk talking. The one who responded looked annoyed. Without actually speaking, with just a grunt and a nod of his head, he pointed directly across the street from where I was standing. It turned out that my hotel was literally within my line of site, but the sign with the hotel's name on it was up on the 29th floor. It hadn't occurred to me to simply look up.

Now, you could say that I wasn't very bright for not looking around and finding the hotel on my own; but, the story is real and I think it is parallel to the stories of the first few days, weeks, or even months on the job for many new employees. How many times do you throw your apprentices into a difficult situation and give them resources, but no context (a map with no dot)? It is no wonder that your apprentice is lost. Even when given a clear goal, if he doesn't know where he is relative to everyone around him, he must either stumble around hoping for the best, or ask for help. Interrupting and asking for directions each time he gets lost will work, given enough time and patience, but it is not the most efficient way to get him involved in his job.

EXPLAINING THE BIG PICTURE

It is very common for people to use the phrase "big picture." For example, they might say, "She's such a big-picture thinker." When I ask those same people to define exactly what they mean by "big-picture thinker," things get a little murky. While they may use many of the same phrases, such as "sees the connections," or "describes the vision well," or "relates the details to the greater purpose," those definitions are pretty vague.

I thought it would be helpful to try to deconstruct the notion of the big picture down to a series of questions that, if answered well, would ensure that your apprentice has the context needed to be able to problem-solve, prioritize, and participate at the highest levels. In Chapter 6, "Leveraging Learning Styles," I describe a learning style in which learning is stalled if this information is not available; essentially, no context means no learning.

Tool 3-2 provides a fairly thorough list of questions you can use to guide your discussions about the big picture with your apprentice. As you read each question, think about how you'd answer it, and how confident you are with your answer. If you're not completely sure of the answer, you may decide that you'd like to discuss this part of the big picture with your manager (and invite your apprentice along).

Tool 3-2 Big Picture Worksheet

Key Elements	Notes/Comments
What is your team's mission or purpose? (What do we do that the larger organization can't live without?)	
How does our work fit with the organization's mission?	
Who are our internal and external customers? How do we prioritize our work for them?	
Who are our competitors (for both the organization overall as well as for the services we provide our internal customers)?	
What are the specific products or services we provide? (What would go on our brochure if we were selling our services internally, to other parts of the organization?)	
Where are we in the product or service cycle (just starting, in full production, or nearly finished)?	
How does the work flow for your job (what happens before and after the work is on your desk)?	

EXAMPLE OF DEFINING THE BIG PICTURE

To illustrate how this works, I'll walk you through the answers I would have given when I was running a training department at Microsoft. Our job was to serve all of the people who shipped software worldwide at Microsoft, using a combination of orientation meetings, technical training, facilitated discussions, best practice sharing, and so on.

- **Team mission and purpose.** Our role is to identify the skills required to ship quality software on time, measure the gap between the requirements and current employees' skill sets, and provide educational programs to bridge the gap.

- **Fit with organizational mission.** We report into the product group business that we serve, rather than the human resources department, because with the growth in staff and so many new technologies coming online, we are the fundamental resource for sharing best practices, improving communication among teams, and leveling out the skills needed to ship great software.

- **Internal and external customers.** Our internal customers are everyone who ships software at Microsoft. Each of my team members owns a subset of that population, including managing the resources available to support that group. While we reach out worldwide and offer support to other training groups from our international operations as resources allow, our primary emphasis is on the Redmond campus. As an internal service organization, we develop a cursory knowledge of Microsoft's customers.

  Internal customer groups (developers, testers, marketers, program managers, etc.) are represented by a handful of people who are influential employees, leaders, and managers in those groups. These advisors help determine the priority of our projects. It is our job to spot the need for training and bring ideas to the advisors, but it would be very unusual to do a major project without their counsel. Every planning exercise starts with this question: Who is the customer, and what is his or her role in ensuring this educational program will be a success? If we can't clearly identify a specific person to serve as the customer, we won't take on a project.

- **Success metrics.** For our team, we measure our success by the number of people who are still in the room at the *end* of one of our educational programs. People are already working crazy hours. Coming to one of our sessions means more overtime, so if they showed up and stayed, when they're not required to do either, then the training session must have been a good use of their time. We also collect evaluations to gather more specific feedback and track average ramp-up time to productivity for our new hire programs.

A more subjective, but no less important, metric is whether the internal customers contact us because they want our help, or we have to chase them down to initiate a project. How often they request our help speaks to our reputation for solving problems, which is a key to our success.

- **Competitors.** Some or all of our work could be outsourced at any time to any number of training companies who would like to serve Microsoft as an external partner. The competition isn't a threat hanging over us; it is a motivation to ensure that we work to earn the job every time there is a new training opportunity. Because there are plenty of external competitors, we develop a project plan and measure customer satisfaction every time we spend company resources.

- **Products and/or services.** Here is a list of the five services that are our primary offerings:

  - **Assessment and consulting.** We can help organizations that are going through major transitions, such as a reorganization after releasing a product, to determine their training needs and develop a plan to solve any problems.

  - **Program delivery using internal resources.** We can take internal subject matter experts who are willing to assist in training, and help them teach their specialties to others, whether in a one-on-one setting, or in a classroom. We provide training and logistical support for these trainers, as needed.

  - **Brown bags.** We define the areas in which panel discussions and Q&A sessions are the best way to deliver content. Then, we recruit for, organize, and facilitate these sessions.

  - **Technical training.** We hire contract trainers to provide courses for the most widely needed technical training.

  - **New employee orientation.** We provide orientation programs for all new hires into the product group.

- **Our relation to the product cycle.** We pay special attention to the needs assessment and consulting work for any given business unit at the beginning of a new product cycle. In that way, we can develop programs that help them prepare for the new technology, new processes, and new team relationships that come when launching a new product. Later in the cycle, as the team is pressed for schedule, our work is primarily over until the product has been shipped.

  We also work closely with recruiting, in order to provide programs that support the hiring cycles. Many of our new employees come to us first as interns. They may also start in the fall, after being hired during the summer. We do a lot of work to help them get on board. During the summer and fall, new hire training is among our highest priorities.

- **Work flow for the job.** In this group most of our work starts in the form of a project. The project can be a one-time training, or the output of the project can become a sustained program. Here is the typical flow of a project:

  - Define the problem to be addressed in one page, using the template provided.

  - Ensure that you have an internal customer signed up and that you have negotiated his or her role.

  - Lay out a plan: including goals, metrics, timeline, and budget. Get approval.

  - Recruit trainers from the subject matter experts or from our team, as needed.

  - Work out all logistics for registration and facilities first. Room availability often drives dates for delivery.

  - Manage the development of the content.

  - Organize delivery of the content.

  - Set up a short review cycle.

  - Write up and deliver post mortem on the results.

  - If appropriate, move into maintenance mode.

CONNECTING THE DOTS

Once you've thought through the big picture questions you can start to get a sense of how people will use the information you provide. In the example from my team, the "Who is the customer?" question often changed our course of action. If one of my program managers whisked into my office with a plan to build a boot camp for new marketers, my first question was always the same: "Who is the customer?" The answer couldn't be, "The marketers." It had to be something like this: "Ruthann is the customer. She's agreed to step up in these specific ways: reviewing the goals, recruiting speakers, delivering the keynote, requiring her people to attend, finding us funding, and attending four key planning meetings." If we didn't have that clear level of customer involvement, the project would be tabled. This may sound harsh, but I learned that without a clear customer, the project was doomed anyway. I chose not even to head down that path. There was no shortage of important work to do, so why not do something that was likely to succeed?

Take a look at the timing for our services. You'll notice that we tended to back away from providing services during the final stages before product release, because we learned that it is a bad time even to try to talk to our customers. By reappearing after release, when they were ready for us, we showed our customers that we understood their business well enough to come in at appropriate times. That definitely added to our credibility and our usefulness.

Knowing the success metrics for your team is another example of a fundamental piece of big picture information. Take Electronic Arts (EA), the video game company, as an example. If I were to ask you what their measure of success is, you might say the game-play has to be realistic, or the characters have to look like they're really sweating, or the performance must be over the top. All of this is true, but their number one measure isn't any of these. It is shipping *on time*. The gaming industry, like the movie industry, markets their product and creates a frenzy surrounding a specific date on which the product will appear. A huge percentage of their revenue comes during the first few weeks after release. If they go to all the trouble to tell the world when it is coming, and then it is late, the customers go elsewhere, and the revenue is simply lost. The impact is similar to what would happen if you had people line up outside the theater for the opening of a movie only to be told, "Sorry, we just didn't finish it on time." How does recognizing timing as the most important metric change the way you'd use your time or run your project?

DOING THE RESEARCH

As you read through this section on the big picture, you probably thought about developing the answers to those questions for your team. As you do that, how confident are you of the answers? If you were to ask your co-workers or your manager these questions, do you think that the answers would be consistent? They should be. As a peer mentor, you may not have any authority to answer these questions, but you can certainly lead a discussion with those who are in charge that is aimed at understanding the answers. Sometimes the answers will flow easily. Sometimes it won't flow at all. Startup leaders often struggle with making these decisions as they shape their businesses. In any event, you have an obligation to ask the questions, and should keep asking them until you feel confident that you have answers that you can use to guide your actions and those of your apprentice.

In class, I often ask how many people got the answers to these questions in the first couple weeks of starting their current jobs. A very small number raise their hands. Then I ask those who raised their hands what having the answers did for them. I often hear, "I knew my priorities and who to talk to. I was focused and sure of our direction." For those who didn't raise their hands, I ask about the result of not getting this information. Their responses include: "I made mistakes because I didn't inform other teams or people about changes." "It took more time to ramp up." Or, "I made some bad decisions on priority." The worst, but still most common answer is, "I'm still unsure about the answers to some of these questions, and I've been here for a year."

My approach to explaining the big picture at Microsoft was to invite one of the vice presidents to a new-hire lunch a couple of times a month. I just asked the questions in Tool 3-2 to get them talking. The executives were great in that forum, because it was free-form and they could just share from their experiences. You could probably invite someone from your organization to lunch with your apprentice and ask these questions, too. It might make it easier on everyone if you warn your guest before springing the questions; but that is all it usually takes to get the information moving.

SUMMARY: PUTTING IT INTO PRACTICE

Think about air, food, and water for the new hire apprentices you mentor and prepare a short list of the information that they can't live, or learn, without. Then make sure that this list is in their hands on their first day. You don't want them to have to spend any time figuring out what they need to get set up and ready to learn or work.

Also think about air, food, and water for the silos of information you own. The list will be shorter, typically just having the right version of the tools, current documentation, permissions or security needed, and vocabulary for the new content. Don't forget that these really are fundamental apprentice needs. If you address them before teaching your specialty, your apprentice will have far fewer roadblocks on the way to learning.

As for the big picture, take a little time to ask and answer the questions in Tool 3-2. The answers will help provide your apprentices with a context through which they can find their own way, and make good choices as they progress.

FROM A MANAGER'S VIEW

As with many of the ideas in this book, the equivalents of Maslow's air, food, and water can easily be determined by your employees. You can make sure that it is a complete list and that it isn't lost in the regular new hire checklist. You can also ensure that the most recent hire updates the list and that the updated list gets handed from new hire to new hire.

Your silo mentors may need more encouragement to think about air, food, and water, because those needs are less obvious when mentoring a more experienced employee. The consequences can be more severe if an existing employee is using the wrong version of the tool or doesn't have the correct documentation. Such employees can go for some time before realizing their error. Clean-up is then time-consuming, expensive, and frustrating.

As for the big picture, I work with a lot of different kinds of companies, from small shops with 25 employees to worldwide operations. I use these big picture questions as measures of the health of an organization. It doesn't take long. In about an hour's time, I can sit with a group of front line employees and quiz them on their highest priority customers, their mission, their services, their success metrics, and their work flow. If they all answer in similar ways, with a strong degree of confidence, then I consider them a healthy organization. You can ask the questions just as I would to see how consistently your people answer them.

I've also been in the room when employees answer these questions with a shrug. They not only don't know the answers, but they're not even sure their manager can answer the questions. When I go upstream to the managers and they, too, seem confused by the questions, I know the organization is in trouble. If I sit with executives who can't confidently answer these questions, I plan either to stay a while and help them figure it out or quietly exit and walk away before they implode. This is a failing company.

If you're a manager, all of your people, including the college student you hired last month, should be able to answer the big picture questions confidently and consistently. If they can't, in my estimation, you're not doing your job. If you're a middle manager and your manager isn't clear with you, then you have an obligation to lead the conversation until you can figure it out. It'll be one of the more important roles you play.

WHEN YOU'RE THE APPRENTICE

Unless your team has also read this book, they obviously won't hand you an air, food, and water checklist. But you can still ask for all of the information in this chapter right off the bat. Be sure to question whether the documentation is current, whether you've been given the most current version of the tools, and if you have all of the security access necessary to do the work. Ask for all of this *before* you let them teach you anything. Then, you can volunteer to create or update any existing new hire checklist and place the air, food, and water list right on top.

Also plan to confirm your understanding of the big picture surrounding your job using the questions in Tool 3-2 so that you are confident of where you fit in and how you can add value. Continue to test yourself and ensure that you can confidently answer the questions. If you can, you'll always be better prepared to solve problems and prioritize with confidence.

4

Developing a Training Plan

What are the skills, measures, resources, and dates needed to do the job?

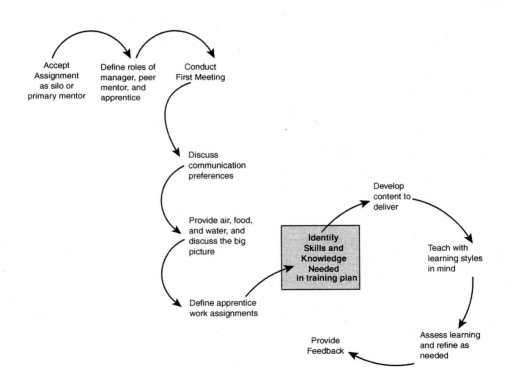

Accept Assignment as silo or primary mentor

Define roles of manager, peer mentor, and apprentice

Conduct First Meeting

Discuss communication preferences

Provide air, food, and water, and discuss the big picture

Identify Skills and Knowledge Needed in training plan

Develop content to deliver

Teach with learning styles in mind

Define apprentice work assignments

Assess learning and refine as needed

Provide Feedback

The training plan is perhaps the most important tool in the entire book. If you take advantage of only one idea, I hope it will be this one. In my experience, it has the greatest potential to get apprentices on the right track quickly. Remember the First Meeting discussion in Chapter 1, "Roles in Peer Mentoring"? I suggested that you say "We've been thinking about you and we have a plan to help you get up to speed." This chapter covers *that* plan.

With the foundation that comes from thinking about Air, Food, and Water and the Big Picture, you're now ready to look at the list of actual skills that you'll teach your apprentice. You'll start by "deconstructing" the job into a list of the things she needs to know how to do. Then you'll figure out the "test" your apprentice will need to pass to prove she has learned, the sequence in which the skills will be presented, the dates by which she should have them completed, and the resources needed to get there. The Training Plan Template provided later in this chapter will give you a way to reverse engineer a job so everyone knows exactly what needs to be known.

Sound daunting? By the end of this chapter, you'll be able to spend about 30 minutes creating a training plan that would take your apprentice at least a week or more to execute. Then, you can spend 15 minutes more each week working with him until you've helped develop all the skills needed to be independent.

TRAINING PLAN TEMPLATE

I want to start this chapter by showing you Tool 4-1a, which is the Training Plan Template. There are five columns, and you can add as many rows as you want. An abbreviated description is provided here, while the remainder of the chapter breaks down each section in more detail so you can complete one for your apprentices.

Tool 4-1a Training Plan Template

Skill/"Do statement"	Sequence	Success measure/"Test" Be able to explain	Accomplish by (date)	Resources

- Column 1 is the skill or task your apprentice needs to know how to do.
- Column 2 is the sequence or order in which you'd suggest the apprentice learn the skills.
- Column 3 is the success metric or test questions that must be answered to prove that your apprentice "knows" the skill. Tool 4-1b (found in the section, "Developing the Test,") provides a list of suggested test questions to be inserted in this column.
- Column 4 is the date by which your apprentice should be able to pass the test.
- Column 5 is the list of resources that are available to help your apprentice learn the information required to pass the test.

WHAT DO YOU KNOW HOW TO DO?

Developing a training plan starts with making a list of all the tasks your apprentice needs to learn how to do. If you plan to replicate your skills completely, so you can have a true peer in your job or so you can retire or move on to another position, you'll think about all of the work you do and make a list of the skills you expect your apprentice to develop. The list could be far shorter if you're just teaching one of your silos of expertise. You're going to break the job into chunks of work that would take roughly one to three hours for you to explain. Of course, she will need more than that amount of time to practice and master the skills, but you can get her going in that time.

How many tasks do you think you know how to do? Some people believe they know thousands of tasks. In my experience, the list isn't nearly as long as you might think. In fact, for most of us, the list will be between 60 and 70 tasks. I've found that even when I'm hired to spend an entire day with multiple people who have the same job and I work to extract as many tasks as possible for a specific position, the list rarely tops 100 skills or tasks. I hope that is comforting. Deconstructing your job so you can train others probably won't be as difficult as you thought.

START WITH THE TOOLS YOU USE

In developing the list, start by thinking about the "tools" you use and what you do with them. If you work at a computer, you have a number of icons on your desktop that represent the software you use. Pick those your apprentice needs to use and write down how he will use them.

Remember, you're looking for chunks of skills or tasks that take about one to three hours for you to go over and teach. Sometimes that will mean lumping a few ideas together. Other times it will mean breaking the skill down into smaller chunks so teaching, and learning, is more manageable. For example, if you use a word processor, you're probably not going to make a list that includes, "Cut and paste in Microsoft Word." You could, however, list "Print and send the monthly newsletter using mail merge and labels." That might be a pretty good chunk to learn.

Make a list of all the tools you use and what you do with them. If you work in an office setting your list might include the following:

- Create pivot tables in your spreadsheet program for quarterlies.
- Develop a project plan in your project management software.
- Post a defect in your defect-tracking software.
- Run a monthly report in your team's database.
- Set up a workstation (desk, computer, phone, etc.).
- Develop an annual budget using the team's template.
- Track billable hours against a project using the team's software.
- Open and assign a customer service ticket in your customer-management software.

If you have a written work plan, annual goals and objectives, or a current job description, reviewing them may trigger thinking about tasks and skills that need to be added to the list. The review may help you to remember skills other than those that are fresh in your mind given upcoming deadlines, work cycles, and so on. Consider having a peer or your manager review this list and help you make sure it falls in line with expectations.

If you work in an industrial setting, such as a professional kitchen or a manufacturing line, you can make a list of your physical tools and think about the things that your apprentice needs to be able to do with each tool. Again, you'll look for chunks of skills that would take one to three hours for you to explain. The list for Boeing's 737 assembly line includes

- Measure Outside Diameters
- Measure Inside Hole Diameters
- Select Jigs and Blocks
- Select Measuring Tools
- Read QA Prints and Specs
- Access QA Prints and Specs

- Tag Pickups
- Create an NCR
- Edit and Attach Documents to an NCR
- Close and Forward an NCR
- Look Up "Jobs for Sale" in A&I

Notice how every phrase starts with a verb that can be used to give direction? You'd literally be able to say to someone, "Go and look up 'jobs for sale' in A&I," and they'd need to be able to do that. Don't say "use," "be familiar with," "understand," "learn," or anything else that is too vague. You'd never ask someone to, "Go *understand* the spreadsheet."

Also notice that none of these items are a characteristic or competency, such as positive attitude, good communication skills, or excellent problem-solver. Save those descriptions for the job postings. Don't put them on this list. Stick with skills your apprentice can do.

Now, think about all the other things you do that your apprentice needs to be able to do as well. Think through your daily, weekly, monthly, quarterly, and yearly tasks and make a list. Start with the things your apprentice needs to do first and keep building the list as time allows. Your list will include the following:

- Meetings that you lead or attend and the role you play
- Documents that you read or write such as monthly sales reports or executive notes
- Problems you have to troubleshoot
- Standards you have to follow
- Data you have to provide or analyze
- Quality reviews you have to conduct
- Systems you have to follow
- Services you provide such as patient intake at a medical clinic, exit interviews for a departing employee, or needs analysis on a new project

Once you've completed this list you already have a great tool for helping your apprentices figure out how to get up to speed. At the very least, you're providing a list of what they don't know, saving them having to scramble to figure that out. If you thought it was hard making your own list, imagine what it is like for your apprentices to try and figure out what they need to learn.

I had a client, Matt, who had hired a new project manager. We were talking several days before the new project manager arrived. He said the new project manager would need to "live" in the bug (defect-tracking) database. When I asked Matt what *skills* the new project manager would need to "live" in the bug database, he was able to go to his list of skills, like the one you just created, and identify nine of them that, together, were what he meant by "live" in the database. He modified the training plan to put these nine skills at the top of the list, in the correct order, and then handed the plan to his apprentice on the first day.

With the plan in place, Matt and his apprentice could work on building those skills before the apprentice was thrown in the deep end on a task. Guess what? By working through the plan during the apprentice's first few days, that new project manager was ramped-up and productive, with very few problems.

Instead of this approach, Matt could have just said, "I need you to live in the bug database. I'm really busy. Sorry it is so crazy around here. See what you can do and let me know if you have any questions...."

Do you have any phrases, like "live in the bug database," that mean something to you, but wouldn't mean anything to a person new to your job or specialty? Here are some phrases that I've heard:

- I need him to "look after" the client when he comes to town.
- You should be able to "fly" between the customer and the team and keep things running smoothly.
- "Stay in front" of that problem.
- You're going to need to "get set up" for that event.
- You'll be the "project manager."

Each of these statements is vague, at best. The worst part is that even you, the peer mentor, don't always know what you mean. You just complete the task instinctively, but have never thought of the skills that make up the whole. For that reason, breaking the job into recognizable chunks is the first step in developing the training plan.

You can find six more examples of training plans in Appendix B, "Sample Training Plan," at the back of the book.

MEASURING KNOWLEDGE: HOW DO YOU KNOW THAT I KNOW?

Once you make the list of skills, then you have to think about how you'll know that your apprentices have developed an appropriate level of competence in a particular area. You need to know that they really "know" the task, not just that they can do the visible work. The most common way that people measure learning is to have an apprentice actually do the task: build the widget, analyze the data, lead the meeting, and so on. Sometimes this is a sufficient metric, but the chances of getting a false sense of security are high. The results are often unpredictable.

For example, my niece learned how to drive a one-ton truck across the farm when she was 13 years old. She could get it into first gear, out to the field, let it idle while hay was loaded, and then get it back to the barn for unloading. She could do it, but was she a driver?

Not in my car!

For drivers, simply being able to get the vehicle in motion isn't sufficient. We need to know that they can handle the myriad situations that drivers face every day, and do it safely and predictably. We test them before we give them a license and let them out on the road. Even when new drivers get their licenses they still do not have a lot of experience. They're bound to make mistakes. Still, we know that they've demonstrated some level of knowledge of the rules, and that they're prepared to handle the most common situations, such as what to do in a school zone, before we let them loose. If they can't pass the test, we don't give them a license to drive on public roads.

Most of your apprentices also need to handle more than the most basic layer of skills, similar to steering, accelerating, and shifting in our driving example. We want to ensure that they also know about a few additional details, such as, to continue the driving example, merging, parallel parking, and traffic laws, and that they can demonstrate competence in those areas *before* being launched into the real job. When you're completely swamped and have very little time to train your apprentice, developing a test is even more important, because you don't have time to monitor all of your apprentice's work at every step. Skip it and you're going to spend an inordinate amount of time cleaning up messes that could have been avoided.

DEVELOPING THE TEST

I want to start this section with a disclaimer. I use the word "test" because I literally want you to get in the habit of orally quizzing your apprentices on the information they've been learning, but I'm not suggesting you get carried away. For example, the test normally does not need to be in writing, nor do the results need to be formally recorded. Just use the quizzing as a direct, but informal way for both of you to know that the knowledge has been transferred at a sufficient level. Your apprentice will be confident she has learned—and you'll be confident that you did your job and can move on.

Also note that if you can create the test before you try to teach, both you and your apprentice can focus on that information first. This practice will allow you to "teach to the test," and for those of you with too many years of experience to count, that'll really help you narrow down what you want to cover.

I suggest you look to history for help in preparing the test. You've probably mentored others on this topic before, so consider what has been a challenge for them. For example,

■ Do the skills on your list have acronyms or terms that an apprentice must understand from the beginning? Have you ever had an apprentice who didn't "speak the language" of your specialty, department, or company and have that lack of understanding cause problems?

- Is there a step-by-step process that you'll teach? If so, are there reasons why each step is important? Are there consequences for missing that step? Would you feel better about your apprentice's competence if he could explain each step in order, and explain why it is important?

- Do new people make the same mistakes every time because they just don't get it? If so, tell them about those mistakes before they make them.

- Is there a work flow they need to know about? Does your skill fit between two other skills? Does your apprentice need to know where to get input and give output?

- Are there common problems to troubleshoot? I know you couldn't teach all of the things that you know about how to troubleshoot. But, could you teach the top three?

- Are there people who apprentices need to consult or keep informed?

- Are there specific guidelines for identifying problems and escalating them in a timely way, meaning neither too early nor too late?

- Could you explain three best practices for the topic? I know you can't teach all of the nuances, but could you give apprentices your top three bits of advice?

- What resources exist to help apprentices pass the test, aside from hanging out in your workspace and asking you?

- Are there choices that an apprentice will have to make as he works through the task? If so, what are the likely choices, and how will he decide which way to go?

- How is quality or success measured for this task? Is the apprentice's work going through a test of some sort? How will it be evaluated?

- Are there any standards such as templates, rules, or even unwritten guidelines that the apprentice must follow?

Pick the issues that really stand out as important for you. Then look through the list of universal questions provided in Tool 4-1b to help you prepare your test.

Pick a handful of questions that, if answered correctly, would allow your apprentice to prove that he has learned enough to be turned loose on the task. Your apprentice should be able to respond to those items.

Tool 4-1b Suggested Measures of Understanding Worksheet

The apprentice should be able to explain the following:

1. The top # vocabulary words
2. The # steps in the process and why each is important
3. The top # things that often go wrong
4. The relationship between x and y (how it fits in the product or service cycle)
5. How to troubleshoot the three most common problems
6. The first # things to check when troubleshooting anything
7. Who is/should be involved/affected/consulted and why
8. How to identify and define a problem versus a crisis in this area
9. How to escalate a problem or crisis in this area
10. The # best practices for this topic
11. Where to find resources (documents, people, samples, web sites, etc.)
12. How to choose between x and y
13. How quality is measured
14. What standards exist and how rigorously they are applied
15. How this skill is relevant to your job

For example, I'm going to go to the list of skills and from that create a scenario to make cinnamon rolls. Then I'm going to go to the list of test questions and decide which of them I'll choose to ask as a way of ensuring that my apprentice is ready to go before sending him off to make the rolls.

Are there any vocabulary words? Sure, I can think of a handful ("start" the yeast; "score" the roll; "baste" the tops with butter; "knead" the dough). If my apprentice has experience in a bakery, I might skip this question. If not, I'll be sure to cover the vocabulary.

Are there steps in the process? Yes, I can think of six steps. Do the steps have to be done in order? Absolutely. Is there a problem with missing any steps? You bet. Baking is chemistry, and must follow exacting standards.

Are there a few common mistakes that people make? Yes, without a doubt. Over- or under-heating the yeast will kill it. Not kneading long enough—or too long—can result in a bad texture.

So, the "test" for the cinnamon roll skill is numbers 1, 2, and 3 on the list of test questions in Tool 4-1b. Now, if I were your apprentice and you taught me the details behind these key points and I was able to explain back each point in detail, would you have more confidence in my ability to bake the rolls? What if I couldn't answer the questions when it was time to turn me loose? How would that affect the degree of independence you'd give me?

Developing this level of clarity gives your apprentices something to work toward. In many cases, they can even do a fair bit of self-study to prepare for the test. In any event, they'll know what to watch and listen for when you're giving them instruction. Equally important, you'll know where to focus your teaching time, because you will have already thought about the core information the apprentice will need right away.

NOTE

There is much more information in Chapter 7, "Assessing Knowledge Transfer," to help you with conducting the test itself. Assessing competency can be as simple as asking the test questions above. But if you want more guidance, that chapter is a great place to look.

RESOURCES TO HELP PASS THE TEST

With a solid list of the skills to be learned and a clear idea of what it means to "know" something about the skill, you can now gather a few resources to help your apprentice pass the test. In some rare instances, the only resource in the resource column of the plan will be you. That happens most often when a peer mentor who has been doing a very specific task for a number of years with no back-up is leaving a position after a long time, often due to retirement. While such situations are not ideal, they do occur.

Usually, there are a number of resources, either formal or informal, to help apprentices take responsibility for their own learning. Some examples include the following:

- Other appropriate peer mentors (By excluding some names, you're limiting the people the apprentice approaches.)
- Classes offered internally or externally, in the classroom or online
- Documentation (Be sure to give guidance on what sections of the documentation are current and reliable.)
- Samples of other people's work
- Regulations, policies, standards, legal requirements, and so on (Include any rules that employees must follow.)

In some instances, especially with regard to some silo topics, your apprentice will be able to research the situation and prepare for the test entirely through self-study. You'll know this was an effective way to get him going because you'll be able to orally quiz him in all of the necessary details.

CUSTOMIZING THE TRAINING PLAN

Up to this point, you've been building a list of skills, measures, and resources that could be used by any potential apprentice. Now you should begin to customize it specifically for the apprentice you're working with right now. Typically, this means working out the sequence in which he will develop the skills, and the date by which you expect him to pass the test.

These two factors are customized for each person because each situation is very different. For example, the order you suggest for tackling the knowledge transfer and the date you expect it to be done will vary depending on if you're training someone who has some experience already (for example if the apprentice is joining you at the end of a project; resources are limited or time-sensitive; the apprentice will replace you entirely) and many other factors.

Let's look back at the "live in the bug database" example from earlier in this chapter. The new project manager was starting his new position at the very end of the product development cycle, when the work was really all about managing the defects in the product before release to manufacturing. Matt (his mentor) had roughly 75 skills on the project manager training plan. Because the apprentice wouldn't need many of them for months, Matt moved them to the bottom of the his apprentice's plan and pushed the nine skills that were critical right away to the top. For the first three weeks, Matt's apprentice focused specifically on those nine skills, which created substantial benefits for everyone. The apprentice was able to stay focused, as opposed to being overwhelmed, and armed with the nine essential skills, was able to make a real contribution to the work of the team.

SAMPLE TRAINING PLAN

Figure 4-1 shows a sample Training Plan completed by a software tester. Once a tester apprentice is identified, the peer mentor should customize this plan to include the suggested sequence for learning the skills, based on prior experience, the priority of need for the skill, and availability of resources. (Together, the peer mentor and apprentice negotiate dates by which the apprentice should be able to pass the test.) You can find more samples of training plans in Appendix B.

Skill / Do Statement"	Sequence	Success Measure / "Test" Be able to explain:	Accomplish By (date)	Resources
Design Functionality Tests (User Interface)		• How quality is measured • What standards exist and how rigorously they are applied • The steps in the process and why each is important • The relevance of this process to my job • The relationship between functionality and structural		Mod 2 in Excellence for New Software Test Engineers
Design Structural Tests		• How quality is measured • What standards exist and how rigorously they are applied • The steps in the process and why each is important • The relevance of this tool/process to my job		Mod 3 in Excellence for New Software Test Engineers
Write stress/security/reliability/ performance/privacy/regression tests		• How quality is measured • What standards exist and how rigorously they are applied • The steps in the process and why each is important • The relevance of this tool/process to my job • The relationship between stress and regression tests (how it fits in the Product Cycle) • The top 3 things that often go wrong • 3 best practices for this topic		Mod 5 in Excellence for New Software Test Engineers

Figure 4-1 Completed Training Plan (continues)

Skill / "Do Statement"	Sequence	Success Measure / "Test" Be able to explain:	Accomplish By (date)	Resources
Define components of a test plan		• The relevance of this tool/process to my job • The relationship between test plan and test cases (how it fits in the Product Cycle) • How "quality" is measured • Who is/should be involved/affected/consulted and why		Class: Test Documentation
Automate test cases using C#/C++		• The top 3 things that often go wrong • How to troubleshoot the three most common problems • 3 best practices for this topic • Define blackbox, whitebox • How to determine when to automate and when not to		• Classes: C++, C# • Introduction to Test Automation—Blackbox Test Design Approach • Introduction to Test Automation—Whitebox Test Design Approach
Manage Bugs: Open, verify bug fix		• Top vocabulary words: priority, severity, # steps in the process and why each is important • What standards exist and how rigorously they are applied • How "quality" is measured • The relevance of this tool/process to my job		• Online class on http://<proprietary> close using <proprietary tool name> • Examples (good/bad) • Handbook • Team template • SME=_____ for your team • Software Tester Trainee Program Manual
Check-in and Update files using <proprietary tool name>		• 3 best practices for this topic • Who is/should be involved/ affected/ consulted and why • The top 3 things that often go wrong • How to troubleshoot the 3 most common problems • The first 4 things to check when troubleshooting anything		• <proprietary tool name> Introduction • Infocenter

Figure 4-1   Completed Training Plan (continued)

SUMMARY: PUTTING IT INTO PRACTICE

Armed with this approach to developing a training plan, look back on how you've handled apprentices in the past. What have you done to give them an idea of the list of skills, metrics, resources, sequences, and deadlines? Or, have you left them to figure this out by wandering around and asking questions?

How many hours per week do you spend cleaning up messes made by people who just don't get it? How many of your apprentices spend months, rather than weeks, getting up to speed? This training plan is the most important tool I'll give you in the entire book for solving this problem.

Whether you're mentoring a new hire or someone new to your specialty, start by spending 10 minutes listing the 10 skills or tasks your apprentice needs to know how to do in the first few days. Put them in sequential order in the left column of a table or spreadsheet.

Next, take out the menu of test questions from Tool 4-1b and spend five minutes picking three to five questions for each skill that would give you a good indication of the apprentice's competence. Put either the text of the question itself or number from the menu in a second column.

Then, spend another five minutes and list the resources that are available to help your apprentice pass the test for each topic. Put them in the last column.

Finally, insert a date by which you want your apprentice to meet with you and answer the test questions in an informal, oral quiz. Following this demonstration of understanding, the apprentice can go to work using the new skill.

Save the table you've just created and have your apprentice add skills to it as they come up. In this way the training plan will become more robust and useful for the next apprentice. It'll be a resource that you can use to bring anyone up to speed. Just pick a few skills, put them in order, set a date, and start working toward them. Sound like a plan?

FROM A MANAGER'S VIEW

From my perspective, every single employee on your team should have a training plan. If they're new, the need is more immediate; but even long-term employees should be both building on their own skill sets and training backups to create redundancy and reduce risk. If they're experienced, the test questions above should be more substantial. For example, ask them to explain how to solve the top 50 problems, instead of the top 3.

Managers can facilitate the development of training plans for the apprentices with some simple questions. You don't have to be an expert in the topic to draw out the list of skills. Just help the peer mentor to deconstruct the job.

Breaking a job into its component parts can be overwhelming for some people. They'll often benefit from you sitting with them and asking them some questions. Start by helping them think about the work that their new apprentice will need to be able to do, and then use the answers to shape the required skill into action language, such as bake cinnamon rolls. Here are some additional questions you can ask:

- What do you spend most of your time doing right now?
- What tools do you use and what do you do with them?
- What do you want or need to stop doing and hand over to the apprentice?
- Which tasks are taking up most of your time? What can your apprentice do to lighten your load?
- What sorts of things do you do on a cyclical basis, weekly, monthly, and so on?
- What kinds of problems are you asked to solve? What do you actually do when you set out to solve them? Can any of that be done by an apprentice?

Look at the list and make sure that each of the skills on the list is worded in such a way that you could send someone off to do it (go, run the report). Remember that no competencies or characteristics, such as being a good communicator, belong on this list.

Also help make sure that no one expects the list to be "complete" before it is put into use. Even a 30-minute effort to build this plan will provide an excellent starting point that can be improved upon with each use.

WHEN YOU'RE THE APPRENTICE

You can use this chapter as a guide and build your own training plan, even if no one else is doing it for you. Follow the same strategy outlined above, but your role will be to ask many questions and draw the answers out of your manager and peer mentors, rather than to try to answer the questions yourself.

Start with asking about the tasks you'll be taking on in the near term. For each task, write down what you'll be doing. Once you have something written down, start asking further questions to break it into manageable chunks. Let's say your manager and/or peer mentor tell you that you're going to set up for the trade show or something similarly vague. You'll dive in and break that general task into the sum of its parts. You might go after it along a timeline by asking if your mentor could walk you through all of the general steps from today until the show is over so that you can write them down. You'll want to know where to start, and then ask what happens next over and over again, until you have a good flow. Your list might look like this, with many steps under each chunk:

- Confirm the location and onsite resources for setup.

- Prepare the booth for shipping.

- Ship the booth.

- Work with onsite union staff to set up the booth.
- Tear down and prepare the booth for shipping.
- Clean and store the booth.

With this list in the "skill" column of your training plan, you can start to ask more questions about how much detail you need to know about each one. You can use the test questions above as a guide or "menu" of information you might need to know. Your questions could sound like this:

- How much detail should I know about each of these chunks of the process? Should I know the steps and why, or just who to call?
- Are there mistakes that new people often make? If so, I'd like to know about those so I can avoid them.
- Is there anyone I should be informing along the way as I do this?
- I see that I'll need to work with the unions who set up the trade show. Are there any other rules or standards that I'll need to know about?

You're working to understand the depth at which you should be competent to handle each task and you're taking responsibility for your own training plan. That will get you the respect of your harried co-workers.

Once you've worked out the test questions, you need to ask about resources available to help you. Your questions may be similar to these:

- Has anyone ever produced any documentation on this? Can I go over it with you to make sure it is current?
- Does the trade show have a web site I can use to get more information on setup?
- Has anyone else on our team ever done this setup?

Once you have drafted a training plan, you have a tool you can use to guide your development. Every time a new task comes your way, you can use the training plan as a shield to manage the flow. Carry it with you and when another new job comes your way. You can pull out your plan and ask for help putting the new skills you'll learn in context. It'll sound something like this:

> I've been making a list of all of the tasks I'm taking on so that I can make sure I'm on top of all of it. Can you help me figure out where your new task, and the associated skills, fit into my list? Is this task a higher priority than the ones that are already listed? If so, I'll work on it first. If not, where does it fit in? If it is much lower, could we wait until I get through the list I already have?

I'm not suggesting for a moment that you should be rigid and linear about how you approach getting up to speed. You may need to multitask and juggle several balls at once; that is the nature of many jobs. Still, if you know how the new tasks and skills relate to those you're already working on, even if that means knowing that three things are considered to be the highest priority, at least you'll be clearer about what is expected and will be able to use that information to your best advantage.

5

Teaching What You Know

*How much should I cover and
how much do I deliver it?*

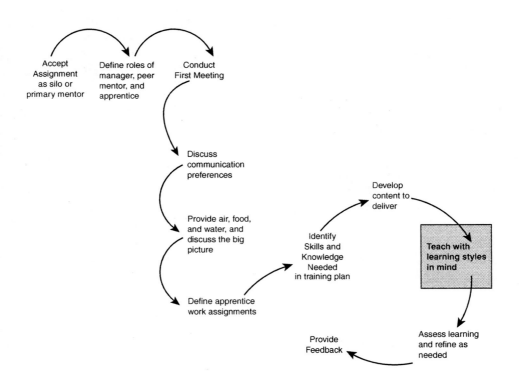

Accept
Assignment
as silo or
primary mentor

Define roles of
manager, peer
mentor, and
apprentice

Conduct
First Meeting

Discuss
communication
preferences

Provide air, food,
and water, and
discuss the big
picture

Define apprentice
work assignments

Identify
Skills and
Knowledge
Needed
in training plan

Develop
content to
deliver

Teach with
learning styles
in mind

Assess learning
and refine as
needed

Provide
Feedback

The first part of this book is devoted to "setting the stage" for the peer mentoring relationship. You've worked to establish roles, set up the work environment, and draft a training plan. Now you can begin executing the training plan. Executing that plan means spending time teaching your apprentice. Your challenge, as a subject matter expert, is determining how much detail you should present. If you were to share all you have learned about a topic during the training phase, you would likely overwhelm your apprentice. So, you'll need to manage the flow of content and do your best to introduce it at a pace that your apprentice can follow.

This is the "Teaching Chapter," and in it you'll find ways to further break your experience into manageable chunks. There are two tools to help you out. The 5-Minute Meeting Plan, which can help you organize a one-hour talk in five minutes, and the Demonstration Technique Worksheet, designed to give you a step-by-step approach to technical demonstration. By the end of this chapter you'll have a handful of strategies you can use to organize and deliver content in a way that will make sense both to you and your apprentice.

It might help to start by giving you a metaphor that offers a (decidedly non-scientific) way of looking at how your brain works.

THE BUCKET AND THE OCEAN

No doubt you already know that you have two kinds of memory, short-term and long-term. Short term memory is finite, like a bucket, in that it can hold a limited amount of information. Long-term memory is more like an ocean, holding seemingly infinite amounts of information. The trouble is that you can't get information directly into your long-term ocean. As shown in Figure 5-1, the information has to go into your short-term bucket first. Then it flows from the bucket to the ocean via a little tiny "tube."

For the most part, this is a good thing, because none of us really wants to remember everything we have ever heard. For example, I for one don't want to recall the room number of the hotel I stayed in last week in Portland. That sort of information should never make it into the ocean. But what about the information that we do want to send to long-term memory? It needs to be organized and sorted out from the extra information that all subject matter experts know, but shouldn't tell.

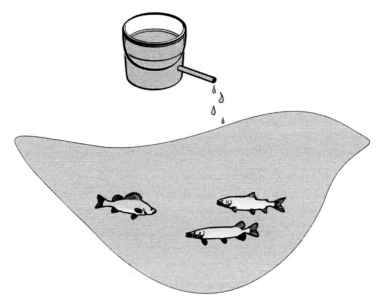

Figure 5-1 Information starts in short-term memory, before making its way into long-term memory.

MANAGING THE SLUDGE

As peer mentors, along with all of the valuable information we share, we deliver lots of information that isn't necessary. I call this "sludge." It is similar to the black stuff sitting at the bottom of the bucket. You know what I am talking about. It's the information you deliver right after saying, "You won't really need to know this right now, but…" Sludge is thick and sticky, and can block up the tube heading to long-term memory. Here are some examples of sludge:

- "If you think the way we do this now is strange, you should hear how we used to do it…"
- "Let me tell you all of the 150 ways this could go wrong…"

- "I did my Ph.D. thesis on this topic. My findings were incredibly interesting..."
- "Did you hear what happened to Walter in accounting this week?"

And here's a classic example of sludge recorded by one of my colleagues:

> The purpose of our meeting today is to learn how to back up a database. I believe you can appreciate the importance of backing up our data, given the number of computer viruses these days. You know, you're also really going to appreciate how easy this administrative tool is to learn. Back in version 1 we had this tool called SAF, System Administration Facility. It was a COW interface, Character-Oriented Windows, which meant you had to type the syntax versus pointing and clicking like we do today. Back then we executed "dump database" not "backup database." But, of course, before you can create a backup, you have to have a file in which to place it. I never could remember if it was the "logical name" or the "physical name" that came after the sp_adddumpdevice stored procedure.
>
> Now, let me demonstrate how easy it is to do today.

All of that, just to learn how to do a backup using a simple, almost completely automated process.

DELIVERING VOLUME

After we dump in some sludge and clog things up, we bring out what I call the "fire hose o' information" and blast it at our poor apprentices! You've all been victims of this, I'm sure. You can probably even picture the over-zealous peer mentor in your life, who went to the white board, cleared his throat, and then launched into his infamous, 90-minute speech that opened with descriptions of how everything worked, random war stories, and the always fascinating tales of how he had persevered through it all. As you can see in Figure 5-2, too much painful and very nearly useless information is a veritable sludge factory with a high-volume fire hose to boot.

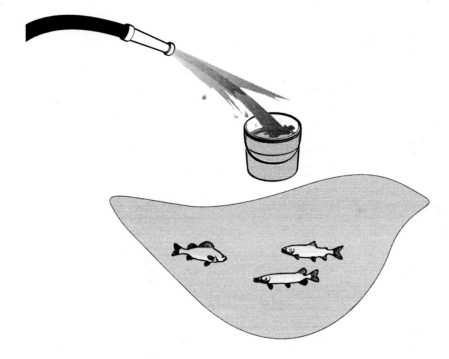

Figure 5-2 Even if you turn up the volume, a one-gallon bucket will still never hold more than one gallon.

Let me ask you this question: How much water will a one-gallon bucket hold, even if you fill it with a fire hose? Right, a gallon, or maybe less, because so much water splashes out. I hope you grasp this concept, because so many peer mentors are guilty of ignoring the fact that conversion of short-term memory into long-term memory has its limits. Mentors often say something like this: "I know you won't get it all on the first pass, but at least you will have heard it." You might as well just say, "I know you can't hear anything I'm saying, but I'll keep talking anyway because I love the sound of my own voice!"

FROM THE BUCKET TO THE OCEAN

You have to do two things to manage the flow of information. Start by paying attention to what you put in the bucket, making sure that it supports your training plan from Chapter 4, "Developing a Training Plan." The plan provides you with focus, prioritization, and a listing of current resources. It can tell you as much about what *not to* cover as it does about what *to* cover. Help your apprentice. Stick to the plan, or choose to modify it by adding topics to the plan in a logical order.

As you use the tools in this chapter to develop the lessons and demonstrations to support the plan you'll want to answer this question: What's the *least* amount of information necessary to make you successful at this task?

For nearly everyone who has some experience, this is a hard question. For instance, I know that I could talk about knowledge transfer and peer mentoring for days, but my class is only one day long. As a result, I have to continually sort through all that I know and cover only the most focused, practical information in the time that I have. The content is still evolving, even after more than 10 years of working on it. You have to select appropriate content and re-evaluate what you teach about your specialty as well.

Focus on the person you're teaching. That will help you pay attention to what you put in the bucket. If you're peer mentoring a new hire, then you're going to deliver different information than you would to an experienced employee learning additional skills. If you're at the beginning of a project, you might not have to cover details about the end of the project. Customize and pare down your "canned speech" whenever possible.

Next, it is important to work very hard to make sure all the information you've carefully placed in your apprentice's bucket makes its way to the ocean for use later. The rest of this book gives you practical ways to make sure that transfer is happening, such as asking assessment questions. By using what you learn in this chapter, you'll be developing a colleague who is predictable in the way he uses the knowledge you've been sharing.

Both these tasks can be achieved through the 5-Minute Meeting Plan and Demonstration Technique Worksheet, which are covered in the remainder of the chapter.

5-MINUTE MEETING PLAN

The 5-Minute Meeting Plan is a tool designed to help you keep your focus on the most important information. It gives you a way to organize your knowledge transfer sessions so that they're as practical as possible—even if you have only 5 minutes to prepare.

See if this scenario sounds familiar: It is Thursday afternoon and your apprentice catches you in the hallway when you're running to an appointment and he asks you a "really big question." You know there is no way you can just spit out an answer on the spot. In fact, from experience with other apprentices, you know that you're going to need roughly 45 minutes or an hour to provide important background information and answer the big question. Now is not the right time. You suggest that your apprentice set up an appointment for the following Tuesday at 3 P.M. You know you have some time free then, and you are also buying yourself an opportunity to be prepared for this important discussion.

Before you can get back to your desk, your apprentice sends you a meeting request for an hour-long appointment at 3 P.M. on Tuesday to answer the big question. You see the meeting request, recognize it from the earlier conversation, and say to yourself, "I have several days to get my act together and prepare to answer the *big question*. This is going to be OK," and you hit "Accept."

When is the next time, realistically, you're going to think about this meeting? For most of us it won't be until the meeting reminder pops up and tells us that we have an appointment in 15 minutes!

At that point, you're in a pickle, because the meeting is coming and you only have 15 minutes to prepare. Before you can even get started thinking through your plan, the phone rings, or someone pops in for a quick question. Even the 15 minutes is eaten away. You look up, and there, standing in your doorway, is your apprentice, ready for the answer. You're trapped. and so you probably do what most people do. You say to yourself, "Oh well, I've done this a million times." You reach into your drawer, pull out your fire hose, and flop it onto the desk. Then you grab the nozzle and prepare to drown your poor apprentice in too much information. Does this sound familiar to you? It happens all the time!

This is the moment of truth. Put down the fire hose, or whiteboard marker, or your favorite handout. Look your apprentice right in the eye and say, "Get out of my office, please" (or substitute a more polite version of asking for some quiet time). "I need five minutes to think before I bury you under too much information. Go get yourself some coffee and I promise I'll be ready for you when you come back."

I know that in a perfect world you would already be prepared and this 5-minute planning session wouldn't be necessary. Unfortunately, that almost never happens. Why? It happens because you have a day job! How can you do your day job, commit to giving your apprentice a whole hour out of an already difficult day, and also prepare in advance? You can't—so you don't. That is where the fire hose problem comes from in the first place.

Once your apprentice has left, you can pull out a list of six action items and begin writing some notes. Tool 5-1 provides the list you'll work from.

Tool 5-1   5-Minute Meeting Plan

1. Define the purpose of the meeting.
2. Explain the relationship to the job.
3. Outline the main points.
4. Note the jargon.
5. Identify practice opportunities.
6. Provide additional resources.

Each action item and associated question is designed to help bring the same focus to your information-sharing that a lesson plan gives to a teacher. There are many side benefits and uses that I'll describe along the way. Here is a detailed description of each of the action items.

1. DEFINE THE PURPOSE OF THE MEETING

I have to confess a bias toward starting every meeting, every time, with a focusing statement, such as, "The purpose of this meeting is..." It reminds both the peer mentor and the apprentice that there is a point to the conversation. Providing a focus for the meeting is especially important for new employees, because they have so little context to begin with. The focusing statement says, "Hey you! Over here! This is what I want you to listen for...."

Here's an example:

> By the end of this meeting I want you to be able to bake cinnamon rolls. You'll be sure that you know how to do it if you can achieve the following:
>
> - Tell me how we use the words knead, baste, and score.
> - Explain the six steps in the process and why each is important.
> - Tell me the three most common mistakes new bakers make on cinnamon rolls.

Can you see the connection between the purpose statement and the training plan we worked on in Chapter 4? The statement comes directly from the training plan. By stating the "cinnamon roll" line item from the training plan in this way, it turns into a specific, measurable learning goal that both you and your apprentice can work on in this session.

If you provide this sort of focus in the first sentence of your meeting, you can expect your apprentice to listen specifically for the information you've called out as crucial. You can also expect him to pass the oral test before you send him off to bake the rolls.

2. EXPLAIN THE RELATIONSHIP TO THE JOB

This next task gives you an opportunity to provide both context and motivation for your apprentice. Most apprentices are bombarded with information as they're coming up to speed. You should help them sort through that information to find the relationships between what you're about to teach them and all the other input they're getting.

Here's how providing the context for your apprentice might sound:

> I'm teaching you how to make cinnamon rolls right now because today is Tuesday, and they're the featured pastry on Wednesdays. We don't make them the rest of the week. Tomorrow, when we come in to work, we'll both spend half of our shift working on making them. Within a couple of weeks, you'll be solely responsible for producing all the cinnamon rolls from this bakery. It is one of our signature products and must be done exactly to the recipe to maintain our reputation.

You can imagine the wheels spinning in your apprentice's brain when you set this sort of context. Here is some of the decoding that is likely to be going on in the apprentice's brain:

- Tomorrow I'll spend half my shift making cinnamon rolls with my peer mentor, so I'll need to know how to do this on my own very soon.
- I'll only get to make the cinnamon rolls once a week. I'd better take good notes so I don't forget what I'm supposed to do before next week.
- Shortly, I'll be on my own so I'd better get this down right away.
- This is an important product with a reputation to protect. I have to bake the rolls exactly as the recipe states. There is no room for creativity on this product.

For different people and different learning styles, the decoding will be at different depths, but everyone will benefit from this context and use it to prepare to learn.

3. OUTLINE THE MAIN POINTS

The next step is to create a quick list of the key points or steps in the process that you're going to cover. The biggest trick here is to list them in order. So often, peer mentors have been doing a task for years, without even thinking about the process. They no longer begin the task by saying, "OK, now, the first thing I need to do is…" They just do it. This makes it difficult for the peer mentor to even identify the first step, let alone remember to explain it. Having time to think about what you actually do before you start teaching it is another reason to carve off five minutes to prepare.

With the baking example I can show you what I mean. Without any preparation, I could imagine the master baker beginning this way:

Step 3:   Take out the recipe. Follow it exactly.

Step 4:   Measure the five dry ingredients into an industrial mixer and mix briefly.

Step 5:   Measure the wet ingredients into the largest bowl.

Step 6:   Add the wet ingredients to the industrial mixer all at once.

Step 7:   Add the "secret" ingredient.

Step 8:   Run mixer for six-and-a-half minutes, and so on.

All of this works perfectly, of course, as the master baker explains and demonstrates the process. However, the next time the apprentice baker makes the rolls, he runs into two major problems. He runs out of the secret ingredient, and makes the wrong kind of rolls. How could this be possible? Well, the master baker started with Step 3 because he forgot about Steps 1 and 2.

It turns out that each morning the master baker walks through the supply room and glances up to check stock of everything that is needed for the next day's shift. If anything is missing, he calls in an order. He's been doing this every day for 20 years and has stopped making the connection between checking the stock and making cinnamon rolls. Because the last apprentice took over making the rolls, the master baker didn't check that stock anymore and they ran out of the secret ingredient.

The other thing the master baker does during morning rounds is to check the "Board" to see what specialty ideas the manager has for this shift. Checking the Board is just part of his routine, and like checking stock, he doesn't connect it to making cinnamon rolls. It turns out the rolls the apprentice is supposed to make are for St. Patrick's Day and the icing is supposed to be green. It says so right on the board. But no one ever told the apprentice about it.

Outlining the main points will not catch every single one of these unconscious steps, but I have found over the years that it does catch quite a few. If you think through your list and edit it a bit before you start teaching, it'll be much easier for your apprentice to follow.

In some instances, you'll be lucky enough to have an established, documented process from which to teach. In that case, you'll just spend this phase of planning the meeting checking the documentation for changes and ensuring that the steps before and after what is covered in the documents are considered as well.

4. NOTE THE JARGON

I once had a new employee tell me that the hardest part about being new is that you don't know enough words to ask an intelligent question. Vocabulary is so important. Yet we, as peer mentors, take it for granted. It really helps to stop and think about your particular job's jargon, acronyms, and shorthand. Every company has its own language, and sometimes that language is even distinct to a team. Plus, the language evolves over time. Then, some people use the old version, while others have moved on to a more recent version. Microsoft is famous for this. I was heading there recently to meet with a client. She told me her building was located at the "Space Labs." Well, because I've been around there forever, I happen to know exactly what she meant. The funny thing is that Space Labs is actually the name of the company that used to occupy the land on which her building now sits. They're long gone, and their building was torn down several years ago, but she still says "Space Labs" to describe it, rather than calling it "Building 142," the current name of the building.

All of you have stories just like this one. What's difficult is that we don't think much about the jargon we choose. It is our language, so how can we "notice" when we're using it? I find that one sure way to stay on top of explaining vocabulary is to look at the outline you created in listing the main points you need to cover (Step 3) and circle any words or acronyms that pop up as potentially confusing. In the case of the cinnamon roll example, we already called out three words in our purpose statement (knead, baste, score), but there may be more as the list develops.

5. IDENTIFY PRACTICE OPPORTUNITIES

In developing a new skill, your apprentice probably needs to get her hands on the work in order to ensure she has really learned. As the peer mentor, you need to control the practice circumstances so the apprentice doesn't do too much damage while still learning. Sometimes, that means you'll put the apprentice directly into the real world to "sink or swim." Other times, you'll have a lab or simulation environment where your apprentice can safely try out her new skill before being put to work in the production environment.

In any event, it helps to think about practice opportunities in advance. In my experience, peer mentors default to the sink or swim option when the risks are far higher than is appropriate. You have to ask yourself how much work would need to be redone if your new apprentice made common mistakes, and whether it would make more sense to monitor the apprentice more closely to avoid redoing the work.

6. PROVIDE ADDITIONAL RESOURCES

Finally, you'll want to think through the resources that are available to help your apprentice when you're not around. If you filled out the resources column in your training plan, you need only to move the resources into your meeting plan. The resource list should include other people who are appropriate to ask for help, any classes that the apprentice can take, and any current documentation or examples that would be useful.

For the bakery example the list might include the following:

- The recipe
- The materials reorder forms
- Other bakers with experience in making cinnamon rolls
- The "Board"

Can you see how making this list would have helped catch the problems noted above? It would have called out the materials reorder form and the "Board."

As you create the resource list, be sure that you're also thinking about any resources that you want to steer your apprentice away from using. For example, are there people on the team who you want the apprentice to avoid using as a resource, either because those individuals are already swamped or you don't want them to pass on their bad habits? You should also offer a warning if any of the documentation is out of date.

CREATING AND USING THE 5-MINUTE MEETING PLAN

Now it's time to try out this idea. If you're like most peer mentors, there is someone (new hire, customer, boss, co-worker outside your team, etc.) who is about to knock on your door and ask you to explain what you know. I'd recommend that you keep Tool 5-1 handy so that you can be prepared to organize your thoughts when they do.

Once you create the meeting plan, you have a resource you can use in a number of ways. For starters, you can use it to guide your conversation with your apprentice. If you give a copy of the meeting plan to your apprentice and keep a copy in front of yourself while you are talking, it will help you stay on track throughout the meeting. You'll think twice before wandering off on a tangent that isn't noted on your plan, and your apprentice will often want to make notes right on the outline. That is a great way to ensure that he is connecting to the new information.

Next, you can have your apprentice improve on the meeting plan by typing up your handwritten notes and adding any important details that he heard you say when you were teaching. This isn't a mere clerical task. It's a way of paraphrasing the content and moving it from the bucket to the ocean. Don't let him get carried away and turn your simple outline into full-fledged documentation, unless there is someone committed to keeping it up-to-date over the long term. In my experience, an outline can be updated on the fly by whichever peer mentor is using it. But once the outline becomes more than a page or two, it often goes onto the "To Do" pile, and never gets updated again.

You can reuse your meeting plan by making it available to other silo mentors and asking them to teach the topic the next time. By preparing the plan, you will have provided a valuable, focusing resource. Often that is enough to encourage others to take on some of the teaching responsibilities.

EXAMPLE OF A MEETING PLAN

Figure 5-3 provides an example of a completed meeting plan from a manufacturing environment. Imagine someone trying to teach this task from memory, without the list. Even if they were able to say everything in the right order, without missing a step or forgetting to explain the jargon, how much easier is it for an apprentice to have this simple list to follow?

Explain Meeting Purpose:

How to communicate priorities to Final Assembly teams

Explain Relationship to Job:

Preparation for the daily 06:00 shift meeting

Outline Main Points:

1. Look up and print out the BOXSCORE in A&I
2. Highlight the flow days and loads for the 6-7-8 and 7-8-Ramp teams
3. Highlight specials, e.g., lavatory and galley configurations
4. Look up and print out NCRs for pickups
5. Discuss behind schedules
6. Discuss how to clear pick ups and sell todays jobs

Note Jargon:

- BOXSCORE — on-line performance dashboard
- A&I — Boeing job tracking system
- Flow Days — bar deadlines
- NCR — non-conforming report
- Pick up — quality rejection
- Sell — submit to QA for approval

Practice Opportunities

- All systems and reports accessible from any computer terminal

Other Resources

- All shift supervisors follow this process; ask them for help
- QA can help with NCRs, pick up and how to sell jobs.
- On-line help available in A&I and NCR

Figure 5-3   A sample meeting plan from a manufacturing job

MEETING PLANS AT SOUTHERN COMPANY

Another good example of meeting planning is from one of the project management teams at Southern Company in Atlanta. Southern Company had about 40 full-time project managers and then another 30–40 employees who didn't report into their structure, but did manage projects on an as-needed basis while doing other jobs in the organization. This flexible staffing was a terrific way to manage the ebb and flow of need for project managers across the organization.

The trouble with having so many non-standard project managers was that they were inconsistent in their approach to project management. Each of the project managers came up with their own system for gathering requirements, writing plans, estimating, scheduling, and so on, which meant that their results were less predictable. There was clearly a need to use the full-time project managers, who were well trained in a formal project management methodology, to peer mentor the lay project managers. Management defined the skills that each lay project manager needed to have, and then (in the resource column) divided the skills among the full-time project managers, setting some up as silo peer mentors for each of the topics.

Each silo peer mentor created a meeting plan using Tool 5-1 for the assigned specialty. This process started very informally, using five-minute windows of time to draft outlines as they were needed. Each time an outline was needed, the silo peer mentor would spend another five minutes improving it. Occasionally the apprentices would also add in pieces of information. None of the outlines were allowed to exceed two pages, so that they'd never be too cumbersome. As the meeting plans began to take shape, they were posted in the resource column of the training plan as the most current and useful documentation for that topic. Then, as the meeting plans stabilized, they could be used by other peer mentors, besides the silo mentors who wrote them, to guide the training of apprentice project managers.

The 5 Minute Meeting Plan allows you to create simple, clear documentation in a matter of minutes. For many of you, there is no formal documentation that describes what you do. You rely on knowledge transfer discussions and real-world experience to bring your apprentices up to speed. For some apprentices, the lack of documentation is just an inconvenience. For others, the lack of structure makes learning extremely difficult and has an enormous negative impact on how quickly they can learn.

EVEN THE AUTHOR NEEDS A REMINDER

As I was writing this book I was asked to train a client who was new to her job on a facilitation technique I'd used many times for her company. She was going to run a planning meeting and wanted the outcome to be in line with the work I had done before she arrived. We set up some time on a Tuesday morning at 11 o'clock for me to give her some tips on how to facilitate the meeting. I had several days to prepare, so you'd think that I would have been ready—but I wasn't. The two meetings I had that morning before we talked ran longer than I expected, and instead of having a half hour before we talked, I was late getting to our call. When I realized that I wasn't prepared, you might guess that I would tell her so, and ask for a few minutes to prepare before I started talking, but I didn't. After all, this was just a simple meeting facilitation, really. The main thing to explain was a couple of questions that needed to be asked over and over to move the group toward a tight plan. How hard could that be to explain?

Instead of taking 5 minutes to think, I got on the phone, pulled out my fire hose, and started blasting. I ran around in circles blabbering about all sorts of things that I hadn't thought of until I started talking. Finally, about 10 minutes into the call, I said, "Ugh!! I know better than to ramble on, unprepared. I teach this stuff. I'm babbling like an idiot. It must be pretty hard for you to follow." The client was polite, but let me know that it wasn't going very smoothly. So, I asked for 5 minutes to prepare right then, in the middle of the call. I put her on hold, whipped out a meeting plan, and e-mailed it to her on the spot. The rest of the call was much clearer and she had an outline that she could use to make her own notes. It was embarrassing to have to do that, but it was much, much better than continuing on when there was little hope of success. The 5-minute time out meant the last 40 minutes of our meeting were far more productive. If I'd taken the time *before* beginning, it would have been an even better meeting.

DEMONSTRATING A TASK

Now we move to the second tool in this chapter. Many peers teach using some form of demonstration, whether that means showing how to use physical tools in an industrial setting, or demonstrating a piece of software in your office. This section provides some advice on how to ensure that your apprentice will leave the demonstration with a known skill set. It should reduce the overall amount of time you spend doing the demonstration and will definitely reduce the amount of work that needs to be redone as your apprentices come up to speed.

The most common way many of us have experienced a demonstration goes something like this scenario: Your apprentice comes into your workspace either by wandering by or with some intention. When you see him you say, "Hey, there you are. I'm working on something that you're going to need to know how to do. Why don't you watch me do this? Here goes...."

You launch into a complete walkthrough of the skill. Next, you jump out of your chair and say, "Great! Now, here, you take over and try it."

At this point, you've put your apprentice into the driver's seat and you're whispering words of encouragement. "Good, more of that. No, not there, over here. That's it. Good going. See, you did it! Now, there's a pile of work waiting for you. Go ahead and get going."

Does this sound familiar? I call this two-step process the "Hey, watch me—here, you do it—school of demonstration."

This type of demonstration works some of the time, but it doesn't work consistently. There is a very real reason why two steps in a demonstration are not enough to consistently move the information from the bucket to the ocean—from short-term to long-term memory.

Advertisers figured out years ago that it takes roughly six exposures to an advertisement's message before the consumer begins to remember the message. That is why you'll commonly see the same McDonald's commercial more than once during a television show.

You'll think to yourself, didn't I just see that commercial, and McDonald's says, "Two! (Only four more exposures to go!)"

How can we use this same information to help your apprentice? You have to plan to expose him to the information more than twice. (Hey, watch me. Here, you do it.) The following discussion provides a flow of information that will get you there.

DEMONSTRATION TECHNIQUE WORKSHEET

This tool can be used every time you sit at a computer or do a demonstration in an industrial setting as a way of teaching. It'll force you to spend a little more time in the demonstration, but it'll guarantee more predictable results. Tool 5-2 provides the steps to a great demonstration

Tool 5-2   Demonstration Technique Worksheet

1. Provide a reason for the demonstration.
2. Talk through the steps.
3. Demonstrate at a normal pace.
4. Demonstrate again and explain the logic behind each step.
5. Have your apprentice talk you through the steps.
6. Provide a practice.

I suggest that you let your apprentice know that you're going to use this technique so he doesn't get nervous along the way. He is probably used to the "Hey watch me—here, you do it" approach to demonstration. Knowing there are six steps will help him feel sure that you're going to do what it takes to make sure he has learned.

STEP 1: PROVIDE A REASON FOR THE DEMONSTRATION

Every demonstration should start by providing motivation for the apprentice. Many adult learners simply cannot learn unless they know why they should care about what you're saying. This doesn't have to be a big motivational speech, but it should give some context. This step should take less than one minute, because you're only making a few opening remarks.

As an example, if I were to say, "I'm going to teach you how to plant a tree," you might look at me as if I were crazy. But, if I told you that I'm teaching you to plant a tree *because* this weekend we're going to have 150 trees delivered to our neighborhood and we're all expected to help get them planted, you'd understand why you should pay attention and learn how to plant a tree.

If your apprentice is going to use the skill you're about to demonstrate in the next few hours or days, or if he is going to use it every day, or if the task will only be completed once but must be done perfectly or someone will suffer the consequences, then tell him.

I'd also include a comment about taking notes. If you're demonstrating something that isn't documented clearly (or maybe even if it is), you should advise your apprentice to pull out pencil and paper and jot down a few ideas because you'll be asking him to talk you through the demonstration in Step 5.

STEP 2: TALK THROUGH THE STEPS

Once you've gotten his attention with the first step, you should tell him what you're going to do once, before showing anything. That means you must look away from your computer or work station and look at your apprentice so you can talk through the demonstration before you give it. For some people, this will seem awkward. You may not be used to looking at anything other than a computer screen. It is, however, important that the focus be on the explanation (the story). Because this is only a verbal account of the demonstration, it should take less than one minute, as well.

Using my tree-planting demonstration as an example, here's how it would sound: "We're going to dig a hole that is twice as wide and twice as deep as the root ball of the tree. Then, we'll put some compost into the bottom of the hole and mix it up. Next, we'll set the tree in the hole, cut the string, and pull the burlap sack out of the way. Finally, we'll fill the hole with water, push the soil back in, do a dance on the soil around the base of the tree, put a stick into the ground, and tie the tree to the stick."

What happens in your apprentice's brain as you read this high-level, quick, run-through of what we're about to do? He gets an image of the process and visualizes the tree being planted. For some, the image is in Technicolor, with green grass, blue skies, and birds flying by. For others, the image consists of stick figures moving in black and white. The image each apprentice sees speaks to that individual's learning style and doesn't really matter at this point. Everyone gets some sort of vision for the process. That is what we're looking for.

WHAT'S GOING ON IN YOUR BRAIN DURING STEPS 1 AND 2?

As I've noted, these first two steps are extremely quick to complete—so quick that they're practically free. For less than a two-minute investment, you can bring your apprentice well down the path toward learning. One reason they're so quick is that they're not very substantive. Your apprentice might not even really notice that you did them. So why even bother? There's a very good reason.

Imagine you are at a footrace—10K or a marathon—and are watching everyone prepare for the race. Some of the runners are on the ground stretching, some are taking off their warm-ups, and some are saying goodbye to their friends. Then, an official says, "Runners on your mark!" This causes everyone to get themselves to the starting line, line up, and get ready to go. Then the official shoots off the gun and everyone runs toward the finish line.

What would happen if, while all the runners were preparing for the race—some on the ground stretching, some taking off their warm-ups and some saying goodbye to their friends—the official simply shot off the gun and yelled, "Go!"? Some people would get it together and figure out where to go and take off. Others would try to go, but would trip and fall and hurt themselves in the confusion. Some would run really fast but in the wrong direction. Some would just give up. The results would be unpredictable. That's why the officials always warn runners that the race is about to begin. Steps 1 and 2 are the equivalent of that warning. In effect, you're saying, "Hey, over here. I'm about to teach you something. It is important. Pay attention...."

STEP 3: DEMONSTRATE AT A NORMAL PACE

Now you're ready to do a version of the "Hey, watch me" step that is how most demonstrations begin. It usually takes a little bit longer, but not so much that you would notice.

You may need to adjust your pace a bit to make it "normal," which is the point of this step. My definition of normal follows:

- **By the book.** I bet you know at least several ways to circumvent the rules surrounding the skill you are presenting. Today is not the day to teach them. Be sure that the first time your apprentice learns a new skill, he learns how to do it exactly as it was intended. Perhaps tomorrow you can teach a few appropriate ways to bend the rules, but not today.

- **No shortcuts or hot keys.** Anyone who's used a computer system long enough has figured out how to move quickly through the myriad layers to get to the work. For some this is hot keys, such as "Ctrl-X" for cut or "Ctrl-V" for paste. Even the "Enter" key is a shortcut for clicking "OK." While it is nice for your apprentice to know that someday he will be as zippy on the system as you are, it isn't helpful for you to show how you can fly through the system when you're teaching. If you're demonstrating software, I recommend that you push the keyboard aside and use the mouse. This will force a slower pace and your apprentice can observe the graphical representation of the story you told in the first step, making it all come to life from beginning to end.

■ **At a pace your apprentice can follow easily.** If your apprentice
has experience with the tool or system and you're just showing a new element of it, then you can move faster. If your
apprentice is new, you have to go slower. The key is that you
select the pace for him, not for yourself.

At this point, I'd plant a tree and let my apprentice watch the
whole thing from beginning to end. I'd take a few questions, but I
wouldn't expect to answer all of them, because this isn't the last
step.

STEP 4: DEMONSTRATE AGAIN, AND EXPLAIN THE LOGIC BEHIND EACH STEP

During this run-down of the content, you'll add an important
element for helping your apprentice remember the steps and troubleshoot any problems that may come up. You're going to demonstrate the entire process again, this time explaining the logic behind
each step. For the purposes of this demonstration, logic explains
why we do the step and/or the consequences of not doing it.

Here's how it would roll out for the tree planting example:

1. Dig the hole twice as wide and twice as deep as the root ball so
   that there is soft soil for the tree's hair roots to settle into.

2. Put compost in the bottom of the hole so the tree has a little
   snack and also to get the top of the root ball up to the height
   of the surrounding ground. If you bury the tree too deep, you
   will ultimately strangle it.

3. Place the tree in the hole, cut the string, and pull the burlap
   sack out of the way so that the tree can get established without having to fight through the burlap sack.

4. Fill the hole with water next, because soaking the root ball can
   reduce transplant shock, and transplant shock can kill the
   tree. The worst part about that is that you won't know the tree
   is dead until you've waited months for Spring to come and can
   see that the tree hasn't leafed out.

5. Push the soil in around the base of the tree and do a dance on the soil so that you can remove the air pockets in the soil. Those air pockets can damage the hair roots, which is bad for the health of the tree.

6. Put a stick in the ground and tie it to the tree so the tree doesn't blow over in the next windstorm.

Can you see that there is a reason for each one of the steps and that none of them is optional? Omitting a couple of the steps could even be fatal. That means that if you did everything right except for one thing, you could still kill the tree. Are you ever just one keystroke (or lever pull, or missed step) from disaster in your job? For many jobs, this is often the case.

Your apprentice will use the logic that you've just given to help remember the steps. He will also use it for problem solving later on—for example, if the tree blew over, I must have forgotten to tie it to the stick.

In my experience, this step often doubles the amount of time spent on the demonstration. While this may sound overwhelming, imagine how much rework and clean-up time you will save when your apprentice makes far fewer mistakes.

STEP 5: HAVE YOUR APPRENTICE TALK YOU THROUGH THE STEPS

By now you've covered the content in detail. Your apprentice should have good notes and a strong grasp of the flow. The only way you'll know for sure, though, is if you ask him to talk you through the steps in the process you've been demonstrating, and tell you what he has learned. This is an "open-book" oral quiz. There is no need for him to have memorized every detail. It is important that he can use the notes as a resource to help him get on track.

Set this step up by saying, "I'd like to stop talking now and give you a chance to tell me what you understand the steps in this process to be. That'll help me make sure that I've been clear in providing you the information. Feel free to use your notes and try to give me the steps, anything that stuck with you regarding why each step is important, and the consequences of missing any of the steps."

It isn't necessary to have the apprentice show you while he's telling you, so this step should be very quick. Just be sure he's doing the talking, not you. You can ask questions along the way to make sure he has the needed depth of understanding:

- Why we do it (the step) that way?
- What would happen if you skipped that?
- Why do people sometimes overlook that detail?
- How much time should you expect to spend on this step?
- What would you do if you got stuck on this step?
- How do you know when the task is complete and that you are meeting the standards?

Don't leave this step until your apprentice can confidently talk you through the entire process. Experience may still be required to make him "skilled." But at this point, your apprentice should have a solid foundation.

STEP 6: PROVIDE A PRACTICE

Now, you're finally ready to put your apprentice in the driver's seat and let him do the work. This step is already familiar to you as an approach, because we always want to get our apprentices to go to work. If Step 5 went well, it may be fine to let your apprentice work alone. But if he had a difficult time, you'll know to monitor his progress more closely.

WHAT IF THE TREE PLANTING PROCESS SOUNDS WRONG?

Many times, when I tell the tree-planting story during the workshop, I get arguments from people who have another way of planting a tree. They argue that adding compost isn't a good idea, that it isn't necessary to take off the burlap sack, or that "dancing on the soil" is actually bad for the root system. These are all examples of personal opinions that differ from the process I've asked them to learn. Does something parallel ever happen in your team? You hire someone with experience and he starts arguing about the differences between his experience and the process you're offering. This happens all of the time. As the peer mentor, you should have a way of handling it. I suggest that you say something like this to your apprentice:

> I know you have experience in this process and it may differ from the way we do things here. I'm going to ask you to listen to our process and then explain it back to me entirely to be sure that you understand how we do things. In return, I'll listen to you explain the differences between our process and the way you're used to working. If there is anything that we need to change at that point, we can decide what to do.

In this way, you can acknowledge that there may be differences in style, ensure that your apprentice still learns from you, and perhaps get some new ideas from your apprentice's experience. It is a win for everyone.

CREATING OPPORTUNITIES TO PRACTICE

In both the "5-Minute Meeting Plan" and the "Demonstration Techniques" sections, I suggest that you give your apprentice a chance to practice the new skill. For some apprentices, this is the most important stage in moving information from their short-term to long-term memory. Here are some rules of thumb for creating practice opportunities.

SET A GOAL FOR THE PRACTICE

It helps to clarify what you're expecting out of the practice. Sometimes you'll look for finished work, while at other times you wouldn't expect the final product to be given to a customer or otherwise put alongside the work of a more experienced employee. If you expect a certain volume of work to be done within a certain time, then say so. Be sure to clarify your expectations so there are no surprises.

DON'T ABANDON YOUR APPRENTICE

Every apprentice wants an opportunity to be independent and do "real" work as soon as possible. Every peer mentor wants the same thing. Just be sure that there is a plan for handling any unforeseen problems that might arise. Be sure that your apprentice knows how to find you and/or someone else who can help if he gets stuck. Telling him when you plan to check back in will also help.

DEFINE BOUNDARIES

Some of your apprentices will be overly cautious and won't dream of doing more than exactly what they're asked to do, which creates its own set of problems. But others will be anxious to prove their capabilities and will take off beyond what you might consider appropriate. You can moderate their performances by providing some guidance. For example, you might tell them what to do if they finish a task early, or which "doors" can and can't be opened. The intent here is to make sure that they stay on the right path, but get as far down the way as possible.

SUMMARY: PUTTING IT INTO PRACTICE

Transferring knowledge to your apprentices through preparing and delivering content is at the heart of the peer mentor–apprentice relationship. There is a flow that, if followed, will make the transfer more consistently successful. Even on your busiest day, you're going to want to find the extra five minutes to prepare using the meeting planner, or you're going to want to pull out the Demonstration Techniques Worksheet and work through it from top to bottom. In exchange, you're going to have a much better shot at successfully transferring knowledge, which will result in fewer mistakes, less rework, and increased productivity.

FROM A MANAGER'S VIEW

As a manager, you'll benefit from the consistency that comes from a prepared peer mentor delivering content. You can encourage the use of the tools presented in this chapter by providing a place to archive the most recently used versions for each task or skill. You can also ask your primary and silo mentors to share their work with each other.

The most common excuse you'll hear for ignoring these ideas is that the mentors are too busy. Don't accept that excuse. The output from the 5-Minute Meeting Plan might be more detailed if your peer mentors spent 30 minutes working up a meeting plan, but they don't really need to do that right away. Spending five minutes preparing an effective transfer of knowledge will give them real results. After all, it isn't hard to imagine that training developed based on five minutes of thought is going to be far better than a session for which no time was devoted to preparation.

WHEN YOU'RE THE APPRENTICE

You can use these tools in reverse to manage any "fire hose" that gets pointed at you. For example, you can take the 5-Minute Meeting Plan and turn all of the points into interview questions:

1. Could you please tell me the purpose of the meeting? What would you like me to be able to do when this meeting is over?

2. How does this skill relate to my job? Will I be doing this soon? Often?

3. Could you outline the main points before you dive into the specifics? It would help me create a complete set of notes.

4. I heard you use a number of words that I'm not familiar with when you outlined the main points. Could you define them for me?

5. I was wondering if there will be a chance to practice this new skill? When and how will we do that?

6. Are there any other resources I should or shouldn't use (other people, web sites, classes, documentation, etc.) to help me learn this topic?

Your peer mentor will see you as someone who is interested in getting the work done and will appreciate your taking an interest in the information.

6

Leveraging Learning Styles

What if we aren't on the same page?

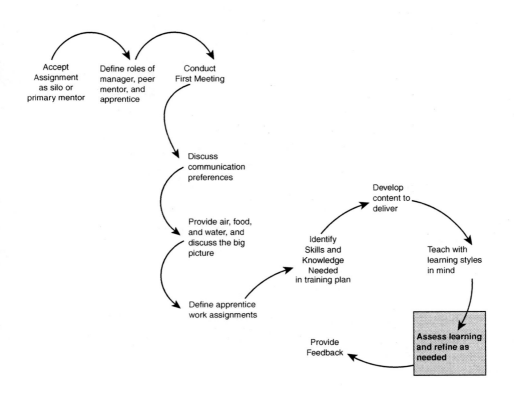

I bet that somewhere along the way you've had the experience of teaching two people at one time using the same approach and one of them "got it" while the other one just didn't. Your gut reaction might be to separate them and declare one is "sharp" and the other is "not." Such perceptions may be mistakes. The truth is that while you may have two different levels of smarts in the two apprentices, you might also have two people who are equally capable, but just learn differently. Part of your job as a peer mentor is to figure this out. Think of this chapter as a form of diversity training—learning how to work with and relate to people who learn differently than you do.

You may have noticed that throughout most of this book the drumbeat is for you, as the peer mentor, to determine how this whole relationship can work best for you. I asked you to think about how you want to be interrupted, how you'd like e-mails to come to you, the best time of day for you to be available to your apprentice, how you'd like to fit this role into your day job, and so on. All of that is about making the relationship work for you. Because you're the finite resource with many issues placing a burden on your time, that makes sense.

In this chapter, though, I suggest that you head the other direction and first look at what your apprentice needs in order to learn best. This means altering the way you deliver content, depending on which apprentice you're teaching. A learning style isn't so much a choice as it is a characteristic of your apprentice's brain. If you can meet on his side of the divide, things will go better.

By the end of this chapter, I want you to know you have a learning style and how to teach to people who are different than you are. I'll give you two simple ways of thinking about this. One tool you can use is a model based loosely on experiential learning and learning styles. The other is an even simpler tool you can use in minutes when you are teaching a task. The second model is also geared toward giving your apprentice a way to identify his own learning style and ask for information in a way that meshes with that style.

There are many ways to become an expert in learning styles, but you don't have to be an expert to take advantage of these ideas. In fact, I won't even get to the learning style model, complete with labels, until the end of the chapter. The goal isn't to be able to put a label on your apprentice. The better approach is to pay attention to doing a few key things to make sure you're a well-rounded teacher. If you are, you'll be able to reach each apprentice, regardless of his learning style.

HOW YOU LEARN AFFECTS HOW YOU TEACH

The first step in thinking about learning styles is to figure out your own learning style. Once you understand yourself, you can begin to understand how you relate to your apprentice. The golden rule is to do unto others as you would have them do unto you. Too often we apply that rule to the way we teach. It shouldn't be surprising that most of us teach in a way that makes sense to us. If your apprentice doesn't learn like you do, this can be a problem.

Here's how it works: If you're the kind of person who likes to learn by being given a really hard problem, a stack of documentation, a quiet corner, and three days left alone to solve the problem on your own, then you're likely to give your apprentice (you guessed it) a really hard problem, a stack of documentation, a quiet corner, and three days left alone to solve the problem on his own. Now, if your apprentice learns like you do, he will think you're a genius and the first person who ever really understood him. If he doesn't learn like you do, you'll be perceived as an antisocial monster who hates his guts. That's two very different responses to the same actions—directly attributable to his learning style.

WHAT IS LEARNING STYLE?

See if one of these scenarios sounds familiar to you. Imagine receiving a new box of software on your desk. How would you go about learning the software? Would you

- Read the entire box so that you could understand why you need the software before you even open it up to check it out?

- Open the box and set everything aside except the manual, which you'd read from cover to cover? You'd learn the whole program before ever booting it up.

- Open the box, install the software, and mess around with it for awhile, and figure out how it works for the most part? You'd go to the documentation and use it to sort out the few details you couldn't discover on your own.

- Boot up the software and then call someone you know who's an expert and ask them to give you some quick tips? You'd listen for a while and get what you need to get started from the conversation.

If one or any combination of these scenarios sounds like your typical approach, then you're on your way to recognizing your own learning style. If any of them sounds like it is definitely not something you'd consider, that is equally important to note. As you read this chapter you'll find more language you can use to define your own style.

QUESTIONS TO ASSESS LEARNING STYLE

You can assess an apprentice's learning style in either a passive or an active fashion. The passive approach is simply to notice the ways you provide content to your apprentice and see what works best for him. For example, if you offer him a chance to read all of the documentation before you teach him anything, and he not only reads what you assign, but asks for more, you have a pretty good indication that reading is one of the ways he learns best. On the other hand, if he sees reading the documentation as a punishment and doesn't refer to it often, that tells you that reading isn't the best option. You can also observe the results. If you're teaching and he is able to answer your questions and demonstrate an understanding of the skills and ideas, then you know you've done a good job of accommodating his learning style. You'll know, because he learned from you.

If you'd like to be more active in addressing this issue, you can ask some questions to assess his learning style and let the apprentice know that you're trying to deliver information in a way that works.

This is another opportunity to explain your desire to be a good peer mentor and let your apprentice take responsibility for helping improve the productivity of the relationship.

Below are some questions you can ask your apprentice to learn more about his learning style. Be sure to start the conversation by explaining why you're asking these questions. You might say, "I know that everyone learns a little differently. For instance, I really like to have some time with the documentation before I listen to the explanation or watch a demonstration. I'd like to know more about your learning style so that I can take that into account as I teach you." Then ask one or more of these questions:

- Tell me about how you learned how to do your last job.
- Who's been most helpful in teaching you how to do your job(s) and what did they do that was so useful?
- Tell me about any examples of people who tried to teach you and it didn't go very well.
- How do you typically use documentation to get yourself up to speed? Do you read every word, occasionally look for specific things, or generally not read much at all?
- If you're learning a new tool or computer program, do you like to discuss the topic first, watch someone else do it, read about it, or try it out yourself first?

You can ask these questions at any stage of the peer mentoring relationship, but there are some obvious benefits to asking them early on. For instance, if you find that your apprentice doesn't typically benefit from reading the documentation and your habit is to always start there, you can change your plan before you've wasted a lot of time. It is just another way to focus on delivering content in the most productive way.

USING LEARNING STYLES

In *Experiential Learning: Experience as the Source of Learning and Development* (Prentice Hall, 1984), David Kolb defines a commonly used model of learning. When I studied it for the first time many years ago, it quickly changed how I taught my students in the classroom and my apprentices on the job. As I deconstructed my own ideas about teaching, with learning styles in mind, I saw that I really did have a lopsided approach. My favorite peer mentors and teachers had always brought plenty of energy and "theater" to my training, seeking to entertain me and keep things lively. They told stories and gave lots of opportunities for interaction and discussion. They provided documentation, I guess, but I never really paid much attention to it because I almost never find it very helpful. Any teacher who merely lectured from a formal outline that was projected on the wall (while all of us tried to figure out what to write in our notes) was, in my opinion, just short of criminally negligent. Who needs all that boring structure?

So, guess how I ordered my own teaching style? I went into each situation thinking that if I "entertain" my students, I will teach them. This approach worked well for all of the people in the room who were just like me. They could follow my anecdotes, laugh at my jokes, and generally come away with a solid understanding of the content. But for the others, my teaching style was painful. Their heads would swim in the unfocused, "random" approach and they'd get frustrated waiting for me to get to the point. The lack of much in the way of outlines or pointers to documentation was most difficult for them, because their brains were looking for that stable structure upon which to build.

Once I understood the concept of learning styles and thought about the differences between myself and some of my students, I made changes to my approach and improved the quality of my delivery, especially for the people who don't learn like I do. While I was applying these ideas in the classroom with my students, I also started to modify them for the one-on-one peer mentoring setting as well.

In the next section, I give you my version of Kolb's work and I apologize, in advance, for the liberties I'm about to take in the interpretation. As I've worked with many peer mentors over the years I've come to believe that the quickest way to take advantage of the research is to reduce it to the actions you can take to help your apprentice. I like to focus on what you can *do* with an understanding of learning styles. I'll try to provide ways you can apply the ideas in your peer mentoring situations.

As you read the following model, notice your own response to the explanations of each section. Whether you find yourself nodding your head and saying, "Yeah, that's the important stuff!" or you read it and say, "What a load of garbage!" your reaction will give you some insight into your own style. Pay particular attention to the sections that you don't find as intuitive, because those areas might be the ones where you have the most opportunity to improve.

TEACHING TO DIFFERENT LEARNERS

This model divides all learners into four main styles with characteristics that must be addressed to help those who fall into that style learn better. It isn't as though your apprentice won't be able to learn at all if you don't get this just right, but you'll certainly improve productivity if you do. I've labeled each style with the first, and most repeated, question they'll likely ask as your apprentice. The "Why?" learner wants to know why he cares; the "What" learner wants to know the facts; the "How does it work" learner wants everything in context, plus an opportunity to try it out; and the "What If" learner wants to know how you decided to do the work in this specific way and if you've considered alternatives.

As you read through each section you may find yourself saying that one or two stand out clearly or that three or even all four sound familiar. Any combination is fine, because you have the potential to have all four learning styles in you. You might find yourself relating to one or another more closely, depending on the topic you're learning, the timing, the resources that are available, and so on. Remember that the goal is not necessarily to become an expert in learning styles or to be able to label yourself and your apprentices (although that can be fun!). The goal is simply to notice the differences in learning styles. You can start by deciding how you believe each of the styles stacks up against the others, in order of preference, so you can start to respond to that.

I also want to point out that none of these styles is "better" than another. This discussion isn't about intelligence or capacity for doing great things. It is just about the learning style you're born with. As I go through the model, I try to poke a little fun at each style, because each has its own foibles.

"WHY?" LEARNERS

"Why?" learners need to know why they're learning this topic at this time, why it is so important, and why they should focus on it versus all of the other input coming in. If you were teaching "Why?" people how to build a bridge they'd likely ask

- Why are we building a bridge?
- Why are you teaching me how to build a bridge right now?
- Why are we doing it before we work on the road?

All of these come down to the biggest question they're really getting at: "Why do I care?"

Some learners simply cannot learn effectively before they get over this hurdle. When you're teaching them, part of their brain is asking these questions and demanding an answer before allowing learning to proceed. Picture yourself as the peer mentor explaining the six steps in the process you're teaching. The script for a "Why?" learner would flow like this:

Mentor: Explaining Step 1...

Apprentice: Thinks, Why do I care? Why are you telling me this right now? Is it important?

Mentor: Explaining Step 2...

Apprentice: Thinks, Why do I care? Why are you telling me this right now? Is it important?

Mentor: Explaining Step 3...

Apprentice: Thinks, Why do I care? Why are you telling me this right now? Is it important?

Mentor: Explaining Step 4...

Apprentice: Thinks, Oh! Now I've heard enough to know why I care about this. I understand why I'm supposed to learn all of this and now I'm ready to go.

Mentor: Explaining Step 5...

Apprentice: Thinks, Wait, I seem to have missed something here! He covered that first part so fast that I'm lost now.

Mentor: Explaining Step 6... OK. Now, do you have any questions?

"Why?" learners use their brains to figure out why they care first. If given enough time, they'll figure it out on their own. While they're working on it, though, they won't be able to focus as much on the true task—learning the skill. Such learners often struggle with missing the first part of every explanation because they're occupied trying to figure out why they're listening in the first place.

Don't think of this as some sort of childish belligerence. They're not actively folding their arms across their chests and daring you to motivate them or else. That may be exactly what is going on inside their brains, but it isn't something they're doing on purpose or to make you crazy. It is just part of their learning style.

My workshop is often attended by apprentices who come to learn how to be mentored. They either come alone, or in the best circumstances, they come with their peer mentors so that they can develop their plan and strategy together. I remember one apprentice who listened to my explanation of "Why?" learners and said, "That is definitely me. I have a really hard time getting engaged in the topic if I don't know why it is important to me. The truth is, I can't imagine how it isn't everyone! Who wouldn't benefit from knowing why they should lock onto a certain chunk of information? Everyone is throwing new stuff at us all day long. It really helps if they tell us which bits we should prioritize before they launch into the details!"

TEACHING TO "WHY?" LEARNERS

As the story illustrates, everyone benefits from knowing why they care about completing a task, so you'll never do any damage by making this part of your repertoire, regardless of who you're teaching. All adult learners seem to appreciate this information and it rarely takes much time. The Peer Mentoring tools I've introduced in this book already support providing context—the "Why."

Remember the first step of the demonstration technique presented in Chapter 5, "Telling What You Know": Give a reason for the demonstration. The example I used was teaching you how to plant a tree—*because* this weekend we're going to have a tree-planting work party in the neighborhood. It isn't hard to picture an apprentice needing to know why I'm teaching him how to plant a tree. Without that simple explanatory sentence, he might spend too much time wondering and never get the information I'm trying to deliver.

Step 4 in the Demonstration Technique Worksheet also says "Demonstrate again and explain the logic behind each step." Logic means why we do it and the consequences of not doing it.

The 5-Minute Meeting Plan also has support for this learner. Step 2 is explaining the relationship to the job, which gives you an opportunity to tell your apprentice how often he will use the skill and how important it is before teaching it. This explanation will definitely help answer "why" questions.

Some of your apprentices will have figured out how important it is to know why they care before they let you teach them. They'll simply ask a few questions at the beginning. You can encourage these questions when they arise. This is the best scenario, because the apprentices can satisfy their needs and you can simply respond with answers.

"WHAT?" LEARNERS

"What?" learners just want the facts without a lot of fluff. Give them the information in the cleanest language possible for the best results. They need documentation or, at least, an outline or an agenda. They really like step-by-step processes. "What?" learners don't do well if you're winging it or talking without a plan. They really appreciate being taught by people who are prepared and focused.

If you were teaching "What?" people how to build a bridge they'd ask the following:

- What kind of a bridge is it?
- Is there anything I can read to be prepared?
- Where is it located?
- What is the plan?
- What are the steps?
- Is there a standard to follow?

All of these come down to the biggest question they're really getting at: "What do I need to know?"

Some learners just do a lot better when everything is in order. That is especially true of "What?" learners. They've been conditioned to expect this sort of information will be available to them, because the traditional educational system caters to them very nicely. Schools are often set up with straight rows of desks. Students learn and regurgitate facts, read and report on findings, analyze data, and apply it to problems. All of these approaches are very comfortable for a "What?" learner.

In fact, many "What?" learners did extremely well in school because the learning environment was so well suited to them. Their report cards reflect their success with lots of A's. When they become peer mentors, many "What?" learners develop a sort of arrogance that comes from those good marks. They draw this conclusion:

I learn by reading.

I got A's in school.

Smart people get A's.

Smart people learn by reading.

You'll even here them say, "I'm surprised you're asking that question. Didn't you read the documentation I gave you? That was covered in the third section." If you're a "What?" learner and you're teaching someone who isn't, you'll likely run into a problem. Remember that this isn't about intelligence or ability. It is about style. Consider working differently with your apprentices, as needed.

"WHAT?" LEARNER EXAMPLE

We worked with a senior engineer who was a "What?" peer mentor for a "How Does It Work?" apprentice. Both worked for a software development company that creates and maintains software for the stock exchanges—high pressure and fast-paced. Up-time is critical. When the company introduces new software, they run old and new systems in parallel, because if their software goes down, trading on the floor stops. This senior engineer, considered to be a genius by many, learned by reading documentation, a true "What?" learner. He could take the software and manual and in less than three days, become an expert. He would not only know how to use the program, he would know all of its limits, capabilities, shortcuts, and potential uses and drawbacks. Because he always read the manual cover-to-cover before he ever used the program, he expected everyone else to learn in the same way.

I overheard him once, when he was chastising an employee who didn't have any prior experience with a new software package and had come into his office after reviewing the manual. The senior engineer started asking the employee questions, difficult questions, and the employee who had started answering with confidence began to hesitate and falter in his responses. Clearly he didn't have the answers. At one point the engineer stood up from his desk and pointed out the window to a homeless person sleeping on a bench in the park a few stories below. "See that bum down there," he bellowed, "He could pick this up faster that you. Now get out of my office! I don't want to see you until you figure it out." The end of the story is that the employee scrambled to get his hands on the software and asked another colleague to give him a demonstration. Once the employee was able to play with the software (like a true "How Does It Work?" learner), he was able to succeed. He just couldn't do it by using the manual. In the end, he demonstrated that he could do the job, but the process was obviously much more painful than it needed to be.

TEACHING TO "WHAT?" LEARNERS

Once again, there is good news here. Everyone benefits from having a peer mentor who is prepared with documentation, lists, plans, standards, and so on. Preparing with "What?" learners in mind won't be a problem for others. If you're a "What?" learner yourself, this will come naturally, but for others, the preparation will need to be a little more deliberate.

It is a good idea to offer any documentation as a matter of course. and then notice how your apprentice takes advantage of it. If he comes back talking about specific sections of the documentation and has questions related to the text, you know you're working with a person who learns by reading. Be sure that before you hand over anything in writing to this sort of learner, you provide a "warning label" for each piece. The warning might include areas to focus on, areas to read with some degree of caution (because they are somewhat out of date), and areas to avoid (because they are irrelevant or hopelessly out of date). This warning is important because the "What?" learner will most likely read whatever he can find. You don't want him to learn the wrong information.

If you use the 5-Minute Meeting Plan in this book to prepare for your peer mentoring sessions, you'll be doing a great service to these learners. Step 3 creates the outline of the content to be presented, in order. Step 6 offers other resources, which often translates to more documentation or reading material. The lesson plan is designed as both an outline from which you can teach in a more linear, focused fashion, and as documentation for use after the session. "What?" learners do much better when they have something to follow when they are learning.

"HOW DOES IT WORK?" LEARNERS

"How Does It Work?" learners need to see the relationships between what they're learning and the big picture. They need to see the context relative to the workflow. They need to get their hands dirty and practice the skills and ideas. For them, the information doesn't line up in neat rows, it comes in connections to ideas and skills they already understand.

If you were teaching "How Does It Work?" people how to build a bridge they'd ask

- Is it like the bridge we built last time?
- Is it going to be part of the state or national highway system?
- Are we replacing or rebuilding an existing structure?
- Who designed it?
- What kind of traffic is expected?
- Which contractors will join the project?
- What is driving the timeframe for finishing it?

As you read through this list you might ask yourself how many of the questions are really about building a bridge. The answer is *all* of them, or *none* of them, depending on your learning style. For a "How Does It Work?" learner, the context and general information that they receive from questions like these are useful in preparing them to learn. For a "What?" learner, this list could be a bunch of random chatter. That is why there is sometimes a disconnect between people with different styles. My colleague, Sherryl, tells a story illustrating the point in the following sidebar.

"HOW DOES IT WORK?" EXAMPLE

I hired a new administrative assistant and asked her to help me with the consolidation of data from a text-based 360-degree performance feedback tool for a senior leadership team. The project involved lots of content: 12 people each had 12 others provide feedback. The administrative assistant had to download the information from the web-based tool, put it into a Microsoft Excel spreadsheet, sort it, create a report template in Microsoft Word, and then paste the content into the report. We were under a time crunch so I thought I was doing the right thing by providing great detail and organizing all the steps in chronological order. I didn't have them all written legibly, but had started an outline. I told her to take notes while we were meeting and to write down all the steps.

I assumed that she was a "What?" learner and that I was doing the right thing by helping create documentation and being cautious to have all of the information in chronological order.

About 10 minutes into the conversation (that I assumed would take about an hour) my new assistant asked me to stop. She said, "I can't do it this way. This is way too much information. I need to get into the tool, see what the data looks like in it's raw form, see what you want the report to look like when it's done, and understand how it's going to be used. I don't want to know all the steps until I do those things. Send me a copy of a similar report, send me the link to the web tool, and I'll call you back in 30 minutes." When she called back, she had a list of questions—really good, thoughtful ones, by the way. She was ready to go. I still don't have my list of chronological steps written legibly, but the project got done, on-time and error free, even though she had never done anything like this before. We were working remotely, and I wasn't very available to help her.

TEACHING TO "HOW DOES IT WORK?" LEARNERS

I am predominately a "How Does It Work?" learner. When I'm learning something new, I sometimes describe my brain as a blank pegboard, similar to the ones they hang tools on in a hardware store. As I approach new content, I ask a lot of questions that give me context. Every time I get another bit of information, it is like putting a peg on the pegboard. When it is time to learn the steps in the process, or the details of the idea, I can take each piece and hang it on a peg. The pegs aren't in any particular order, so the steps I learn don't line up in any linear fashion. The information, nonetheless, finds a home on one of the pegs and I learn it.

If I don't get enough contextual information early on in any learning process, I have a hard time finding a place to put the new content. I look for the pegs, but if there aren't enough of them, the content doesn't have a place to "hang" and it falls away. Because of that, I might not remember it.

"How Does It Work?" people need that context, so it makes sense that when they're peer mentoring they tend to deliver a lot of big picture information to their apprentices. This is great for the other "How Does It Work?" learners, but can be a real burden for apprentices who need less of it.

If you're teaching "How Does It Work?" learners then you can use the "Explaining the Big Picture" from Chapter 3, "Focusing on the Most Important Information," to guide you. Remember that these learners like to see the connections and put themselves "on the map."

The 5-Minute Meeting Plan has two steps to support the "How Does It Work?" learner. Step 2, "Explain the relationship to the job," provides context, and Step 5, "Identify practice opportunities," reminds peer mentors that these learners need plenty of opportunity to experience the tools or processes first hand. They often have trouble learning without hands-on practices.

"WHAT IF?" LEARNERS

"What If?" learners learn by testing your ideas while you're teaching. Leave room for them to discuss some of the options you considered. They want to know if you've tried any of the ideas they might have come up with, and then, if you have, what happened. They're often called the "devil's advocate" because they're always poking around trying to find a better way of doing a task—even if there is a smooth, established way of doing that task. Often you aren't particularly interested in their opinions, but they will still ask challenging questions.

If you were teaching "What If?" people how to build a bridge they'd ask the following:

- What if we built a ferry boat?

- Have you considered how much faster and cheaper a boat would be?

- What if we put two boats on line? Then we'd have double the capacity.
- What if we skipped Step 3 in the bridge-building process?
- What would happen if we put Step 2 before Step 1?

Each question is about understanding the boundaries and the options that were considered in shaping the information presented. The questions don't often sound like that to the peer mentor who hears them. Instead, they can sound judgmental, arrogant, and completely off-topic. It is hard for some peer mentors to keep from feeling defensive when questioned in this manner. They start to protect themselves whenever they sit down to teach a "What If?" learner. You'll hear the peer mentor say

- Can we take questions like that off-line? (But there never seems to be an "off-line" time.)
- Let's put that question in the "parking lot."
- Let's try to stay on the topic and be a little less random.

After explaining this concept in the classroom one time, one of my students shot up her hand and said, "I'm a 'What If?' learner and people hate me! Every time I ask a question so that I can try to figure out what is going on, I get shot down. I always thought there was something wrong with me!"

One group from a manufacturing client heard the explanation and then there was a big pause in the room. One of the managers said, "We don't have any 'What If?' people. We killed them." He said the last several people who had quit or been fired were all people who seemed to question the status quo and couldn't stay "on task" well enough. In reality they were all probably just trying to learn their jobs, but were going about it in a way that was different from the "What?"-oriented managers in front of them. Imagine what a loss it was for that company to miss out on all of the great ideas and creative solutions that would have come from this line approach to learning.

TEACHING TO "WHAT IF?" LEARNERS

Perhaps more than the other learning styles, "What If?" learners need you to talk with them about their learning style and come to an understanding about how you'll work together to transfer knowledge. If you're working with a "What If?" learner in a professional setting, that means they somehow survived the more "What?" oriented world of formal education. They had to have adapted in order to get a high school diploma and/or a college degree.

If "What?" people got A's in school, then "What If?" people probably got detention! They just don't line up and do things in an orderly fashion very often. Still, if they survived school, that means they can probably survive learning how to do their job by making the best of whatever way you teach them. It will just be more fun and more efficient if you work with them somewhat on their own terms.

When I asked people who present themselves as having this learning style how best to teach them, they usually give me a few consistent answers. Some simply want to be given more than "no time at all" to ask their questions. Once they've been labeled as "the guy who asks the crazy questions," people pre-empt them and shut them down before the first question flies. They don't get to ask any questions at all. What would happen if you gave your "What If?" apprentice three minutes at the beginning of a meeting, or even the three minutes prior to it starting, to ask a few questions to get his head in the game? While this apprentice might like more time, a few minutes to ask questions is better than no time at all and will probably make a big difference.

Sometimes the best ways to teach to this style of learner is to have an agenda or outline as a focusing tool. If your "What If?" learner asks a question in topic four that you know you're going to address in topic eight, you can use this three-step technique:

1. Acknowledge the question: I am going to address your question.
2. State exactly where, specifically you'll answer it: I'm going to talk about it in Step 8.

3. Give permission for the "What If?" learner to ask the question again: If I don't answer your question in Step 8, will you please raise it again?

I've also heard "What If?" learners ask to be put on challenging problems as a way of learning. Such learners do well with scenario-based questions: How could you improve this process? Or, how else could you use this tool? They like turning the problem around in their minds and considering all the ways it could be solved. They can talk with you about their thinking, and you can guide them toward the right approach. Be sure to listen to their ideas along the way! They're often very creative; you might just hear something that is an improvement.

ROUNDING OUT YOUR TEACHING STYLE

Once you've begun to think about your own learning style and considered the learning styles of your apprentices, you might be overwhelmed trying to get this just right. Everyone is a little different and it might seem crazy to try to analyze each one so you can hit the mark.

There are two solutions that will ensure you reach apprentices with differing styles. One solution is to hand this chapter to your apprentice and have a frank discussion about what works and what doesn't for him. It won't take long, and you're bound to learn something from each other. At the very least, you'll give your apprentice language that he can use to speak up and give you feedback. The last thing you want is to have him be a victim of your approach to teaching.

The second thing you can do is even better. You can round yourself out as a teacher, so you accommodate all learning styles all the time. All types of learners benefit from each type of information described. If you provide that information, you won't be wasting time. It'll just mean that no matter whom you're teaching, you'll have a much better shot at hitting the mark. Using the list in Tool 6-1 will help round out your style.

Tool 6-1 Learning Styles Model

- For the "Why?" Learner: Explain the benefits and purpose of the information you're teaching.
- For the "What?" Learner: Develop an outline and provide documentation.
- For the "How Does It Work?" Learner: Provide plenty of hands-on experience and discuss the big picture relationships.
- For the "What If?" Learner: Be prepared to discuss the possibilities.

Go through this list and think about what you do already. If you're already good at saying why and explaining the big picture, then maybe you could add in some practice opportunities and some documentation. If you're already good at documentation, maybe you could leave more time to talk over the possibilities. The more you can do to round out your teaching style, the less important learning styles will be. You'll already be meeting your apprentice's needs, no matter which styles he favors.

Remember, the tool that gives you the most support for rounding out your teaching style is the 5-Minute Meeting Plan. The only learner who isn't obviously addressed is the "What If?" learner. However, having the agenda as a focusing tool, or better yet, e-mailing the agenda as part of your meeting request, is excellent for "What If?" learners. They're typically not shy. They'll look at the agenda and e-mail you back with questions, such as, "Are you going to talk about x?"

The following sidebar provides an even easier way to talk about learning styles. Take the noted four words to work with you tomorrow and ask your apprentice to put them in order of his preference.

LEARNING STYLES AT WORK IN AN INDUSTRIAL SETTING

One of my manufacturing clients was orienting a large number of new people over a very short period of time. The company was struggling with the mistakes that the new employees and contractors were making. I met with some of the new employees and asked them to try to help me explain this phenomenon. They talked with some frustration about the "foot-thick" manuals that were thrust on them on their first days on the job. After spending some time with the manuals, they were sent to watch someone else do the work. Then, they were expected to do the work themselves. Only then did they have the opportunity to ask questions and discuss quality and other issues of importance. Everyone went through this process in exactly the same way.

I broke down this training pattern flow as follows:

Read—read the documentation

Show—watch someone do the work

Do—try to do the work yourself

Talk—Discuss the big picture, quality issues, best practices, and so on.

A few days later I was teaching Peer Mentoring to this group of manufacturing personnel (engineers as well as operators who work on the shop floor). When I got to the chapter on learning styles I wrote the four words (read, show, do, talk) on the whiteboard and briefly explained what I meant by each one. Then I asked everyone in the room to reorganize this list into the way they'd prefer to learn and the way they think they'd learn best. The whole process, from explaining the four words to having them all think about their own preferences to making their own lists, took less than five minutes.

When I asked for a show of hands to determine how many people left the four options in the original order, about 25% of the hands went up. Guess who those people were? You're right; it was the engineers who designed the training program! They all had a "What?" learning style. Reading first made perfect sense to them. In fact all of the grumbling about having to read the manuals was a real sore spot for them. They felt that the operators and others who didn't want to read first were just lazy or undisciplined.

For those who didn't raise their hands, I asked them to tell me the order they'd like to use to learn new content. All of the different permutations of the four choices came out: Show, Do, Talk, Read; Talk, Read, Show, Do; and Talk, Show, Do, Read, and so on. The implications of having someone read first when they'd prefer to read last should be obvious. It doesn't work.

The solution was as simple as the idea. Every employee in the plant was already taking the Peer Mentoring course; so, while they were in the classroom, they learned that they were responsible for telling anyone who was teaching them (their peer mentors) about their learning preferences using the four words. It was no longer necessary to suffer through an approach that wasn't working. In fact, it became the apprentices' responsibility to ask for what they wanted. Primary or silo peer mentors decided that they should ask about "the four learning styles" before diving into teaching a topic.

To support all of this, we created cards the size of the security badges everyone wore on a lanyard around their necks. It was very cheap to customize and laminate cards for each employee. When the maintenance technician planned to train an operator on the nightly maintenance task, he could simply walk up, flip the card over, and see that this employee wanted to Talk, Show, Read, Do. With that information, he could tailor the training and dive into an oral overview of the task, demonstrate it, and then hand over the documentation. Later he could return to set up the operator to do the work and monitor progress. This process instantly changed the way all employees were trained. The consequences were felt throughout the plant. The cost was about 40 cents per employee to make up the cards.

SUMMARY: PUTTING IT INTO PRACTICE

Knowing that you have a particular style of learning, and that it affects both how you gather information and how you teach, is very important to being a good peer mentor. Even if you never label any of your apprentices, you can do a great deal better at teaching them by being open to the differences you'll likely encounter. Don't forget that while each of us can benefit from multiple approaches to learning, we do have preferences that will make knowledge transfer more efficient. With this awareness, you can look for ways to round yourself out as a teacher. You can be sure that you explain why you're covering a topic before you start. You can offer documentation, or at least an outline, before you dive into new content. You can explain the big picture and provide hands-on practices, and you can be ready to discuss the possibilities. The more you're able to be versatile in your approaches to teaching, the more successful you'll be.

FROM A MANAGER'S VIEW

Managers can help their teams develop an awareness and appreciation of the different styles represented on a team and pay attention to rounding out the way that content is delivered. If all of your team's apprentices are expected to read as a first line of learning, be sure to discuss this with them and ensure that process works well for them. You might be surprised to find that fewer than half would choose to read first. The others may benefit from knowing why they're learning the topic at hand, seeing how it fits into the big picture, discussing the possibilities that were considered in shaping the material you'll be teaching, and getting a chance to practice them. If, as the manager, you open the door to this conversation, you'll increase the efficiency of knowledge transfer while supporting diversity in your team.

WHEN YOU'RE THE APPRENTICE

Everyone should develop some self-awareness about the ways they learn best. As an apprentice, you shouldn't be shy about asking to be trained in a way that works well for you. It would be a much bigger problem if you were to sit quietly while your peer mentor wasted time going in the wrong direction. Instead, you can explain what works better for you.

My colleague, Stacey, had an intern one year who was working on a project for her. She didn't have the benefit of this book then. Stacey realizes now that the intern was very much a "What?" learner, while she's mostly a "What If?" learner. She would stop by his office to see how he was doing. He wanted to ask her one question. He truly wanted the answer to only that one question. But, of course, Stacey would fly into brainstorm mode: "What a great idea. What if we did this? And what about that?" Later she found out from his office mate that her intern would look dazed when she left the room. He would say, "You know when Stacey leaves the room, I just want to take a deep breath!" She wishes he had spoken up sooner, so she could have made it easier on him from the start.

If you're a "What?" learner and there is no documentation, use the 5-Minute Meeting Plan to help your mentor create an outline. If you're offered documentation, and you're more of a "How Does It Work?" learner, then you might ask to see a quick demonstration and have some time working with the tool or idea before you spend time reading about it. If you're a "Why?" learner, you should always ask for a quick description of the importance of the content to your job. If you're a "What If?" learner, work with your mentor to carve off a few minutes to discuss the possibilities; and then stay focused on using the time well and finishing as planned.

If you take responsibility for supporting your own learning style, your peer mentors will be more likely to give you what you need.

Assessing Knowledge Transfer

How do I know if they are learning anything?

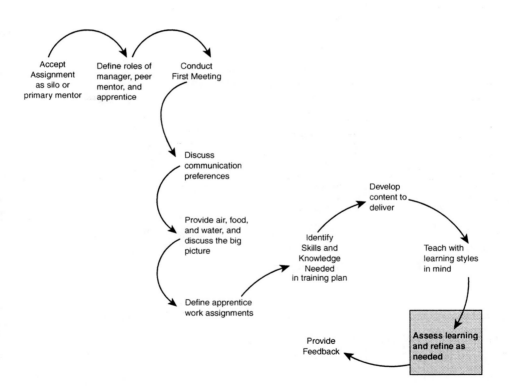

Accept Assignment as silo or primary mentor

Define roles of manager, peer mentor, and apprentice

Conduct First Meeting

Discuss communication preferences

Provide air, food, and water, and discuss the big picture

Define apprentice work assignments

Identify Skills and Knowledge Needed in training plan

Develop content to deliver

Teach with learning styles in mind

Assess learning and refine as needed

Provide Feedback

If you've ever had the experience of spending an hour carefully explaining a subject and then having your apprentice prove, moments later, that he didn't learn a thing, this is the chapter for you. There are many ways your apprentice can demonstrate a lack of understanding. He can ask the same question again and again, or ask the same question of someone in the next cube over. He can make a lot of mistakes and cause rework. He can do something entirely different than what you asked, or anything less than you expected. These are all familiar ways that our apprentices drive us crazy.

There is a simple remedy for this problem, but it may require stepping slightly out of your normal relationship with your apprentice. It involves asking open-ended assessment questions at key junctures along the way to make sure that you're both on the same page.

By the end of this chapter, you should have three universal questions that you can use as a tool to assess your apprentice's learning. You'll see many different choices. I recommend you start by choosing three questions, one for each stage. The first question helps you figure out where to begin in teaching your apprentice; the second question ensures your apprentice is learning from you along the way; and the third question confirms that he will do what you are expecting after you're done teaching. You may find that you've picked up a broader set of questions than just three, but that isn't necessary to make the assessment work.

I believe that "Questions While You're Teaching" is one of the most important sections of the entire book. It shows you how to prove knowledge transfer is happening so you get more consistent, predictable results.

BEWARE OF THE NOD AND SMILE

One of the most common ways that many peer mentors assess the learning of their apprentices is to watch body language. Apparently, it is possible for some insightful people to just "read" their apprentices and be certain the knowledge is successfully transferred. Well, in my experience, the outcomes from this approach are fairly inconsistent. There's a good reason for the inconsistencies. Most people learn very early in life to control their body language and mask the truth when someone is teaching them.

I learned this on the fourth day of my first week in kindergarten. It was the day that I realized that all of the marketing hype about school was completely overrated. I'd always been told that I'd be going to school one day and it would be so awesome and exciting—the best experience ever. I was expecting Disneyland. When the day finally came, I was shocked to find hard chairs in straight rows, recess outside restricted to only a short time twice a day, no snacks, and no messing around. Sitting still clearly mattered to my teacher. I handled my disappointment by daydreaming. I'd sit in the chair, but fly out of my body, chasing birds in the sky, soaring in imaginary rockets, and picturing myself swinging from the trees.

One afternoon, as I was landing back in my body to see if it was snack time, I tuned in just in time to hear a question that my teacher was asking of the entire class. Of course, because I'd been daydreaming, I didn't know if she was talking about reading or math and made a face that said so. You can imagine what happened when my teacher saw the confused look on my face—she called on me. I was already a smart aleck, so of course, I popped off with a comment that got me sent to the corner. Now, I learned a very important lesson from that experience: You never leave your face unattended when you're "out of the room." If you look confused, you're going to get called on, and that is generally something you want to avoid. Before you zone out, strap on a facial screensaver otherwise known as the "smile and nod."

This definitely worked for me and I know it has worked for you. It is the expression we create that says, "You're a terrific teacher/communicator/spouse/preacher/person and everything you're saying is just fascinating. I'm getting it all so you don't need to call on me. Find someone else to pick on. And, oh, by the way, you look lovely today!"

So, you have to ask yourself, "What do you really know when your apprentice is smiling and nodding at you?" The answer is that you don't know anything. Many people smile and nod when they're really, truly understanding. Some smile and nod when they think they're understanding. Those are the worst kind of apprentices to work with because they take their false confidence and charge into the work with gusto, only to make huge mistakes. Some people smile and nod because they can't bear the sound of your voice for even one more minute and are plotting their exit while you're talking. And finally, there are those who actually look confused. Their look of confusion usually means that they're so confused they just can't fake it anymore! You didn't just lose them a moment ago. They've been lost for a while, but held it together until they couldn't fake it anymore.

Instead of trusting body language, trust something much more predictable. Use open-ended assessment questions. Tool 7-1 provides some simple examples, with more to follow throughout this chapter.

Tool 7-1 Assessment Questions

 Ask open-ended questions at the

- Beginning: What do you already know about the topic?
- Middle: What did you hear me say?
- End: What are you going to do when you leave my office?

QUESTIONS FOR BEFORE YOU TEACH

If you're going to help an apprentice build a skill set that replicates yours, you have to find out what he already knows so that you can begin at the beginning for him. If you don't assess where you should start with your teaching, you'll start by teaching things he already knows, or by making assumptions about what he knows and starting over his head.

Let's say that you got a call from your best friend, visiting from out of town, who was trying to find your apartment after coming off of the subway in New York City. You've lived there for years and know your neighborhood very well, so this should be a snap. He calls you from his cell phone as soon as he gets off the train and is coming up to the sidewalk. You tell him the first thing he'll see is a newsstand, where he should turn left, walk three blocks, take a right, then another left, etc. You can't miss it. He calls you again 15 minutes later, hopelessly lost. How could that be? You gave him perfect directions. Well, it turns out that you assumed he was at the 57th Street exit from the subway, because that's the one you always take. Your friend, however, came up across the street on the Broadway side of the exit. Coincidentally, there was a newsstand at the top of both exits. As a result, the rest of the directions took him off track. You never really knew where he was to begin with, so your careful directions were useless.

I was frustrated by receiving useless directions over and over again when I was new at Microsoft. I was hired for my management and international experience, not my technical experience. Even though I never tried to hide the fact that I came to the job barely knowing how to double-click, people assumed that I already knew a lot of technical information. I can't tell you how many times I'd carefully write down all the steps I was given for a task, such as setting up a computer for a new employee or getting them a new account on a server, only to find that the instructions didn't work. I'd go back to my colleague so frustrated. He'd say, "Of course it didn't work, you forgot to do x, y, and z." The truth was that I "forgot" those three things because he never told me to do them. He assumed I already knew.

YOU'VE DONE THIS BEFORE, RIGHT?

Finding out where to begin is as simple as asking a few open-ended questions. Unfortunately, peer mentors often skip this step or choose questions that don't provide enough information. There are many closed-ended questions that aren't as useful, such as the following:

- Have you ever done this before?
- You've done this before, right?
- You have some experience in this area, don't you?
- Didn't you used to take care of this?
- Your resume said you did this in your old job, didn't it?

If your apprentice answers any of these questions with a "yes," you would make some assumptions about him. Some of the time, you'll be right on. But there will be many times when your assumptions are off-base. The cost of those incorrect assumptions and the mistakes they lead to is too high.

WHAT DO YOU ALREADY KNOW?

Instead of asking a question that has a yes or no answer, try a question that will get your apprentice talking a bit. I always start by thinking about my assumptions and asking a question that allows me to test them.

If you're an experienced employee, I assume that you already know something from your experience at the company; so I ask, "Tell me about your recent experience with (fill in the topic)."

If you're a new employee with industry experience, I assume that you already know something from your experience in the industry; so I ask, "Tell me about your experience with (fill in the topic)."

If you're a new hire with no experience in the industry, I assume you learned something relevant from your other jobs, internships, training, or whatever got you this job in the first place; so I ask, "Tell me about your experience with (fill in the topic)."

I'm guessing that you noticed a trend here. You can ask the same question at the beginning of any knowledge transfer session and save yourself the trouble of starting at the wrong spot. You'll also give yourself, and your apprentice, a moment to push aside all the other information that you're juggling and focus on the topic at hand. The answer you get may not surprise you at all. But if it does, even once in a while, the one minute you invested asking this question and listening to the answer will be well worth the investment.

QUESTIONS WHILE YOU'RE TEACHING

I wish I could put a huge neon sign on this page and call it out with sirens and confetti. The idea that you should ask questions to assess learning while you teach is the second most important concept I'll cover in this entire book. (My choice for the most important concept is the training plan from Chapter 4, "Developing a Training Plan.") The idea is to stop talking or demonstrating once in a while and ask a question to ensure that what you've been covering is making its way from your apprentice's short-term memory to his or her long-term memory. If you hear the sound of your own voice for 10 minutes straight, stop and ask for a paraphrase to ensure that your apprentice is learning. The paraphrase request sounds something like this:

> Hey, I've been talking awhile. Why don't you read your notes back to me so I can make sure I've been clear?

> I'm going to give you a minute to talk me through those last few steps to make sure I've covered them clearly.

> Please explain back the main points you've heard me cover.

Assessing understanding after 10 minutes of instruction is a good rule of thumb. If your apprentice isn't able to answer your question at that point, your team has only lost 20 minutes (10 minutes per person). You can start over without feeling too discouraged. If you go on for a whole hour and wrongly assume that your apprentice is following you, you've not only wasted the 2 hours (1 hour per person), but you'll also have to teach the same information again and clean up the messes your apprentice made because he didn't learn from you the first time.

How many hours did you spend this week cleaning up messes made by people who didn't "get it" the first time? Do you see why assessing learning is so important?

Recently, when I was teaching at a fast-growing software company that had hired 25 percent of their team over the last year, I asked for a show of hands saying, "How many hours per week do you spend fixing mistakes made by others?" The lowest estimate I heard was 4 hours. For some in that group, the estimate was 15–20 hours, or even more. The answers were nearly identical when I asked, "How many hours of overtime are you working on average?" It was clear these employees needed to work overtime to solve problems that could have been avoided.

Let's go back to the tree-planting example from our discussion of demonstration techniques in Chapter 5, "Telling What You Know." Imagine that I taught my apprentice how to plant a tree and then skipped Step 5: "Have your apprentice talk you through the steps." Here's one of the possible outcomes. My apprentice was able to plant the tree. When I walked by the site, it actually looked pretty good: The tree was in the right spot and the stick was there holding it up. When springtime rolled around, the tree was dead. Why? Because he missed a couple of steps in the process. If I had said, "OK, talk me through the steps to plant the tree and tell me why each step matters," he would have given me these answers.

1. Dig the whole twice as wide and twice as deep so that there is soft soil around the hair roots.
2. Put the compost in the hole to get the tree to the right height and provide a "snack" for later.
3. Put the tree in the hole and push the soil in around the tree.
4. Stake and tie the tree so it doesn't blow over.

Now, this isn't a crazy list. It is actually pretty logical. You can imagine many people thinking that these steps are sufficient. In the end, the tree actually looks the same as a properly planted tree, because all of the missing steps are covered up. In this case the apprentice forgot to take off the burlap sack (roots were bound), forgot to soak the root ball (transplant shock), and forgot to tamp the soil down around the base of the tree (air pockets damage the hair roots). Each of these omissions has an impact on the tree's health. In this case, the combination of missed steps actually killed the tree. If I had just stopped to quiz him before letting him work alone, we'd be enjoying spring blossoms instead of digging up a dead tree and replacing it using the proper steps.

REMEMBER TO BE QUIET, OCCASIONALLY

What happens to your "fire hose" when you ask a question? Right, it turns off. Picture this: You've been talking and going on for a while and your apprentice's "bucket" is filling and filling and filling. As it gets close to full, the tension starts to build. You can imagine the water getting to the rim of the bucket and pushing up in the middle to create a dome just before bursting and going over the top. Just at that moment, right before it blows, you turn off the fire hose and ask a question. Your apprentice, in answering the question, moves information from the "bucket" to the "ocean." Then, there is room for more information at the top of the bucket. Excellent! Now you can deliver more information, being careful to stop along the way and give your apprentice a chance to move it through to long-term memory. This is an example of a knowledge transfer machine at work. You're pouring knowledge in and your apprentice is pulling knowledge through. Everyone is playing a part, and together you're making rapid progress toward your apprentice's independence.

DO YOU UNDERSTAND?

There are plenty of closed-ended questions for this stage of the training process, too. We use them all the time to give ourselves confidence that things are going well. I'm sure you could come up with a few. Here's my list of some I've heard over the years:

- Did you get it?
- Are you with me?
- Do you follow me?
- Do you understand?
- Is this working for you?
- Are you on top of this?
- Is this making sense to you?
- Are you OK here?
- Any questions?

You ask all these questions while nodding your head "yes," as though that is the only acceptable answer. Maybe it is. Have you ever had an apprentice answer any of these questions by saying, "No, I don't follow you. I don't get it. I have no idea what you're talking about. This doesn't make sense, and I'm not following a word you're saying"?

I didn't think so. So, why bother asking them at all? You'll just get a nod and smile anyway. What a huge waste of time! Instead, ask for a paraphrase and get to the heart of the matter.

WHY PEER MENTORS DON'T ASK FOR PARAPHRASES

Before I give you a number of ways to ask for paraphrases without ever saying, "Can you paraphrase that for me" (although there is nothing wrong with that question either), I want to address the barriers that keep many peer mentors from this line of questioning.

There are a number of excuses I've heard:

- I wouldn't want to put my apprentice on the spot. It might make him uncomfortable if I "test" him. I'd rather just see if he can do what I've said. (Translation: I'd rather send him into the deep end with an anchor instead of a life ring.)

- I don't have time to listen to the answer. (Translation: I prefer the sound of my own voice to the sound of my apprentice's; or I prefer to do the rework and re-teach the topic, rather than get him to do the job right the first time; or I'm a control freak and don't want to let my apprentice have the "floor" when we're together.)

- I'm very intuitive. I don't need to ask, because I can tell by my apprentice's body language when he's getting it. (Translation: I believe I'm psychic and can see through the "nod and smile" even though I'm proven wrong on a regular basis.)

- What if the apprentice didn't get it and can't answer the question? That would be awkward for both of us. (Translation: I prefer to live in denial. If I ask the question, I'd have incontrovertible evidence that he didn't get it—and that would be too hard to ignore.)

None of these excuses make sense when you really think about them. Yet it isn't hard to imagine that most peer mentors believe one of them to be true, and enough of a reason to skip this approach.

Here's a quick story from my colleague Sherryl, who is an instructor for the Peer Mentoring Workshop.

ASSESSMENT QUESTIONS IN ACTION

I think of the time I was preparing to teach the workshop for the first time. Steve and I were going to Boeing for another project. Because we were riding in the car for some time, we decided to use the time to make sure I was ready to teach the following week. After starting by doing a high-volume data dump, he stopped, took a breath and then said, "Why don't you tell me what you would say about the first chapter? Hit the main points for each topic." It was my first exposure to being on the other side of the question, and I was really uncomfortable. I knew it was critically important to us (and me) to do a good job but it made me squirm. I knew I couldn't fake it any longer; the rubber was about to meet the road, so to speak. I remember that situation frequently when I am teaching others, because it was so powerful and so vital to our success. I now not only make a point of warning people when I am going to "test" them (to relieve some of the discomfort), I make sure that I never back off of asking the questions. It really is the *only* way, not just the best and quickest way, to make sure people get it. I'm not only a trainer these days, I'm a consistent practitioner!

WHY YOUR APPRENTICES WOULD LOVE TO BE ASSESSED

If you're not comfortable with asking questions for one of the aforementioned reasons, maybe you're looking at it the wrong way. Consider all the reasons why your apprentice might really appreciate your taking a moment to ask a question. Here are some of the reasons why apprentices are grateful for the questions:

- When I'm asked a question, it tells me that the information must be important or my peer mentor wouldn't be checking that I got it.
- It really helps me to know for sure that I learned it. Sometimes I think I did, but I'm not sure until I go through it again from my notes.
- I often find that I missed something. It is so much better to get that figured out before I cause any trouble!
- It is a lot easier to let the information sink in if I don't have to do it while you're endlessly giving me more information.
- Since I'm not a native English speaker, it makes it much easier to manage the translation in my head if you pause once in a while.
- It makes me feel like my mentors are really concerned that I learn the new information and I appreciate that support.

WARNINGS ARE IMPORTANT, MAYBE ESSENTIAL

If you're really concerned about asking assessment questions, the easiest way to get over the discomfort is to let your apprentice in on the secret. Tell them something like this:

I'm about to cover some information that you're going to need to know to do your job. You'll need to be able to do it perfectly every time so that there aren't any problems. There isn't any up-to-date documentation on this, so I suggest you take some notes. As we're going along, I'll stop and have you read your notes back to me to make sure I've been clear.

This warning would go over much better than randomly stopping and yelling, "Pop quiz!" Such an approach would be annoying and not at all welcome. Don't forget how you felt and how successful you were as a student when you had a little warning. When you're told there is going to be a "test," you listen differently, take better notes, and have a greater chance of success.

TELL ME WHAT YOU HEARD ME SAY

Hopefully, you're now open to the idea that there is no better way to test understanding before you send your apprentice off to actually do the work than to ask open-ended questions. A little assessment can reduce the need to clean up messes later.

To develop the questions you'll use while you are teaching, remember why you're asking the questions—to test whether or not the information you thought you delivered was, in fact, received by your apprentice. You're checking the connections to make sure the wiring is working properly.

There are several ways you can go about checking in. Pick one of these to use most of the time, and keep a couple of others for special occasions. Remember, you don't need to come up with a distinct question every time. If you've warned your apprentice in advance, you can ask the same one every time.

- Could you talk me through those last few steps?
- Why don't you read your notes back to me to make sure I was clear?
- Before I go on, why don't I let you go back over what I've just covered and explain it to me?
- Tell me what you heard me say. (I know, this doesn't sound very friendly, but it is quick and efficient, and works perfectly because the apprentices have been warned. It isn't a surprise.)

> ### USE THE TEST QUESTIONS FROM THE TRAINING PLAN
>
> Remember, you should also ask the assessment questions you picked out for the training plan in Chapter 4:
>
> Explain:
>
> - The top (number of) vocabulary words.
> - The (number of) steps in the process and why each is important.
> - The top (number of) things that often go wrong.
> - The relationship between x and y (how it fits in the product or service cycle).
> - How to troubleshoot the three most common problems.
>
> And so on.
>
> You thought about this notion of quizzing when you chose questions from this menu. Just ask those questions and you'll learn a great deal. When you use them you're not merely asking for a paraphrase, you're asking the apprentices to be able to apply the knowledge they've learned and demonstrate their confidence with the content. Because you set up answering those questions as determining how the apprentice will know that he knows, it make sense that you'd double-check the ability to answer them.

MAGIC KNOWLEDGE TRANSFER MACHINE

This magic machine is made up of the collaboration between you and your apprentice, each taking on a distinct role and working to move knowledge and skills methodically from your head to his. It can be as predictable as a conveyor belt if you're both doing your parts.

Here's how the machine works:

1. Start with a learning goal and a warning to your apprentice, such as, "By the end of the shift you're going to be able to bake cinnamon rolls according to a very exacting recipe and standard for production. You'll want to take notes on every step in

the process. Every 10 minutes or so I'm going to stop and have you read your notes back to make sure I've been clear."

2. Deliver content for no more than 10 minutes.

3. Stop and ask your question. For this one, I'd say, "OK, why don't you read me your notes on the first phase of the process?" Or I'd simply ask, "Why don't you tell me what you heard me say?"

4. Listen to the answer and offer suggestions if there is anything missing or incorrectly stated. If the apprentice doesn't have any notes at all, give some examples of what you expected him to have and start over. Don't worry about it if there are a couple of false starts as he learns how to be your apprentice. You'll likely be working together for a while and it is worth the investment.

Repeat Steps 2, 3, and 4 three times. Then here's where the magic comes. By the time you've warned your apprentice that you'll ask for a paraphrase and then followed through with it three times, on the fourth round, something will change. You'll deliver the content as before, but somewhere along the way, your apprentice will stop you and say, "Before you go on, let me stop a minute and *tell you what I heard you say*."

Your apprentice will take over the job of proving that he learned from you and will do it when needed. For some apprentices that might be after 6 minutes some of the time, or after 14 minutes at other times. The timing will be up to him, not you. The important thing will be that he will be driving the learning—you just taught him how to do that. You're moving information into his bucket and he is pulling it through to his ocean like a machine. That's magic!

If you can make this happen, you'll move the burden of ensuring that your apprentice is learning from your shoulders to his—and that is exactly where it belongs!

QUESTIONS FOR WHEN YOU'RE DONE TEACHING

There is a moment that every peer mentor loves. It is when your apprentice, who's been at your workstation for an hour learning from you, slides to the edge of the chair, picks up and straightens his notes, and says, "Well then, I guess I'll be going." This is known as "leave-taking behavior." You're relieved to have the meeting done and are glad to be able to get back to your own tasks. But you can't let him go just yet. You need to double-check that he is about to go and do exactly what you expect. Most of us have had an apprentice leave our workstation and miss something important, do something out of order, or do something inappropriate. This is your chance to fix that before problems arise.

This isn't a rehash of the steps in the process. The apprentice has already proven that he understands how to do the work. This is all of the larger steps around that. When you're done teaching, he needs to do things, such as contact other people, set up meetings, write reports, send e-mails and, of course, complete and submit the work you just covered. There is an order in which these things must be done. It is not acceptable to skip any of the larger steps, so you have to make sure he really got them all.

ARE YOU GOOD TO GO?

For most of us, the sight of our apprentice about to leave is so welcome that we want to just jump up and help him out the door. We say the following:

- Now then, any more questions before you take off?
- Are you ready to go tackle this project?
- Great job getting this down; don't hesitate to come by with any more questions.
- I'm looking forward to seeing your work when it is done.

You're seeing a trend here—the same as before. These are all closed-ended questions or statements that leave no room for your apprentice to confirm his understanding. Each of the questions might make you, as the peer mentor, feel as though you've done your job, but none of them tests whether or not you have.

WHAT ARE YOU GOING TO DO NOW?

When you see your apprentice prepare to go, just stop and ask one of these open-ended questions:

- Before you go, could you talk me through your next steps?
- What are your action items from this meeting?
- What are you going to do when you leave my office?
- Do you have any comments for me? Would you mind walking through your action items so I know what to expect?

This last example is great if you are worried about sounding offensive when you ask your apprentice to let you know what he is going to do. The first time you ask, your apprentice may have to think about what he or she is going to do. You may have to tell him again to make sure he got it all. After you review what he should do next, you'll be much more likely to get what you want in the end—predictable results.

I used to have a mentor at Microsoft who was the director of development. I'd wander into his office on occasion and ask for his help in getting a project done. While he was senior to me in the organization, he wasn't my boss or even in my department. I really treated him as if he were my peer mentor and spoke to him as such. He was really smart and would give me context and pointers on how to navigate the company. I remember two things about our interactions. He had great ideas that got me thinking, and he always ended our conversations with the same question: "OK, Trautman, what are you going to do when you leave my office?"

The first time he said it, I froze. I didn't know what to say! I hadn't really thought about it, I guess. Once he asked his question, I came up with a few things as a response. He generally commented on my ideas, after which I did whatever he suggested in his follow-up comments. Looking back, I know that there were many times just asking me that simple question caused me to sign up for more than I ever would have done on my own. It was a powerful way to manage me without ever having any authority to follow up.

GOAL-ORIENTED LANGUAGE

The power of this last question is that you're asking for a commitment. When your apprentice answers, he will be setting a goal. He will say, "I'm going to *do* something by a certain time." You should be able to depend on that. Wouldn't it be great if every team had a shorthand method for setting goals that was as simple as this? Later in the book we'll talk about how to give feedback when your apprentice meets, exceeds, or fails to meet this goal.

THE THREE QUESTIONS IN ACTION

I have many great stories of this concept in use. One of them started with my taking on a project at Microsoft a year or so after leaving the company as a full-time employee and starting my consulting practice. I was asked to serve as a part-time manager to cover a project for a client who was on maternity leave. I was to manage the worldwide rollout of a week-long technical training class. We shipped computers, materials, and trainers to locations all over the planet. Students flew into regional hubs to take the class. It was a very expensive program designed to promote a new technology. A one-week class could cost up to $100,000 dollars to deliver.

A stellar contract admin (administrative assistant) was assigned to work with me. After a short time working together, she was handling the bulk of the project on campus, while I did my part remotely and by attending meetings. We were an excellent team. For two months of the three-month contract, things went smoothly. Then one morning I got three calls at my home office before 10 A.M.

The first call was from my admin's manager saying that she had eloped over the weekend and would never be coming back. Ouch!

The second call was from the same manager (now following up for the missing admin) telling me that we had a big problem with an upcoming class in India. The instructor who was planning to go was very ill and could not make it. There was another instructor available, but he'd never taught the class before, and there would only be a couple of days to get the materials in his hands so he could prepare to cover it.

The third phone call was from a woman who said, "Hi, I'm your new admin." Her name was Kim. I'd never met her before, but she was on-site at Microsoft, with access to everything we needed to solve this problem. I was not. I needed her to do some very specific things to take care of the situation in India or I'd have to drop everything and scramble to do it myself. She was clearly my apprentice at that moment, so I kicked into gear.

STAGE 1: BEFORE YOU TEACH

My first question was, "Hi, Kim, nice to meet you. Can you tell me about your experience at Microsoft?" Without missing a beat, she said, "I've been a contract admin here for two-and-a-half years and I just finished covering a three-month maternity leave on the PowerPoint team." Now I knew the company very well and was confident that anyone who'd survived those experiences would certainly be able to do the work I needed her to do. She wouldn't still be around if she couldn't. If she had told me today was her first day, then I would have treated the situation differently. With the background she described, I decided to plow forward and see how she would do.

Then I said, "Sounds great! Grab a pen and put me on speakerphone. I need you to do a few things quickly to save this project in India. If we don't get it right, it'll cost $100 grand, and that would be a shame." Then I launched into a series of detailed instructions including the following:

1. Look up the new instructor's contact information.
2. Call the travel desk and book his travel.
3. Go to the warehouse and pack a box.
4. Go to server x.
5. Using password y,
6. Find file z, the Course Materials in PowerPoint, and open it.
7. Print out the instructor notes.

8. Fax the printout to him directly.
9. Check on the hotel location.
10. Ship the box to his hotel.

STAGE 2: WHILE YOU'RE TEACHING

I was on full tilt for nearly two minutes, giving her important detailed information. Then, I asked for a paraphrase. I said, "OK, can you read your notes back to me to make sure I've been clear?" And so she did. This is what came back:

1. Look up the new instructor's contact information.
2. Call the travel desk and book his travel.
3. Go to the warehouse and pack a box.
4. Go to server x.
5. Using password y,
6. Find file z, the Course Materials in PowerPoint, and open it.
7. Print out the slides.
8. Fax the printout to him directly.
9. Check on the hotel location.
10. Ship the box to his hotel.

The amazing thing about her paraphrase was that she got every single detail perfectly, except for one. Can you see it in the list? She said she was going to fax the PowerPoint *slides,* when I had asked her to print out the *notes.* That would have meant that the new instructor, who would need to be on a plane immediately, would likely have gotten the slides without getting the notes on all that he'd have to say during the class. Given the tight timeframes, he probably wouldn't have been prepared on time, and the $100,000 expense and a great deal of attendee time would be lost. Moreover, the reputation of our department, and likely Kim's job, were at risk. She missed only one word, and all of it could have fallen apart. But it didn't, because I just said, "Everything is perfect, except you'll want to fax the instructor *notes*." She interrupted me mid-sentence and said, "Of course, he'll need those, because he hasn't taught this material before." She even knew the difference; she'd just missed it in the rush. How often are your apprentices nearly perfect, but the one missed keystroke is enough to create a disaster?

STAGE 3: WHEN YOU'RE DONE TEACHING

Then I followed up with the final type of question, and asked, "What are you going to do now?" Kim told me she'd fax the notes, book the travel, double-back and make sure the hardware was all on track, take care of a few other details to support the new instructor, and assured me we'd be good to go. This was all right on target, so I hung up the phone and finished my coffee. No fire drill. No drama. This was just a clear solution to a difficult situation. In the end, Kim handled the whole thing better than I could have if I'd taken the time to scramble and do it myself. It can work just like this for you, too.

SUMMARY: PUTTING IT INTO PRACTICE

I strongly suggest that you write down your version of the three types of questions in Tool 7-1 and post them somewhere visible in your workstation so that you can reach for them every time you need them. Be sure you have one question for the beginning that helps you assess your apprentice's experience; one for the middle that helps you assess what he has learned; and one for the end that helps you confirm what he's going to do.

Don't forget to bring your apprentice in on the secret. Let him know that you're going to ask these questions. Explain why you think it will help both of you and that you're in no way trying to make him uncomfortable. He will be your teammate, then, in transferring knowledge, rather than just a vessel waiting for you to fill him up.

FROM A MANAGER'S VIEW

Managers can help this process in a number of ways. Once you've identified the peer mentor and apprentice relationship and you're clear on the skill they'll be working on together, you can model these questions and demonstrate their value.

Start by telling the peer mentor and apprentice that you're going to help them ensure that they're as efficient as possible and that you'll expect them to work this way even when you're not watching. (It would be ideal for you to share this chapter with them so they know what is coming.)

Then ask the peer mentor to describe the apprentice's experience relative to this task. This models the behavior because you're testing the peer mentor in the way you want the peer mentor to test the apprentice later. The apprentice will listen to the answer and fill in any gaps. The peer mentor could be right on target or a mile off. Just make sure they see how important it is to know where to begin.

Next, listen in while the peer mentor covers about 10 minutes of information. You don't need to be a subject matter expert on the content to observe. Just let the peer mentor work while you listen. Then, interrupt the conversation and ask the apprentice to go over all of the information he just learned. Be sure that he knows it is OK to use notes or any handouts given as support. Ask the peer mentor to give the apprentice feedback and then let them continue with new content.

Repeat this step one more time after another 10 minutes. Then ask that they work together in this way from now on, paraphrasing every 10 minutes to ensure that the apprentice is moving information from short-term to long-term memory.

Finally, ask the apprentice to stop by your office at the end of the session. Tell him that you're going to ask him to explain any action items from the meeting. Encourage him to work with the peer mentor on what he is going to tell you. Alternatively, you could have him send this information in an e-mail. Don't trust that the apprentice is connecting the training with the end result you want to see. Ask for some proof. Remember that this is the goal language he will be using to make commitments. You want to ensure this gets done.

Your total investment for these steps is less than half an hour. I predict that if you took these steps twice during the early stages of the peer mentor/apprentice relationship, you would instill in them an approach that will pay dividends forever.

Don't forget to notice and reward this behavior. Mention the assessment question process in performance reviews, noting when it is used effectively and when asking assessment questions would have reduced rework, frustration, costs, missed deadlines, etc. You want to build a discipline around this skill throughout your team.

WHEN YOU'RE THE APPRENTICE

These questions are uniquely suited to being driven by the apprentice. You don't have to wait for any of them to be asked. You can answer them anyway.

Before you settle in to learn a new skill, be sure to speak up and let your peer mentor know about your background. I remember working through my first substantial budgeting process as a general manager (GM) at Expedia.com. My peer mentor on the topic was a colleague from finance. She assumed that I'd already worked on budgets many times before or they wouldn't have promoted me to the GM position. That wasn't the case at all. So, I stopped her before she started and said, "Don't underestimate my lack of experience in this area. I've sat in on a number of budgeting processes, but I've never led one as the GM. I'm going to need you to start by explaining the process, the vocabulary, the templates, and the expected outputs before you do anything else." She was a little surprised, but glad that I'd told her of my lack of experience up front. She quickly switched gears, and we didn't waste a minute.

While you're listening and learning from your peer mentor, don't let the volume of new information overwhelm you. Stop after no more than 10 minutes (or even two or three minutes) and double-check that you're really getting the information. You could say, "Before I let you go on, I'd like to quickly go back over the notes I've taken to make sure I've got it all. Is that OK?" Your peer mentor will be pleased that you're showing that kind of initiative.

Finally, you should always double-check your action items before you leave any mentoring situation. You have a responsibility to understand the expectations and to communicate your goals so you can always deliver consistently. Just say, "Here are my action items from this conversation. I'll be doing "task" by "timeframe" and making sure it is well done by watching out for "quality measure."

In this way, you're never a victim of inadequate peer mentoring. You can drive the whole relationship to your best advantage.

8

Giving and Getting Peer-Appropriate Feedback

When and how should I say what I'm thinking?

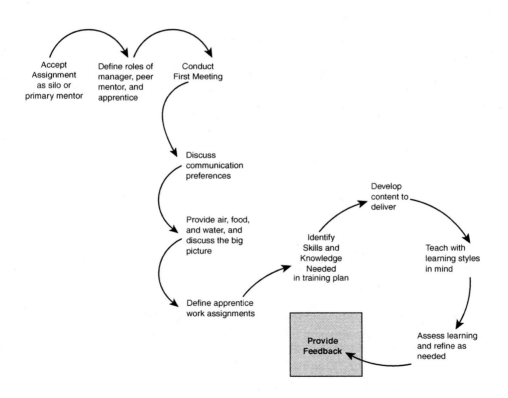

"If only my people would talk to each other." This is one of the most common messages I receive from managers at all levels. Managers know that productivity and quality go up when a team is cohesive enough to help each other look for ways to improve. Peers are in an excellent position to notice the strengths and weaknesses of their colleagues, yet they often shy away from speaking up. It isn't hard to imagine why this is true. Telling a co-worker what you think can be awkward. You might wonder, "Who am I to judge? What if he is offended? Will it give my colleague license to pick me apart later?" For some, these concerns are enough to keep them quiet.

Ask yourself why your peers would welcome feedback. If you offer them a chance to hear what you have to say (either positive or critical feedback), how many of them would take you up on it? Delivered in the right spirit, peer feedback can be some of the most valuable feedback available. This is especially true for critical feedback. Many people would rather hear criticism from a co-worker than from a manager, because it gives them a chance to make the change before it affects their standing in the workplace.

By the end of this chapter, you'll have a pair of tools you can use in giving and requesting feedback. The first tool, called the Feedback Worksheet, is used to give peer-appropriate feedback. The second tool, called the Apprentice Feedback Request Worksheet, is located in the "When You're the Apprentice" section of this chapter. I'll suggest that your apprentice never go a whole week without hearing feedback from you. Ideally, he will hear from you more often, but once a week is a good minimum. Managers can certainly use both worksheets as well; however, they were specifically designed for those without authority who are looking for a way to give or get feedback.

I want to be clear up front that this feedback model is not going to "fix" peers who are poor performers. If you provide critical feedback and your co-worker continues to repeat the problematic behavior or actively ignores your sound advice, you should ask your manager to step in and help out. Most of the time, this will not be the case. You'll say what you see, you'll offer suggestions, your co-worker will make some changes, and you'll both be the better for it.

LOOKING OUT FOR YOUR COLLEAGUES

My friend and colleague, Sherryl, tells a story that illustrates this concept very well. She was washing her hands in the ladies room at the airport when she looked up and saw another woman walking back onto the concourse. This woman was dressed up. She had everything going on. Picture the hair, the nails, the clothes, the shoes, the jewelry, the suitcase to match, and…her skirt was stuck in her pantyhose, leaving her exposed. Sherryl only saw her as she was walking out the door. The ladies room was long and narrow, crowded with other travelers, and Sherryl was at the far back. To add to the difficulty, the woman turned left and Sherryl's gate was to the right. The lady was walking fast. Sherryl was both late for her flight and exhausted from a hard day, so she just let her go on walking down the concourse with her skirt tucked in her pantyhose.

Sherryl will tell you that it has been several years since that happened—and she still feels awful. She really could have made the effort to catch up to the woman and tell her about her skirt. The woman would have been embarrassed, but incredibly grateful. Sherryl would have wanted nothing less from anyone who found her in the same predicament, yet she let it go, because at the time it was just too much of an effort.

Do you have any colleagues who are normally on top of their game and "dressed to kill," but can't see a flaw because they don't have eyes in the back of their heads? That is what you're there for. That's what teammates do. They look out for each other and speak up; they don't leave each other exposed, even if it takes a little extra effort.

FOCUS ON THE GOAL

Peer-appropriate feedback can be defined as a specific response to a specific action. If you want to say what you think, it helps to be disciplined about the language you use, so that you can avoid being emotional or setting your apprentice up to be defensive. In my opinion peers do not need to give feedback on attitude, work ethic, or personal characteristics, unless they have a long-standing and trusting relationship with their colleague. Managers should be responsible for that type of feedback. There are plenty of useful times to speak up without stepping over that line. Besides, if you focus your feedback on work, it is easier, less risky, and more likely to elicit a positive response. In short, let the manager manage the attitudes; peers can give feedback to each other on the work and the results.

The best way to stay specific is to focus your feedback on the apprentice's goals and say what you notice about the degree to which he met, exceeded, or failed to meet a particular goal. Because we don't normally identify ourselves through our goals, they can be written down and discussed. We can all look at them and talk about them without getting too personal.

USE GOAL LANGUAGE AND STANDARDS

In this book, I've given you several ways to introduce goal-oriented language into your relationship. If you use the Status Report Worksheet from Chapter 2, "Managing Time and Communication," you'll encourage your apprentice to say not only what he plans to do during the week (his goals), but also what he did (his output). If you use the Training Plan Template from Chapter 4, "Developing a Training Plan," you'll set learning goals for your apprentice (e.g., the date by which he can "pass the test"). If you assess him at the end of a peer mentoring session and say, "What are your action items?" you'll be asking for new goals as a result of the conversation. In each of these situations, your apprentice is making a commitment, which provides you with an opportunity to give feedback whether he meets the goal, exceeds the goal, or fails to meet the goal.

The other opportunity to give feedback is after observing how your apprentice responds to the standards you've set. The standards could involve rules for following a process, measures of quality, consistency of communication, and so on. If you give clear directions and explain the reasons why each standard has been set, you can then notice when he is meeting, exceeding, or failing to meet the standards.

In each of these examples, the focus is always on the work, not the person. That makes the exchange of feedback more natural, and therefore more likely to be accepted and used in a peer relationship.

LANGUAGE AND TONE FOR PEER FEEDBACK

If you plan to focus on the work when you give feedback, you'll avoid many of the pitfalls, but there are still plenty of reasons that people feel awkward. How feedback is received often comes down to the intent you communicate. The worst thing a peer can do is play a game of "gotcha!" You should never be perceived as lurking in the corner just waiting for your apprentice to make a mistake so you can point out his errors. Rather than "gotcha!" your apprentice should hear, "I've got your back," and "I'm looking out for you." After all, you'd hope to have the same level of support from your peers when you need feedback, too. Before you give any feedback, you should think about what you're really trying to communicate and how you're going to go about it.

POSITIVE FEEDBACK FIRST?

There are many schools of thought about whether or not you should give positive feedback before you give critical feedback. If you're a manager sitting down to give an annual performance review, and you're going to spend 30 minutes just giving your employee feedback, it makes perfect sense to start with complimenting strengths and then move to discussing weaknesses. For peers giving feedback in a real-time work environment, this flow doesn't work. If you feel a need to say something nice before offering critical feedback, it is going to sound like this, "I think you're really a terrific person, *but* the work you've done here is all wrong."

Someone once called this the "but sandwich." It doesn't matter what you say in front of "but," because it is all negated as soon as you give the critical piece. You might think you're being polite or trying to soften the blow. You're not fooling anyone. Your feedback could even be perceived as patronizing, which could make things worse. The piece of positive feedback you offered at the beginning of the phrase might be really solid and important. If it is, you don't want it to get lost.

Give lots of positive feedback. A good rule of thumb is that you should have a 4:1 ratio of positive to critical feedback. Practice giving only positive feedback for a few weeks, until you get the hang of things. Be as specific and disciplined about giving positive feedback as you are when you give critical feedback. It'll make the positive feedback much more powerful. As you resume giving critical feedback, don't feel like you have to say something positive just so that you can provide feedback on a missed goal or broken standard.

ALWAYS AND NEVER

"Always" and "never" are words that are the mortal enemies of "specific." They're superlatives that cast such a wide net that they're difficult to prove. When you're giving critical feedback, "always" and "never" can also be fighting words. Nothing pushes our defensive buttons more than being given critical feedback that is exaggerated. "You *always* forget to fill in that field on the form," is likely to be rebutted by your apprentice. He can say, "Now hold on there! I don't *always* miss it. I've been trying to do my best to remember; and I was pretty good about it for awhile there and…"

The whole conversation is shifted from the empty field on the form to whether or not the apprentice *ever* got it right. Who cares if he ever got it right? All you care about is that the field in the form is empty right now, and there is a consequence to that. You want him to change his behavior for the future, so focus on that. Even if you are sure he has been making the same mistake for weeks, you don't need to say so to get your point across. Instead of focusing on the long history, just say what is true right now. "Today, I noticed that the field on the form is empty…."

The same is true for using "always" and "never" when you're giving positive feedback. Again, being specific is very important. For many people hearing, "You're always so great!" is nice, but not at all substantive. It is cotton candy, where a steak would be much better. "You never seem to get upset" is feedback that ignores the reality that nearly everyone gets upset once in a while.

Instead of being vague when you give positive feedback, try being very specific. You might say, "I want you to know that your idea saved me two hours last night. I went home early for the first time in a month." You can imagine your apprentice really appreciating knowing the specific benefit of his actions. It is much harder to say, "Oh, you're just saying that!" when someone gives you a specific result from your efforts.

KEEP IT TIMELY

Feedback isn't very useful if you give it long after the fact, yet there are many reasons peer mentors wait. You might think the problem will blow over or that the mistake was a one-time issue, so you don't speak up. You might feel embarrassed or awkward or that you're too busy to take the time to give feedback. I'm sure you could come up with more excuses, if needed. They're all some version of the same thing: You don't give feedback because it feels harder to give feedback than to skip it.

That is why the timing is so important. Here are some definitions of "timely":

- Right now
- Maybe tomorrow
- Not next week

If your apprentice exceeds or misses a goal and it is simple and clear to see, you should provide feedback on the spot. Why wait? Right now is the right time.

If you're getting a little hot under the collar and are afraid you might get too frustrated or emotional, it is appropriate to wait and prepare your thoughts. Maybe tomorrow would be better.

Under no circumstances should you wait until next week. Your apprentice shouldn't hear about a problem from a week ago when there is no longer any way to rectify the situation. That just isn't fair.

Timing is also important when delivering positive feedback. Apprentices, especially newly hired peers, need to know when they've hit the target expectations so they can begin to develop their confidence levels. I've had a great deal of experience working with orientation and onboarding programs. If you interview a manager or a peer mentor and ask how the new hire is doing, you might hear plenty of positives. But, if you ask the same new hire how she thinks things are going, she will often be cautious and self-critical, because no one has said that she should think otherwise. You should be confident that if I interviewed your apprentice, at any point in your relationship, she would answer that question the same way you would.

MAKE SURE YOUR APPRENTICE CAN TAKE ACTION

If you think about critical feedback as an opportunity to help your apprentice improve her game, you should explain both the area of concern and provide a suggested solution. One without the other is just complaining. As you think through the problem area, consider how you've handled similar stumbling blocks in the past and whether any of your strategies would work for her. You might also think about another employee who faced this problem and solicit solutions there. If you have no idea what to do, you can at least sit with your apprentice and your manager, brainstorm the best possible solutions, and plan to follow up with your apprentice to help her with the change. The Feedback Worksheet will give you a framework for this.

FEEDBACK WORKSHEET

There seems to be a good deal of mystery surrounding giving peer-appropriate feedback. I'd like to introduce some language that you can use to make it less challenging. Peers should know how to bring about change quickly by noticing the issue, explaining the impact, asking for permission to give feedback, and then providing guidance in the right direction. The same process works for giving positive feedback. We all benefit when we support the strongest behaviors by calling them out for the value they provide.

Tool 8-1 provides a feedback worksheet that you can use to organize your thoughts.

Tool 8-1   Feedback Worksheet

■ I noticed that _____.
   (fill in this blank with something irrefutable)

■ The impact of that is _____.
   (fill in this blank with something measurable)

■ I have some suggestions for solving the problem. Can I tell you about them? My recommendation is _____.
   (fill in this blank with something that is actionable)

Let's take a look at each one of these elements separately.

I NOTICED THAT_____

When you fill in this blank, you have to narrow the issue down to the *specific* reason for giving the feedback. You'll know it is specific and focused enough if, when you say it out loud, you know that no one could argue with you. It is true and irrefutable. Even if you hired 11 accountants from Ernst and Young to audit the facts, they'd all agree that your point is true. Your apprentice most certainly would have to agree with you, even if grudgingly. For positive feedback, this is equally important. You don't want your apprentice to brush off your feedback with, "Oh, you're just saying that."

Here are some examples of statements that are appropriate:

■ I noticed that you finished the project two days ahead of schedule.

- I noticed that you didn't complete Part 4 of the worksheet.
- I noticed that your code was checked in without comments.
- I noticed that Step 3 from the procedure wasn't followed.
- I noticed that a signature was missing from your approvals list.
- I noticed that you were ten minutes late to the meeting today.
- I noticed that you sent the meeting notes three days after the meeting.
- I noticed that your scrap bin has four broken plates in it.
- I noticed that three different people are using your idea.

You can see that all of these statements are completely provable and that none of them address your feelings or your opinion. They all speak to facts that are part of the work landscape. Your apprentice would not be able to say, "You're just being picky, I *feel* like I did fill in that field on the form." He would have to agree with the facts. Without agreement on the facts, the feedback that follows won't be effective.

Managers often need to give feedback that is much less specific, such as addressing work ethic, attitude, communication habits, personal hygiene, and so on. It is rarely appropriate for a peer to cross into that territory. Usually, if the peer can't get specific enough in their feedback, it is because they haven't really worked to connect to the data that exists.

Not long ago a peer mentor told me, "My apprentice is not writing code fast enough." That certainly isn't very specific. So I asked, "How do you know?" and "What's that based on?" until the peer mentor came up with some facts that might have been refutable, but were at least a starting point. His responses started with ideas like, "Well I've been doing this long enough that I just know," and "I just have a gut feel for it." After a short time we landed on a message that was much clearer, if not perfect. When he met with his apprentice, he said, "Successful developers on our team average X lines of code per day. Right now you are generating Y. Would you like to talk about some ideas on how to close the gap?" It took a little work to get to the specifics. In the end, the feedback was much clearer than simply telling the apprentice he wasn't fast enough.

THE IMPACT IS _____

Once you've established the behavior you want to address, think about the consequences or impact of that behavior. The impact statement should be specific and measurable. You'll know it is measurable if you can put a number on it. Usually this number will appear in the form of dollars spent or saved, time wasted or saved, or specific quality measures, such as customer up or down time, stability or instability of a product, or other such measures.

Describing the impact of an action makes positive feedback much more substantial than the typical "way to go" statements that are often thrown around. If you say, "I noticed that the problem-solving question checklist you implemented in the customer care center has reduced average call length by 15 percent," you're really showing the value your co-worker added. The feedback is extremely potent and likely to encourage more of the same kind of behavior. Another example might be, "I noticed that you finished the project two days ahead of schedule. Now we won't need to work all day Saturday, as I thought we would, to stay on schedule."

The process is the same for critical feedback. Being specific about the behavior and the impact gives weight to the issue and helps your apprentice understand the consequences of the behavior, so he can make the appropriate changes. You might say the following:

- I noticed that Part 4 wasn't completed in the worksheet and the impact is that we had to stop production for one hour to get that information. That put us four hours behind on our plan for the week.

- I noticed that your code was checked in without comments and the impact is that I spent two hours debugging your code on what should have been a 15-minute fix.

- I noticed that Step 3 from the procedure wasn't followed and the impact is that the customer backup failed. When they called for it this morning, we had to tell them they'd need to redo a whole day of work.

- I noticed that a signature was missing from your approvals list and the impact is that the contract couldn't be signed on Friday. The penalty for being late was $5,000.

■ I noticed that you were 15 minutes late to the meeting today (the other four of us were on time) and the impact was that we had to cover the opening statements twice and this put us 20 minutes behind. We didn't finish the agenda and had to schedule another meeting. It costs roughly $400/hour for five of us to be in that room together.

If you're giving positive feedback, you could be done now. You would have laid out the facts, quantified the impact, and let the apprentice know that he is definitely on the right track (no more wondering about performance). You may want to continue to the next step if you have a suggestion for encouraging more of the positive behavior or want him to share his approach with others. If you've delivered critical feedback, you're ready to start helping your apprentice figure out what he can do to improve his game.

I HAVE SOME IDEAS; DO YOU WANT TO TALK THEM OVER NOW?

Before you can offer feedback to your peers, you need to double-check that they're open to listening to you. It would be good if managers followed this same model, but their position on the organizational chart implies that they don't need to ask permission to provide feedback. For peers, it is a show of respect to check in before offering your help. You'll say, "I have some ideas. Do you want to talk them over now?" Your apprentice may have any of a number of responses:

■ Sure. What do you think?

■ I'm really exhausted (and a little embarrassed) right now. If you try to tell me anything, I'm going to get defensive. How about tomorrow morning? Hint: Your reply is going to be, "Great, I'll buy the coffee."

■ No, thanks. I can take care of this myself. Hint: Your response is to back off. If the problem goes away, that's great. If the problem doesn't go away, you don't have a peer-mentoring problem; you have a management problem and should ask for help from your manager in dealing with the situation. In either case, you've done your part to help.

By asking permission to give feedback, you're also allowing your apprentice a moment to collect his thoughts and prepare to hear you. If he looks up and tells you he is ready, you'll feel more confident that your offer to collaborate will be well received. That will make giving feedback easier for you, too. Now you've set the stage to help figure out the solution.

WHAT ARE YOUR IDEAS? I SUGGEST _____

If your apprentice has experience and has been working with you for a while, you might start this part of the feedback with brainstorming instead of making suggestions. You might say, "What are your ideas for fixing this problem?" He might respond, "Oh, yeah. Now that you pointed it out, I realize that I'll need to (do something differently) in the future." If the idea is sound, then you're off the hook and can move on. If it isn't, you might offer another impact statement, such as, "When I've seen that approach tried, the impact was...." Remember, you need to be open to the solution your apprentice presents. You're not his manager. He should have some autonomy, within reason. Still, the whole point of the conversation is to change his behavior and get him on the right track. It makes sense that you should continue working on options until he has a better approach in mind for the future.

When your apprentice is less experienced, you may need to come up with all of the ideas. In many instances, the suggestion is going to be obvious to you. Because you're peers, you're likely to be giving feedback on goals that you, yourself, have met many times before. You've probably stumbled in the same way as your apprentice just did. You probably figured out a strategy to reduce the errors or hit the deadlines. It is from that well of experience that you'll draw in giving feedback. Be sure that you offer suggestions your apprentice can act upon. It doesn't help if your feedback is, "I suggest you get it done on time from now on;" or "Read the documentation and do what it says, for heaven's sake;" or my personal favorite, "Just don't do it anymore." This may be exactly what you're thinking, but remember that you're working from a level of experience that makes the answer seem obvious. Your apprentice doesn't have that same experience to draw on, so the solution isn't as straightforward.

When you offer suggestions, try to think about ways that you can provide ideas to help change the behavior. This often means introducing some sort of a workplace job aid or handout to remind your apprentice of what is expected. Here are some examples:

■ I noticed that you finished the project two days ahead of schedule. The impact is that we won't need to work all day Saturday to stay on schedule, as I'd planned. I wonder if you would be willing to share your approach to dealing with that issue at the next team meeting? Hint: For all positive feedback, you're asking some version of, "Please teach the rest of us how you did whatever you did so well."

■ I noticed that Part 4 wasn't completed in the worksheet and the impact is that we had to stop production for one hour to get that information. That put us four hours behind on our plan for the week. I have a suggestion; do you want to hear it now? I post a checklist on my workstation and double-check it before I turn in my work. Do you want to see how I set it up?

■ I noticed that your code was checked in without comments and the impact is that I spent two hours debugging your code on what should have been a 15-minute fix. I have a suggestion; do you want to hear it now? I suggest that you write or change your comments before you do the work on the code. It'll organize your thinking as well and then you won't have to remember to do it after the fact.

■ I noticed that Step 3 from the procedure wasn't followed and the impact is that the customer backup failed. When they called for it this morning, we had to tell them they'd need to redo a whole day of work. I have a suggestion; do you want to hear it now? I'd like you to get either Mike or me to review your work for another week before you submit it as complete so that we can help you ensure you've covered all the steps. Or, I have this little song I sing in my head that reminds me of all the points I have to double-check before I submit the work... 'A' is for the...

- I noticed that your work was due today and it isn't complete. Since I wasn't aware that you were behind, the impact is that we'll both need to work for two hours this evening to get you caught up or our team won't make Friday's deadline. I have a suggestion; do you want to hear it now? I suggest that we set up more milestones during the project to check on your progress before it becomes a crisis. Then I can help you sooner if needed rather than this last-minute scramble. I also suggest that if you think you're going to miss a deadline that you let me know at least two days in advance so I can help you figure out what to do.

- I noticed that you were 15 minutes late to the meeting today, while the other four of us were on time. The impact was that we had to cover the opening statements twice, which put us 20 minutes behind. We didn't finish the agenda and had to schedule another meeting. It costs roughly $500/hour for five of us to be in that room together. I have a suggestion; do you want to hear it now? I suggest that you block out the half-hour before this meeting so that you can be prepared and get here on time. There aren't very many meetings in the week that are as important as this one.

You may have noticed that none of these ideas is particularly dramatic. Most peer feedback isn't. The feedback just helps your peer get into a rhythm of consistently hitting or exceeding the goals and expectations for his role. If you think of peer feedback as just holding up a mirror and helping your co-worker see that his "skirt is in his pantyhose," you won't be as concerned about overstepping boundaries.

BUT THIS TOOL FEELS STUFFY

You may be thinking that this approach may sound fine when you read it in a book, but you can't imagine ever saying "I noticed that…and the impact is…" in the real world. It just sounds too academic or like something out of a politically correct training manual. All true, really, and yet I'm going to suggest you use it anyway. The trick for some has been to "bring the apprentice in on the joke" with this tool (as well as all of the other tools, for that matter).

That means telling your apprentice that you want to make sure that she knows you'll be doing your best to give both positive and critical feedback on a regular basis and that you expect the same treatment, so you can improve as well. Introduce her to this tool so she knows what to expect. Encourage her to be honest when you ask if she wants to hear it now. By having this discussion, you'll remove most of the awkwardness up front.

The best example I've ever seen of this approach came in a voice mail a few years ago. I had taught a class at Boeing. The room was filled with a mixture of peer mentors and apprentices learning how to work better together. I had one student (Joe) who told me that he had been at the company over 30 years and had "247 days until retirement." He was there to learn how to pass on his "wisdom" to the 40-year-old "kid" (Mike), who was sitting next to him. Joe had a very good sense of humor and we bantered back and forth throughout the class. When we got to this module, he laughed out loud and gave me a good-natured hard time. He said that this sounded like "girly man" stuff and that he wasn't likely to even try it. About three weeks later I got this voice mail from him:

> Steve, I had to let you know what happened when I tried one of your ideas. Remember that kid, Mike, who was sitting next to me in the class? I really like Mike and want to see him do well here. There were a couple of things that Mike was doing that I thought he'd stop doing once we worked together for a while. I'd call them "career-limiting moves." Despite some subtle prodding, he wasn't budging. So, I decided to buy him lunch and talk to him. I started the conversation by saying, "Mike, I'm having an **'I noticed that'** moment." Since he'd taken your class, too, he knew that I was about to give him feedback and looked a little surprised. He laughed a bit, but was eager to hear what I had to say. When we finished the conversation, he thanked me several times for helping him out. I thought you'd like to hear that even a gruff old guy like me can do this and make it work.

I'll never forget that story because I think it was such a terrific approach. Joe took all of the mystery out of the situation and used humor ("I'm having a…"moment") to bring Mike in. Mike was grateful that Joe would look after him in this way and was very receptive to the ideas. That is exactly how it should work.

SUMMARY: PUTTING IT INTO PRACTICE

Be sure your apprentice hears from you every single week with specific feedback that has a measurable impact and actionable next steps. This is what teammates in healthy working relationships do for each other. If you think of peer feedback as just holding up a mirror and helping your apprentice see that his "skirt is in his pantyhose," then you won't be as concerned about overstepping boundaries. You'll be more worried about how disappointed he would be if you just "kept walking" and left him alone.

It will also help if you address the issue of feedback in your First Meeting or in a team meeting with the whole team. Tell your co-workers about the language you're going to use so that when they hear, "I noticed that," they'll know that you're trying to help them. Ask them all to do the same for you. You'd want nothing less. If you make that much of an effort to support each other, it'll pay off over time.

FROM A MANAGER'S VIEW

As a manager you really do want to foster improved feedback among the people on your team. Start by thinking about examples of problems that have come up in recent weeks that could have been averted if your employees had been watching each other's work and looking for opportunities to give feedback. Do they have to redo much work? Do they miss deadlines because of bottlenecks? Is the quality of their work consistent from one person to the next? Your job is to look for areas in which improved peer feedback would improve the overall productivity of the team.

Once you identify specific areas in which you want team members to talk to each other more, you can offer this model in a team meeting and can talk through several scenarios where improved feedback would have produced better results. Ideally, you'll have at least one or two situations where improved feedback would have made their lives easier (e.g., they didn't have to stay late to clean up a mess). This will get their attention and help them see the value of talking to each other more.

Have everyone read this chapter and have them talk through examples of what would have been appropriate feedback for the past situations you identified. When those situations reoccur, they'll be ready. This exercise will help to give them all permission, or even better, to help them feel an obligation to offer feedback when they see an issue come up. You can also use team meetings as an opportunity to share feedback that would be more broadly useful.

Be sure your silo peer mentors know your expectations for giving feedback. If you want them to be active in monitoring the quality of the work being done by others within their specific area of expertise, then say so. Brainstorm between three and five situations in which there is a need to move others toward the standards, so the silo knows how far you expect him to go. Then tell everyone else that they can expect feedback from the silo mentor because you've asked him to give it. This deputizes the silo and sets everyone's expectations. Preparing your team in this manner will go a long way toward alleviating people's discomfort.

Finally, don't forget to model this behavior yourself. The best way to bring this idea to your team is to have them hear the words come out of your mouth regularly. A good rule of thumb for a manager is that every one of your employees should hear you say "I noticed that…" at least once a week. It doesn't even matter if the feedback is positive or critical. What matters is that the feedback is specific, has measurable results, and includes action steps when there is something to fix.

WHEN YOU'RE THE APPRENTICE

Apprentices often want more feedback than they're getting. If that is your situation, you should get good at asking for feedback. Usually this comes out as "How am I doing?" Unfortunately, that question rarely gets you more than a "You're doing fine," which isn't very helpful.

To get specific feedback, ask specific questions like the ones listed in Tool 8-2.

Tool 8-2   Apprentice Feedback Request Template

- I have been trying to_____.
  (fill this in with something specific, such as hit deadlines, meet the quality requirements, participate in meetings, design a new interface, or complete the problem-solving exercises)
- How does that appear to be working?
- Do you have any suggestions for improvement?

By using this worksheet, you can get your manager or peers to stop and think about the specific area you'd like them to assess. They can then try to give you ideas that will help you improve in that area.

Be sure that if you ask, you're prepared to listen to the answer and ask follow-up questions. If you appear defensive in any way, you're going to discourage honest feedback. A good way to prove you're listening and to help give you time to internalize what you're hearing is to paraphrase the feedback. "So, it sounds like you'd suggest I…" This always helps you get the most out of the interaction.

9

Peer Mentoring from a Distance

What if I rarely or never see my apprentice?

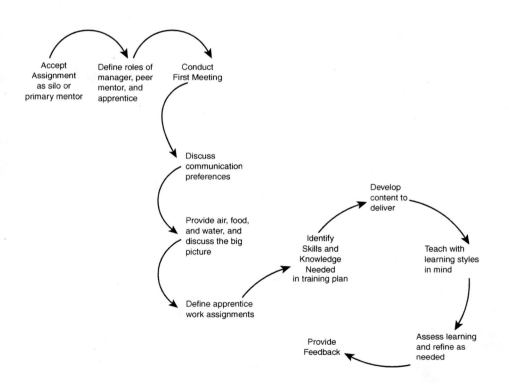

Accept Assignment as silo or primary mentor

Define roles of manager, peer mentor, and apprentice

Conduct First Meeting

Discuss communication preferences

Provide air, food, and water, and discuss the big picture

Define apprentice work assignments

Identify Skills and Knowledge Needed in training plan

Develop content to deliver

Teach with learning styles in mind

Assess learning and refine as needed

Provide Feedback

Many of us have had the experience of working with a team that was really humming along: productive, consistent, and fun. Then something starts to go awry, but no one can put their finger on why. I often get invited in to consult at this stage, to help organizations work on their knowledge transfer, communication, and leadership issues. Many times I've heard managers tell me, "Everything was great, until recently."

At this point, I ask questions to uncover what recently changed. I've found that there is almost always an element of physical space and distance to the story that includes adding offices, taking over another floor, or adding another building. Even just moving down the hall changes the dynamic. People typically notice the challenges long before they can figure out what causes them. Add the distances associated with outsourcing and multinational organizations to the complications of simply adding space locally, and you've got a problem to solve.

Communication and knowledge transfer are different when there is little or no physical connection. This difference in process needs to be addressed to maintain the steady flow of information. By the end of this chapter you should be able to use the tools you've already read about in this book to mitigate the challenges you face when you're mentoring outside of arm's reach. If you recognize this issue in your organization, you'll need to be more disciplined about how you manage the relationship than in any other knowledge transfer situation.

DISTANCE AFFECTS FLOW

When I was running the advertising business unit at Expedia.com, I remember four of us being packed into one office for a time with no cube walls or other separation. There was plenty of togetherness. I had never worked in such an open environment. While there were many drawbacks, the flow of information was complete and took no real effort. It just happened as a consequence of the space we shared. As our team grew, I moved to a separate office and, even though it was only two doors away, I remember how much it changed the team dynamics. I had to be intentional about getting information. I had to set up more meetings and ask for more regular status reports. I had to put more systems in place to keep on top of our work together.

Take that simple problem, my moving two doors down, and think about it in relation to the distance issues that are commonplace today. I have clients who manage "teams" that span companies, time zones, continents, languages, and cultures. These folks need to share ideas, hand work back and forth, collaborate on problem-solving, and develop products as though they were across the hall. When team members are located in both Asia and North America, there may not even be one hour during a regular business day when team members from both locations are in the office at the same time. In this situation the vast majority of exchanges have to be in writing and when there is a question, it takes a minimum of 12 hours to get an answer.

If you're called on to be a peer mentor from a distance you may want to know about the famous "magic bullet" for transferring knowledge across these boundaries. I hear requests for this all the time. Clients ask, "What's the magic bullet for communicating with the outsource partners, the company we just bought, the team with whom we have to collaborate, and so on." The solution you're looking for is known but there is no magic in it. The answer is— drum roll please…

Do *everything* in this book *consistently*.

Ta da! Feel better now? Maybe not. I'm sorry, that answer may not be the one you wanted to hear. Implementing all of the ideas in a whole book may sound too difficult, but don't forget that all of them are short and sweet. It really won't be too difficult. I'll outline a flow shortly.

When you're working from a distance, you really have to be disciplined about the way you manage the flow, because you can't rely on any of the informal, serendipitous ways that information and knowledge are transferred. Even if you're just mentoring someone on another floor, you'll have fewer opportunities for hallway conversations, discussions over breaks, popping over the cube wall with a "quick question," observations, brainstorming, and so on. When you're really far away, you have none of those easy wins. You have to be intentional every step of the way.

SHANGHAI TO WASHINGTON STATE

I watched mentoring from a distance work with an engineering design team at Intel that was based primarily in the U.S., but was growing additional headcount in Shanghai, China. I received a call from Bill Fishburn, the team's human resources business partner, on a Tuesday saying that there were seven new engineers coming from Shanghai to Washington State on the following Tuesday. They were all new to their jobs and were hired to help with the workload of the U.S. team. Some of the new engineers came from inside the company, some from competitors, and some were fresh out of university. All of them were coming to the U.S. for the very first time. They were going to be training with their U.S. counterparts for six weeks before returning home to China.

During that six weeks the Chinese engineers needed to learn their new jobs, vocabulary, tools, standards, work processes, and so on. In addition, they also had to figure out, from scratch, how to partner with a team they'd never met. The catch was, they needed to do all of this while the U.S. team was in the middle of one of its busiest times ever.

I asked some questions about the expectations of the Chinese employees: What roles would each of them play? Who would be responsible for training them? What would they need to be able to do when they returned home? How would they partner with their U.S. counterparts over the long term? How were their systems for security and communication linked up?

I asked what plans already existed to orient these new employees. The answer to the last question was not surprising, but it was definitely a concern. There were no plans. The new engineers would be arriving in a few days and no one really knew what they'd do with them when they appeared. In some ways, that made it easier. We were free to build a plan from scratch.

A LITTLE PLANNING

OK, we needed to do more than a little planning but there wasn't much time, so we had to move quickly. All day Thursday (two days after the initial call) we began to follow the recommendations I've set forth in earlier chapters of this book. We worked to get our hands around the expectations of these new engineers. By the end of the day, we had determined that there were five different job descriptions represented by the seven engineers and had identified a rough list of skills that each job required. We had identified resources for each skill that included online training, classroom training, current documentation, silo mentors, samples, and so on. Then, for each person, we customized a training plan that included the order in which we recommended they develop the skills, as well as the dates by which they needed to be able to complete them in order to finish within the six-week window. Finally, we identified a primary mentor for each of them to ensure that they had a one-to-one relationship with a peer who could help them survive the aggressive schedule that they were about to receive.

On Friday of that week, I introduced the Peer Mentoring tools to all the primary and silo peer mentors. In the workshop, they learned how to use the tools to manage the relationship so that they could both help their new colleagues get up to speed and still get their own substantial workloads finished on time.

The next Monday, all of the peer mentors spent some time using what they learned on Friday to clean up the training plans. They also talked with their managers about the expectations of the relationship they were about to start. The manager of the Chinese team was already in town, so he was incorporated into the entire conversation. While the preparation of this peer mentoring team was rushed because of the limited time, we were still able to ask and answer the initial questions. The peer mentors all felt ready for the next step.

SET EXPECTATIONS

That next step came in the form of seven engineers arriving on Tuesday morning, ready to get to work. They were greeted by a First Meeting (outlined in Chapter 2, "Managing Time and Communication") and a peer mentor and manager who said, "Hi, welcome, we're glad you're here. We knew you were coming. We've been thinking about you and have a plan to help you get up to speed." Just a few days earlier they would only have been prepared to say, "Ouch, are you here already? Sorry, but we've been really busy and, well, we really don't know what we're going to do with you. Sit tight. We'll think of something."

The plans weren't perfect, but they were clear enough to serve as a starting point. The Chinese manager was involved in the Peer Mentoring Workshop. At my urging, he briefed his team on the idea of a training plan, a First Meeting, and some of the other tools. In effect, he brought them into the game so they could take as much responsibility as possible for their own training. During that first week, each peer mentor met with his new apprentice and gave advice on the best way to tackle learning the new content, communicate and stay in touch on progress, bring problems or concerns, and measure progress during the training period. They also warned their apprentices that, because they were already under the gun, they wouldn't be able to provide a lot of hand-holding. All of this was laid out in a very straightforward way. Then everyone went to work.

FOLLOW UP

I had done my part so I disappeared for three weeks. When I went back, I held two meetings: one with the peer mentors and one with the apprentices. I asked the peer mentors how they thought things were going. Their basic response was, "No one is dying. The new guys are pretty good and we're making progress." Now, if you've ever worked with a team of engineers, you have to know that this is akin to doing the "wave" at a championship game. They were comfortable moving forward, with both their own workloads and their responsibilities for orienting their apprentices. No one's hair was on fire—so that felt great!

Then, I met with the seven Chinese engineers and asked them how they were doing. Each was able to pull out his training plan and identify which skills he had mastered, because he could pass the test, and which skills needed more work. They all agreed that they were doing well but that they wouldn't finish on time. The plan had been too aggressive (big surprise). They asked for two more weeks to finish their training. Their request was reasonable, and because there was plenty of time to arrange it, they were allowed the additional training time. At the end of the eight weeks, they still had not completed everything, but were able to determine exactly what each of the new engineers knew how to do, and perhaps more important, what they didn't know how to do. In effect, they were going home with a known skill set. Because everyone knew what they had and had not mastered, it was easy for them to plan to continue building those skills before they left.

During the last week, before the engineers returned to China, the teams worked out strategies for communication, escalation, problem-solving, status-reporting, and so on. They also decided which of the new engineers would take on silo mentor responsibilities for the growing team in Shanghai.

In preparation for this book, I contacted Bill Fishburn again and had him read this story to make sure I got it right. In reply he said, "If I hadn't lived through it, I'd have said it was impossible. That team was a real testament to your tools and practices."

SOMETIMES THEY COME ON-SITE

Now, I know that having eight weeks on-site to train an offshore counterpart is truly a luxury. Many of you won't see your colleagues in person at all, let alone have that much time. Still, you can use the principles we used in this example from a distance. The issues are the same. Having distance between you and your colleagues just means that you need to work diligently, using the communication tools at your disposal.

Let's take a look at the ideas addressed throughout this book and see how much more smoothly the distance issues could flow if you set up simple systems to make them work. To show you how, I've broken the peer mentoring process down into three phases:

- Setting the stage
- Managing the flow
- Following up

As you read through each phase, you'll see which tools apply and get some ideas on how to apply them for peer mentoring across a distance.

PHASE 1: SETTING THE STAGE

At the beginning of any working relationship, it is often uncomfortable while the parties figure out how they'll work together. Much of the work needed to understand one another occurs informally, which is why physical proximity really helps move the relationships along. When you're working across a distance, the same issues are present but there is no informal system on which to rely. So, you'd better set up a specific conversation to clarify how you'll work together. Remember, the root of most frustrations is unmet expectations. Distance can be a huge factor in muddying the waters and making it more difficult to meet expectations. Be sure to work through these worksheets methodically to combat this problem. If you set expectations up front you'll deal with less disappointment.

ROLE DEFINITION WORKSHEETS

These worksheets are designed to establish the differences between the roles of the peer mentor and the manager and to give the apprentice tips on how to be successful. (See the "Identifying Your Preferences" section in Chapter 2 for details.)

Start by discussing the situation with your manager and defining the roles. What does the manager expect of you, with regard to your remote colleague? Are you a primary mentor, silo mentor, apprentice, or a combination of all three? If your colleague works for a different manager, you or your manager should loop that manager in on the conversation so that you're all on the same page. If you're serving as a mentor, be sure to understand if you're actively driving the relationship or just passively making yourself available to your apprentice.

You'll know you're on the right track if the peer mentors and managers involved describe each role, the general deliverables, and success metrics for your work together in the same way.

FIRST MEETING TEMPLATE

The First Meeting among the three players in the relationship (manager, peer mentor, and apprentice) is sometimes called the "triangle meeting." It functions as a "kickoff" meeting and is used to set expectations, clarify roles, and set goals for the apprentice/ mentor team. (See the "Conduct a First Meeting" section in Chapter 1, "Roles in Peer Mentoring," for more information.)

If you can't be face-to-face, even for a short time, set up a video teleconference for the meeting if at all possible. The technology will allow you to put a face to the voice mails and e-mails. At the very least, hold your First Meeting on a conference call so that you can make the best personal connection. During the call, each of you should share what you believe to be your role; how you'll work together; how you will provide each other with feedback; and the deliverables that are expected. This is also a good time to clarify what information will be shared with others, who those "others" are, and how the information will be shared. For example, if you are intending to share your apprentice's status report with your manager (as suggested later in the "Status Report" section), make sure your apprentice knows that. Again, manage expectations on the front end so there are no surprises.

When you're having a First Meeting to set up a distance peer mentoring relationship, you should definitely add an element of risk assessment to the conversation. Brainstorm and talk over the problems that could arise as a byproduct of the distance and decide how you'll work together to mitigate them. Be sure that you have an escalation plan in place in the event that any of these risks you've identified come to pass. For instance, what will you do if one of you is stuck and the other isn't available? Leave as little to chance as possible.

TELLING ABOUT YOURSELF WORKSHEET

The Telling About Yourself Worksheet provides a framework for defining the best ways to stay in touch with each other, including the best time of day to reach each party; the best way to send and receive questions, comments, and concerns; and the best way to hand off work and communicate progress. (See the "Telling About Yourself" section of Chapter 2 for more information.)

Telling about yourself from a distance means you have to be explicit. Your apprentice won't have the opportunity to figure you out on his own. He won't be able to notice that you're grumpy (and therefore to be avoided) first thing in the morning or that you're always swamped and unavailable on Tuesday afternoons because of the big assignment you have to deliver on Tuesday evenings. He can't wait until you're sitting at your workstation and then stop by for a quick question—he can't see you're there.

In mentoring relationships that span multiple time zones, your apprentice won't know what to do if there is an emergency in the middle of his workday while you're asleep at home. How do you distinguish the "find me wherever I am" issues from the "important, but not mission critical" ones? What are your expectations on how to contact you in each of those situations?

Do you and your apprentice speak a different primary language? If so, is it more comfortable and effective to communicate in writing rather than by speaking? How do you expect follow-up to happen? For example, is the Status Report enough or do you want a summary e-mail after each meeting?

This is an opportunity to really set the stage for the kind of fluid communication that you'll want for the entire relationship.

AIR, FOOD, AND WATER CHECKLIST

The Air, Food, and Water Checklist is the list of information, connections, tools, and setup that your apprentice "can't live without." It is the foundation for all other learning and working that is to come and must be handled completely on one of the first days of your peer mentoring relationship. (See the "Start with Air, Food, and Water" section in Chapter 3, "Focusing on the Most Important Information," for more information.)

The air, food, and water concept is often overlooked, even for apprentices who share an office with their peer mentors. It is easy to forget to make sure that the apprentice has the right security clearance, has the correct physical or technical tools, meets the right people, gets access to the right documentation, and understands some of the core vocabulary. In many cases the peer mentor assumes that because the apprentice is working out of another office, all of this information is being covered by someone else.

The most common area of concern is often compatibility of security and tools. For example, returning to the previous story of the engineers from Shanghai, we all assumed that their laptops would work just fine when they visited Washington State, because everyone worked for the same company. That turned out not to be the case. They lost roughly three days at the beginning of their visit sorting out the compatibility issues.

In distance mentoring, the technology for communicating also becomes an important part of the Air, Food, and Water Checklist. Do you use video conferencing equipment? If so, when? Who is responsible for managing and troubleshooting the equipment? How does the apprentice schedule use of the equipment on his end? Are you going to ensure the equipment is working before the meeting or during the meeting? What web-based software or other tools will you use during meetings to capture thoughts and ideas in a way that everyone participating in the meeting can see them? How will the apprentice learn to use the tools? How does he get into the directory so he can participate? How much meeting time can be squandered on managing the technology instead of conducting the meeting? As the peer mentor you should check in on that assumption in the First Meeting and follow up as needed.

BIG PICTURE DISCUSSION

For an apprentice to really get the "big picture," she needs an explanation of how her role fits into the larger organization, who the team serves (the customer), what the team "produces," how success is measured, and so on. All of this will put her "on the map." She will use this information to make decisions, set priorities, and focus efforts. (See the "Explaining the Big Picture" section in Chapter 3 for more information.)

The big picture is another area where a peer mentor could easily assume that a distant apprentice is getting this background from the local manager. Some local managers might explain the big picture; however, I strongly suggest you not take it for granted that the apprentice really understands these issues. The good news is that you can test big picture knowledge by questioning the apprentice about the issues outlined in the big picture discussion in Chapter 3. Just ask her to talk about her understanding of her role, product, customer, and success metrics. If the phone line goes silent, you know that she is not fully equipped and that there will be problems with how she prioritizes and solves problems. Once you assess the problem, you can team up with your manager and the apprentice's manager to make sure that the apprentice is briefed.

PHASE 2: MANAGING THE FLOW

Once you've established some baseline connection to your apprentice, you'll move into the core of the relationship and go to work. During this time, you'll be developing a training plan to outline the skills she needs, assessing what she already knows, providing training, handing off work once she has shown competency, and making yourself available for questions. There are a number of peer mentoring tools that will dramatically reduce the risks you face during this time. Depending on your responsibilities in monitoring your apprentice's work (or even just relying on her output) you'll want to track what is going on in a way that isn't too difficult for either of you. Think about applying each one of the tools highlighted in the following five sections. Plan to use them all unless there is a specific reason not to.

STATUS REPORT TEMPLATE

The suggested status report requires answers to four questions every week in order to stay in touch with others (peer mentors, managers, other colleagues, etc.):

- What did you say you would do?
- What did you do?
- What help do you need?
- What are you going to do next?

Your apprentice should never have to spend more than 10 minutes, nor write more than one screen in e-mail to complete this report. As a result, completing it won't be perceived as an undue burden. (See the "Writing Quick Status Reports" section in Chapter 2 for more information.)

The status report can be an invaluable resource for both you and your apprentice, because it is a way for her to clearly communicate commitments, results, and concerns. Many of your remote apprentices will be from another culture. This tool gives them a safe and respectful way to let you know what is going on. Don't forget to copy your manager(s) on your reply. Be sure to send your status report to your apprentice every week as well. This sharing of reports not only keeps you all in touch while you're working together, but it documents the relationship in case there is any need to follow up later on.

HANDSHAKE E-MAIL AND ANATOMY OF A PROBLEM-SOLVING QUESTION

The Handshake E-mail Worksheet gives guidance on the best format for your apprentice to use in composing an e-mail to send to you. It also outlines your commitment to respond to e-mails if he follows the format you've requested. Using the Problem-Solving Question is the best way for an apprentice to organize his question before sending it to you. (See the "Anatomy of a Good Problem-Solving Question" section in Chapter 2 for more information.)

When your apprentice is far away, and especially when he is outside of your time zone, you must rely on written communication to a large degree. To mitigate the problems this causes, you'll want to discuss a format for e-mails. This discussion should include an explanation of the kind of information you need to receive when he is asking for your help (this is where the anatomy of a problem-solving question comes in), as well as guidance on how to communicate specific action items and urgency via e-mail. You might show your apprentice some examples from others in his position that illustrate both good and bad e-mail messages to provide some idea of what you want. If you go to the trouble of explaining the best way to communicate in writing with you and asking the same questions of him, you'll be surprised at how much more efficient your correspondence will be.

TRAINING PLAN WORKSHEET

The Training Plan outlines the skills your apprentice will need, the "test" questions he should be able to answer to prove that he has learned the skill, the resources he can use to pass the test, the order in which he should learn the skills, and the date by which he should demonstrate proficiency. (See the "Customizing the Training Plan" section in Chapter 4, "Developing a Training Plan," for more information.)

The Training Plan is particularly important to establish early on because the learning needs to be fully intentional. Distant apprentices can't absorb knowledge by simply being next door. Each aspect of their training must be outlined so they can know what they don't know and then do the work to develop themselves for the position. I suggest you pull out the Training Plan on a weekly basis and discuss, over the phone, what your apprentice has learned (get him to talk over the test questions) and what he is working on at the moment. This will continue to refocus him, expedite his learning, and help you assess risk along the way.

THE 5-MINUTE MEETING PLAN

The lesson planner helps you develop an outline for any lecture you'll deliver before you start talking. It keeps you focused on the content you've decided to cover and makes sure you don't leave out any of the main points. (See "The 5-Minute Meeting Plan" section in Chapter 5, "Teaching What You Know," for more information.)

In many instances you will not have formal documentation for the content you're describing over the phone. That means your apprentice has to listen and hope that he is getting the salient points of your talk. For some apprentices, this methodology works at a certain level, but the truth is that everyone would benefit from having an outline in front of them when they're trying to learn. Use the lesson planner to prepare beforehand and e-mail the outline to your apprentice in advance of your meeting. It'll help him see what is important and will help you stay on track.

LEARNING STYLES MODEL

Understanding your apprentice's learning style gives you insight into the best way to teach him. Which does he prefer to do first: read, see a demonstration, try the skill out on his own, talk about how the skill fits into the big picture, or discuss the possibilities? (See the "Questions to Assess Learning Style" section in Chapter 6, "Leveraging Learning Styles," for more information.)

The easiest way to approach learning styles, whether your apprentice is across the world or across the hall, is to talk about them. In the beginning, you can ask your apprentice how he likes to learn. Let him read Chapter 6 if he doesn't know. Check in along the way to see if your approach is working for him. Generally speaking, the physical distance between you is going to force more of the training to take place through reading. Unfortunately, a significant portion of the population doesn't learn well from reading. If you're prepared to modify your approach in response to your apprentice's preferences, you'll improve the likelihood that he learns faster.

PHASE 3: FOLLOWING UP

Throughout the peer mentoring relationship you should take specific steps to monitor progress. When you're working from a distance, plan to check in and ensure that all is going as you expected. The assessment questions and feedback models presented in this book will give you tools that you can use to follow up. If you introduce the ideas to your apprentice early in training, you can get him to take some responsibility for using them as well.

ASSESSMENT QUESTIONS

The assessment questions are designed to ensure that you and your apprentice are always on the same page. You'll use them to ensure that you start at the right place ("Tell me what you already know about..."), that your apprentice is staying with you ("Tell me what you heard me say"), and that, when you're done with a topic, he will take action in the way you expect ("Tell me what you're going to do now"). (See "The Three Questions in Action" in Chapter 7, "Assessing Knowledge Transfer," for more information.)

When peer mentoring from a distance, it is a good idea to ask your apprentice's permission to check in along the way. You might say, "I'm going to be covering a lot of information on our calls and in e-mails because of the distance between us. There will be plenty of opportunity for me to lose you. To make our work together easier, I'll be asking you some questions along the way to make sure that I've been clear. How does that work for you?"

In this way you can be certain that your time is well spent and will be able to reduce the risk that your apprentice missed some portion of what you covered. In addition, you are again managing expectations so that you don't unintentionally violate any personal or cultural preferences by asking questions that could, potentially, create some discomfort.

FEEDBACK MODEL

The Feedback model is designed to provide simple language that a peer can use in giving feedback to another peer. It goes something like this: "I noticed that... The impact is.... I have some suggestions. Do you want to hear them now? My recommendation is..." (See "The Feedback Template" section in Chapter 8, "Giving and Getting Peer-Appropriate Feedback," for more information.)

Because you'll be collaborating with your apprentice on work that is passed back and forth between you, you'll be in a unique position to assess quality, adherence to standards, and whether or not the goals you've set together have been met. But, because you'll be working remotely, you may feel even less comfortable in giving your apprentice feedback than if you were working side-by-side.

This is another example where the best way to combat the effects of distance is to set the stage early in the relationship. Discuss the idea of feedback at the First Meeting and then again after a week or so. Let your apprentice know that he can count on you to look out for him and make sure he is on the right track. You'll be letting him know whether you think his work is on track. If you see any problems, you'll give him some ideas for fixing those problems. He'll be glad to know that you're on his side.

Don't wait until the first big problem comes up before using the feedback model. This is especially true if time zones do not permit giving feedback over the phone. Sometimes a critical e-mail can sound far harsher than you intended. If your apprentice receives regular, balanced feedback, he will trust you right off the bat. The sooner he hears "I noticed that...," the more comfortable he will get with the idea of feedback. Then, if a real problem arises, you'll already have a system for handling it.

SUMMARY: PUTTING IT INTO PRACTICE

This chapter serves as a summary of everything you've read so far. While picking a handful of the tools can work well if your apprentice is nearby, the magic bullet of mentoring at a distance is to use *all* of the tools described in the previous chapters. There are just too many opportunities to waste time and energy on the wrong things when peer mentors and apprentices don't see each other day-to-day.

The key to making mentoring from a distance work is to be more disciplined right from the start and to ensure that expectations are clearly understood by all parties involved. If you take the time to set the stage, manage the flow of information as you would manage any other project, and then follow up to ensure you've been successful, you'll reduce the frustration and the quality problems that are so common to teams working from a distance.

FROM A MANAGER'S VIEW

As a manager, you have to identify and control risks every day. You need to continually look at the work your team must produce, the resources that are available to produce that work, and the likelihood that it is going to get done. If your team is spread out, the risks associated with inconsistent communication and delivery expand exponentially. You can mitigate those risks by helping your employees set up the systems described in this book. Don't leave proactively preparing to work across a long distance to chance. Check in with both peer mentors and apprentices regularly to ensure information is flowing.

WHEN YOU'RE THE APPRENTICE

If you're the one who is located remotely and you need to rely on peer mentors to transfer knowledge to you from a distance, you have an even greater need to develop a plan for your own development. You can ask for and drive a First Meeting; ask about the best ways to stay in touch, send e-mails, escalate, and ask problem-solving questions; clarify the foundations you'll need to get set up using the Air, Food, and Water and Big Picture templates; develop a training plan for yourself; and get input from your peer mentor. With each step you take to clarify the expectations between you and your peer mentor, you'll improve your chances of success.

10

Peer Mentoring in Practice

What am I going to do with what I've learned?

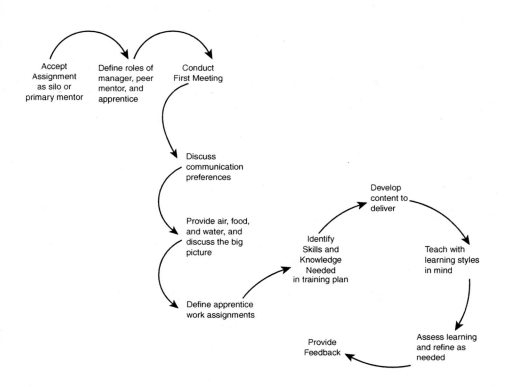

Accept Assignment as silo or primary mentor

Define roles of manager, peer mentor, and apprentice

Conduct First Meeting

Discuss communication preferences

Provide air, food, and water, and discuss the big picture

Define apprentice work assignments

Identify Skills and Knowledge Needed in training plan

Develop content to deliver

Teach with learning styles in mind

Assess learning and refine as needed

Provide Feedback

Welcome to the last chapter. We're almost done here, and by now you may have noticed a funny thing about this book. There aren't any new ideas in it. As you've been reading along, I'm sure that many times you've thought, "I already do that," or "I know somebody who already does that." For the ideas you haven't already seen, they seem so straightforward that you might imagine them to be familiar anyway. That familiarity is comfortable, so you bob along through the book, pleased with yourself for already being on top of so much of this. Or, it could be that you read the book and found a twist that was interesting to you. You said, "Well, now. There's something to think about. I should try that." At this point, "thinking about it" is as far as you've gone.

All of these sentiments are the loud, screaming voice of *inertia* masquerading as a whisper in your ear. It is telling you to nod knowingly and then step away from the book that might cause you to take action. Adult humans generally don't like to change anyway so we start subconsciously working on ourselves whenever we sense movement coming along. Inertia will start as a mumbling sound that will get noisier as you think about these new ideas and will, if possible, drown out any hope of change and keep you right where you are. Inertia is also telling you that if you just had enough time, you could be as proactive and on the ball as this book suggests. You're busier than most people, after all, so you can't really use the ideas, but it sure would be nice. If only your boss could free up some time in your schedule, you'd get right on it. If only you didn't have so many deadlines right around the corner, this would be perfect. Well, now is a good time to notice those excuses. Get ready to resist inertia and take action.

Every idea in this book is common sense, designed to stand alone and to be implemented in minutes. You can make progress by taking just one idea and applying it. If you string together a series of ideas over the course of a few weeks, months, or years, you'll see immediate and compounding results. You certainly don't need a Ph.D. in knowledge transfer or peer mentoring to make this happen. You just need a plan.

To illustrate how the Peer Mentoring toolkit can be put to use in the "real world," the end of this chapter features a tried and true story of one of my clients. The story is of how Electronic Arts (EA), the largest video game company in the world, rolled out the Peer Mentoring Workshop in its Vancouver, British Columbia studios to help manage overwhelming growth. You'll see a flow for using all the tools in this book together to maximize their impact.

By the end of this chapter, you should be able to identify the tools you'll use and develop a strategy for returning to this book to build on your development as a peer mentor, manager, and/or apprentice over time.

SCOPE OUT YOUR ENVIRONMENT

Start thinking about using the tools from this book by looking around you and deciding what you want to see happen through improving knowledge transfer. Of course the easiest place to start is by looking in a mirror, but you're more likely to create movement if you enlist some help. This book was written with the assumption that you'd need to manage your manager, as well as the relationships with your peers, so look as broadly as you dare. In the example at the end of this chapter, you'll see that just one relatively junior employee from Electronic Arts took the Peer Mentoring Workshop and before long hundreds of her colleagues (internationally) had been trained to use these ideas! You have more power to effect change than you think.

WHO ARE THE PLAYERS?

Consider the people who would benefit from working with you to improve knowledge transfer. Then, think about which of the tools and ideas you could share with them. You should look at the following:

- Your manager/supervisor
- Your apprentice(s)
- Other co-workers who could be primary or silo peer mentors
- Your customers
- Other collaborative teams
- Your project manager

- Your project teammates
- Your human resource or training contacts

As you think about this, make a list of the names of the people you'd like to collaborate with to improve knowledge transfer. At the very least, you should determine the names of the three people who would attend the First Meeting (refer to Chapter 1, "Roles in Peer Mentoring"): the manager, the peer mentor, and the apprentice in your "triangle." You can definitely build on that triangle if you are one of those three people.

If you have a long list of names, you might be inclined to call a meeting and get them all on board right away. Generally, I'd discourage you from calling that meeting. It could feel as if you were creating a "knowledge transfer committee." Unless you're the president of the company and can dictate what happens, I encourage you to resist the temptation to start by creating a committee of any kind. Committees are expensive, time-consuming, and can create even more inertia, because it feels like you're doing something when all you're really doing is talking about doing something.

PICK YOUR TOP PROSPECTS

Instead of creating a committee, look at your list and rank all of the players in order. At the top, put those who have the following traits:

- The highest combination of need (they would really benefit from the improvement in knowledge transfer).
- The desire or openness to change (they have a habit of heading toward ideas like these, rather than resisting them).

Need and frustration are great motivators. Often, even the surliest among us will look for solutions if we've been banging our heads on the wall long enough. Openness and desire are additional traits that will give your efforts more gusto.

Now, look at your list and set all but the top three to five people (including those in the triangle) aside. These three to five people are the ones you should plan to work with to improve knowledge transfer right now. Chances are, you're in a position to influence that group right away. You'll most likely benefit personally from your efforts. Don't bite off more than you can chew on the first pass. I want you to make progress for yourself before you think about tackling the larger opportunity. After you've experienced some success in transferring knowledge, you can bring ideas to the others in your original list, along with stories of the results you've seen.

In the meantime, you can put this book in the hands of the others, or point them to my website (www.practicalleader.com) to sign up for the Peer Mentoring Workshop. Some people learn better in a classroom.

WHAT IS YOUR ROLE IN THE TRANSITIONS YOU FACE?

Think about the changes that are going on in your organization. For example, are there any new employees coming in? Have you launched any new technologies or processes? Do you have new customers or products? You'll find a long list of potential transitions in the introduction of this book. Which ones relate to you? Take a minute to jot down those that are likely to affect you the most. If you're the primary peer mentor or are apprenticed to someone who is, do you know what is expected of you? You should be able to answer these questions confidently. The Role Definition Worksheet and the First Meeting Worksheet from Chapter 1 will help you.

PLAN YOUR APPROACH TO PEER MENTORING

Now that you have a snapshot of your environment, you can start to build a firm strategy for the way you'll move information and skills around. Spend some time now deciding which of the ideas from this book you'd like to implement yourself and which ones you'll introduce to the key colleagues from the list you defined earlier. See a complete list of the peer mentoring tools in Appendix A, "Peer Mentoring Tools at a Glance."

PICK THE COMMUNICATION TOOLS

Start with developing communication plans. So much of a healthy peer mentoring relationship is based on staying in touch, without overdoing it. Of course, you have to define exactly what that means to you. Take into account the expectations, location, work requirements, frequency of interaction, risk, and personal preferences that will affect the way you and your apprentice will work together. Then, shape a strategy for staying in touch with the managers, peer mentors, and apprentices you outlined earlier. You'll want to look for a balance between being available to them as much as possible and still having enough time to get your "day job" done.

You can use the Telling About Yourself Worksheet, Status Report Worksheet, Handshake E-mail Worksheet, and Anatomy of a Problem-Solving Question Worksheet from Chapter 2, "Managing Time and Communication," to shape the way you communicate. You will be more likely to be successful if you share some of these tools with your colleagues and ask them to use the worksheets, too.

DEVELOP THE STRUCTURE

Next, you should set the foundation for doing the work. Chapters 3, "Focusing on the Most Important Information," and 4, "Developing a Training Plan," provide tools that help you with this. Begin with defining Air, Food, and Water so that you have the foundation (workstation, tools, vocabulary, security/access, relationships, etc.) you'll need to either teach or learn. Then develop your understanding of the Big Picture so that you're able to describe the relationships between your products, customers, process, collaborators, success metrics, and so on. The most important part of this step is to develop the Training Plan, a list of the skills, test questions, and resources, sorted by sequence and date.

DEVELOP AND DELIVER THE CONTENT

Once you've set up the structure for the peer mentoring relationship, you should break it down further, organize it into manageable chunks, and deliver it using the tools from Chapter 5, "Teaching What You Know." The 5-Minute Meeting Plan will help you prepare informal documentation and an agenda for the times you need to lecture. The Demonstration Technique Worksheet will help you prepare to explain a tool or a process.

As you put together all the content you plan to use, keep in mind that you may be dealing with a variety of approaches to learning. You can respond to your apprentice's learning style by using the model in Chapter 6, "Leveraging Learning Styles."

FOLLOW UP

It isn't enough to just develop and deliver solid content. You'll want to have a plan to ensure that the information is received as intended. Chapter 7, "Assessing Knowledge Transfer," offers Assessment Questions you can use to check in along the way. For the time it takes to ask and answer one question at each stage (before you teach, while you're teaching, and after you teach), you can make sure you're never off track.

Finally, make sure that you are always clear about the progress being made. The Feedback Worksheet in Chapter 8, "Giving and Getting Peer-Appropriate Feedback," offers language that can be used to make sure that everyone knows how they're doing.

This flow works for most peer mentoring situations. If you follow it, the results won't disappoint you. Sometimes I get questions about different combinations of tools for different sorts of peer mentoring scenarios. What follows are some ideas on that.

STRATEGIES FOR DIFFERENT PEER MENTORING SCENARIOS

Look in this section for the subtitle that best describes your situation and then read it for specific guidance. This section is designed to help you if you're trying to introduce these tools to others. It'll help you put your finger on their role and give them some quick guidance that they can put to work right away.

PRIMARY PEER MENTOR FOR A NEW EMPLOYEE

Every new employee—regardless of the level of chaos he walks into at your company, no matter how busy everyone is, no matter where he comes from, no matter what day of the week it is—should get five things during the first three days on the job:

- A primary peer mentor who's been briefed on expectations for the role
- An Air, Food, and Water list of the minimum setup requirements
- A First Meeting to set expectations
- A Training Plan that will take at least two weeks to implement (You don't have to have the whole job laid out, but always try to stay one or two weeks ahead.)
- A Big Picture conversation so the apprentice knows where he fits in

These five items can be delivered in a matter of a couple of hours and will shave off up to 50 percent of the ramp-up time to productivity. If it normally takes six weeks to get a new employee up to speed and working independently, you can cut that to three to four weeks by delivering these five items. It's the most powerful training investment you'll ever make.

PRIMARY PEER MENTOR CROSS TRAINING AN EXISTING EMPLOYEE

If you're cross training an existing employee so that you can take a vacation without your beeper or just reduce the number of times you're called in the middle of the night, you probably have someone with a baseline of skills. There are still some important tools to introduce:

- The existing employee still needs a peer mentor so she knows whom to emulate.
- This apprentice needs a Training Plan to make sure she knows which skills to build, in what order, and by when.

- She needs a First Meeting to ensure that everyone is clear about expectations. This meeting "deputizes" a primary mentor to lead the relationship and helps clarify the expected outcomes for the apprentice.

It is especially important to manage expectations with cross training because the assumptions people make could be all over the map. Remember, the heart of most frustrations is unmet expectations.

PRIMARY PEER MENTOR TRAINING AN "EXTENDED" TEAM MEMBER

If you're responsible for training a person who doesn't work for your manager, either because they work in another part of your company, are an outsource partner, or are a client partner, you can use these tools to get off on the right foot and manage the relationship successfully.

- Use the Role Definition Worksheet with your manager to better understand what is expected of you.

- Be sure to set up a First Meeting that includes you, your manager, your apprentice, and his manager. It doesn't have to be a lengthy meeting, but it is a great time to test assumptions and clarify a plan.

- Be sure that you fill out the Training Plan and discuss it with your apprentice to make sure you both agree on the skill set you're transferring.

Because you're not working for the same manager, there is another variable: the other manager. That "other" manager makes all of this up-front work even more important. As the peer mentor, you can help reduce surprises and problems by using this framework.

SILO PEER MENTOR

If you are a subject matter expert, the most important thing you need to do is understand what your manager and team expect of you so you can deliver it.

- Use the Role Definition Worksheet to clarify expectations with your manager. Be sure to address whether you're actively mentoring your apprentices or just passively making yourself available.

- Use the Training Plan to clarify which skills you're expected to be able to teach.

- Use the First Meeting to meet with your manager and apprentice(s). Be sure to clarify in this meeting whether you're actively pursuing your apprentices and ensuring they learn from you or passively waiting for them to come to you.

- Customize the Training Plan for each of your apprentices.

- Use the Telling About Yourself Worksheet to ensure that you can be available to your apprentices and still get your "day job" done.

- Silo mentors are often problem solvers. Be sure to introduce the Anatomy of a Problem-Solving Question Worksheet.

Remember that as a silo mentor you often have responsibility for the consistency of your team's quality within your specialty. Use these tools to clarify exactly what that means so you can stay on top of it.

EMPLOYEE LEAVING A POSITION

If you're leaving your job, you become a primary peer mentor either for a new employee or for someone cross training. (See the earlier apprentice sections.) The big difference in this situation is that if you're leaving the company entirely, you need to work more diligently on the Training Plan and complete it at the beginning, rather than just keeping a couple of weeks ahead of your apprentice. I recommend that you keep the Training Plan at your side and continue to build on it during all of your final days on the job.

Every time you start a new task, answer a question, solve a problem, look after a customer, run a process, and so on, put it on your list. Even if you can't teach all the skills on the Training Plan before you depart, at least your apprentice will "know what he doesn't know" and can work on the skills you've identified after you leave.

APPRENTICE

If you're the apprentice, I've been writing a sidebar at the end of every chapter for you. Read them and look for advice on how to drive your own training. If you read the sidebars, you'll probably notice that they are basically the content from the chapter, but in reverse. For example, instead of waiting to be asked for a paraphrase, the sidebar guides you to give a paraphrase proactively. In this way you can take more responsibility for getting yourself up to speed. Your peer mentors and manager are really just resources you can use to help yourself get going. If you see the process in that way, you'll impress those around you as a self-starter and a great addition to the team.

FIRST LINE LEAD, SUPERVISOR, OR MANAGER

If you lead a team, I've been writing a sidebar at the end of every chapter for you, "From a Manager's View." Read those sidebars for advice on how to bring these ideas into your team. This book was written for people who are literally *peers*, meaning that they don't have any authority to "make" their colleagues do anything. As a manager, you not only have the authority to introduce these tools and make them stick, you also have a responsibility to improve communication and knowledge transfer within your team.

You can definitely use the tools to define roles, set expectations for the mentor's success and, ideally, drive the First Meeting yourself. Having peers train their own backups is a great way to work on distributing and balancing the workload on your team. It removes the risk of "single points of failure" on the team when an employee has a three-week medical or family emergency that brings your work to a screeching halt. I also recommend that you share this book with everyone on your team and pick the tools you'll implement together. Then, follow up with each team member to ensure they're adopting the ideas.

PROJECT MANAGER

Project teams often have members who come and go as their specialty is needed. When a contractor builds a house, he'll often have a core group of carpenters who stay on the job the entire time and will bring in people like plumbers, electricians, and carpet installers as they're needed. If you manage a team with changing membership, treat every specialist as either the new employee or cross training employee referenced earlier. Every additional member of a project team brings a higher degree of risk along with his extra pair of hands. Make sure that you don't take anything for granted in orienting the new apprentice. The orientation cycle might be shorter but should be no less thoughtfully developed than the orientation of any other new employee.

HUMAN RESOURCE OR TRAINING MANAGER

Human resource professionals should see peer mentoring skills as a supplement to a robust formal training offering. A well-run classroom experience is still the best way to deliver one-to-many training. No matter how large your training budget, you'll still come up short because so many skills (more than 70 percent by some accounts) must be learned on the job. You can use this book and the ideas presented to support your internal clients and help them build an "army of trainers" in your company. For every formal training program, there should be silo mentors trained to follow up with on-the-job training support.

SENIOR MANAGER OR EXECUTIVE

Many books have been written to help executives think about the way information moves around their companies. As an executive, you've no doubt spent a few sleepless nights reading and thinking about this issue. If you're still not satisfied that your people are talking to each other consistently and sharing their skills and knowledge, you may be stuck thinking about knowledge transfer at too theoretical a level. I suggest that executives start to use these tools, just like every other subject matter expert in the company. When you start to notice that you're more effective at communicating and managing knowledge transfer, you can begin to tell about your own experiences. Believe me, there is no more powerful testimonial for change than when an executive says, "I learned something." When you have learned something, put this book into the hands of others in your company and talk with them about the changes you expect. You'll start to see the real results you're looking for.

IF YOU CAN'T FIND YOURSELF ON THIS LIST

I've spent the past 15 years customizing these ideas for many different situations. If you've just read this list and still can't find yourself, you might be thinking, "I'm a little different than any of the people you described here." If so, please contact me directly through my website (www.practicalleader.com) and ask for advice. I love hearing from people who are trying to solve their knowledge-transfer problem and will be glad to help. Just be warned, I might use you as an example in my next class!

ELECTRONIC ARTS CANADA CASE STUDY: THE TOOLKIT PUT TOGETHER

I've been working on improving how people transfer knowledge in the workplace since the early '90s. During that time, I've had a chance to work with a number of different types of organizations, each one faced with a different version of the same problem: "How do we get our employees to communicate with and teach each other with more predictable results?" This wasn't a new question when I started—and there is still much work to do on the subject. The results so far are worth sharing because you can definitely replicate them in your situation.

There are many stories sprinkled throughout the book explaining how different kinds of organizations have used and adapted the tools presented. In this section, the focus is on how one company used the Peer Mentoring toolkit to improve the experience of their employees.

Electronic Arts Canada (EAC) is the largest and most profitable studio in the Electronic Arts (EA) video game family. In preparation for writing this case study, I spent a day interviewing people from EAC who have been involved in implementing the peer mentoring framework and tools for more than a year as leaders, peer mentors, apprentices, and executives.

The word that they used over and over again to describe peer mentoring was "framework." Brad Herbert (EA's worldwide vice president for human resources) and Jeff Ryan (EAC's senior director for human resources) both described the peer mentoring tools as a framework for future training at Electronic Arts worldwide. "If you think that peer mentoring is only about onboarding, then you haven't even scratched the surface," said Herbert.

INITIATING A PLAN

When my colleagues and I started working with EAC in November 2004, the studio had been growing at an incredible clip, hiring more than 600 full-time employees in the prior 2 years, to bring their total number of employees to more than 1,400. The growth was at all levels of the organization, across all disciplines, including software engineers, game producers, artists, animators, designers, project managers, and testers. Video game development is a relatively new industry so there are many young people involved. The youthful employees managed their grueling 70-plus hour work weeks, at least for a time, by sheer determination and lots of Coke and pizza.

For me, the culture I encountered when I first visited EAC felt very similar to what I experienced in the early days of Microsoft: very smart people on the cutting edge of technology, passionate about their work, and committed to getting it done at all costs. On top of all the new hires (more than 60 percent on some teams), EAC was also facing familiar transitions, including integrating a company they'd acquired, adding additional office space, reorganizing the art teams into a centralized unit, and rolling out a new standard for game development., To top it all off, they were in the final stages of releasing a new gaming platform. For many employees, the familiar technical environment was giving way to a far more complicated future. Oh, and did I mention they were also shipping games? The situation was defined by new people, new thinking, and new technology on top of increasingly aggressive competition and backbreaking deadlines.

The challenge, of course, was that the pace wasn't sustainable. There were some cracks opening up that put the organization at risk. Burnout was increasing, turnover was becoming a problem, and Electronic Arts' reputation in the marketplace for being a "sweatshop" was hampering their ability to recruit new talent.

Hiring continued through all of this. New employees were a cause of real concern because they were both desperately needed and at real risk of failure. They could, potentially, even do more harm than good. New people were brought on board with limited orientation beyond signing up for benefits and getting a tour of the facility. The dedicated in-house training resources were primarily coming from headquarters in Redwood Shores, California. Those training resources were focused on technical training and a few leadership programs. The Vancouver Studio (EAC) had grown so quickly and was focusing so heavily on shipping games that they hadn't begun to develop any orientation programs to help new hires get up to speed. With so few hands and so much work, each new recruit was thrown into the deep end with a "sink or swim" mentality.

I want to be clear that I didn't advocate taking away the "edginess" that made working at EAC exciting. As is the case in many companies, starting a new job at EAC will never be a completely "controlled" situation because of the nature of the work. In my opinion, taking the "sink or swim" approach isn't even all that bad, unless you also hand the new employee an *anchor* (all of the challenges noted above). That makes survival too difficult. I think that if you're going to throw new employees into the deep end, you need to make sure they have a good shot at living through the experience; throw the employee a life-preserver in the form of support from a solid peer mentor.

MOVING TOWARD A SOLUTION

In August of that year, a member of EAC's technical team met me at a workshop I was teaching in Vancouver. She referred me to an in-house contact to talk about customizing a program for them. One of the things that impressed me right away about EAC was how quickly they could make decisions and move me through the ranks to arrange meetings with Brad Herbert, Jerry Bowerman (their chief operating officer), and other executives and senior managers. Jerry was working to stabilize the game development process and set standards that would help the game teams to get more done in less time. Brad wanted to talk about two main issues: work-life balance and growing leaders quickly enough to help his studio stay in front of the wave of growth. "We needed a framework that we could build on to create a predictable talent pipeline and a better working environment for our people," said Herbert.

SETTING GOALS FOR PEER MENTORING

One of EAC's business issues was very clear. They had enormous potential in the marketplace and a very talented group of people assembled to tap into it. Their leadership was solid, but strained, and they needed to get a lot of people "skilled up" to handle all of the work. Just hiring all those new people wasn't going to be enough. The new hires needed to get up to speed using their peers as resources—in an incredibly challenging environment. We set the following goals to help focus our Peer Mentoring efforts to help address the problem:

1. Ensure a consistent, predictable onboarding experience for 100 percent of the new employees joining the studio in Vancouver.

2. Develop a Training Plan for each job family so that every employee can customize it and see a clear list of skills he or she needed to develop.

3. Develop knowledge-transfer skills in both the experienced employees and the new employees to expedite ramp-up to productivity by teaching the Peer Mentoring Workshop to more than 500 people.

4. Identify and support a pool of leadership talent that could develop into managers as needed.

The first goal was to solve the immediate problem of taking care of the new talent entering the building. We believed we could reduce the time it took them to ramp up by half and also make them less likely to burn out in the process.

The second goal was to "deconstruct" each position into the sum of the skills that were needed to do the job in its entirety. We could then take each new employee and have them work on the subset of the larger list that they would be need for the work at hand. Everyone else could view the list as a barometer of their progress in becoming truly skilled in their role.

The third goal involved developing the kind of "culture" of communication and knowledge transfer that we needed to improve the consistent development of all the employees. We would bring them together in teams and teach them the tools to improve the flow of information.

The final goal took into account that identifying good peer mentors was a way of identifying and developing good potential managers. Because we expected more than 30 percent growth in the studio, EAC needed a pool of leaders to draw into the management ranks.

CUSTOMIZING THE PROGRAM

Once we knew what we hoped to accomplish, we set about customizing the tools for the audience. We conducted a day of focus groups at all levels of the organization to better understand the vocabulary they used to describe the situation, the areas of most intense frustration, the specific skills and tools that were most commonly an issue (so we could make them into examples), and the motivations of the employees. We included recently hired employees in the conversations right away, because they were such an area of concern. We asked them about their greatest challenges in getting themselves going and what they'd recommend to help those still coming onboard. The picture that emerged was helpful in planning next steps.

RUNNING THE WORKSHOP

Some of the game teams were having more trouble than others because they had up to 60 percent new employees. When there are so few experienced people, the burden can't lie entirely on the peer mentors; there just aren't enough of them. Sometimes we had to recruit the silo mentors for specific subjects from other teams because no one on the target team had the skill. Of course, the other teams were plenty busy managing their own projects so the situation required some help.

We decided, wherever possible, to teach the Peer Mentoring tools to whole teams at once, or at least to include multiple groups from a team in one session. This meant that we were teaching not only the experienced peer mentors, but also the apprentices and their managers all at the same time. We figured that if we had so many new people, we needed them to take as much responsibility as possible for their own development. We also needed some of them to become silo mentors—while they were, themselves, apprentices on the same topic. It may sound crazy, but it was far less crazy than simply throwing the new hires into the deep end and hoping for the best.

The workshop gave the team a common vocabulary and a process they could follow. In each class, the team would talk over which of the tools they'd like to have everyone use consistently in order to improve overall communication. They also figured out who would be the silo peer mentor for each subject (technology, process, documents, meetings, relationships, etc.) and what was expected of each of them. Because they were in the room with the producer (the most senior manager) who ran their team, they could get some guidance from him or her about how the team would implement the ideas. These sessions always improved morale because people could see a solution to some of their concerns.

One of the senior producers recently remarked that 50 percent of his current team has not taken the workshop. He's at the beginning of another game development cycle and has decided to run all his employees through the workshop again as a way of resetting expectations and ensuring that everyone is prepared to use the ideas to work together on the coming project.

INDIVIDUALS TOOK ACTION

After the workshop, it was up to the individuals to take action and put the tools to work. Nothing gets better without making some changes in behavior. We tried to map out the specific changes we expected. For new hires, we picked five ideas from Peer Mentoring that would help us toward our first goal, "a consistent predictable onboarding experience for every new hire." Following are the five ideas we agreed to guarantee for every new hire:

- A designated primary mentor who was introduced on the first day
- A First Meeting to set expectations
- A customized Training Plan that was filled out at least two weeks into the future, if not more
- An Air, Food, and Water checklist to make sure the new hire wasn't tripping up because of missing basics
- A Big Picture conversation to ensure they got the lay of the land and understood their place in it

Even without many formal training resources, we found that making sure these five ideas happened consistently had a huge impact on the experience of the new hires. Later on, as more formal training became available, these resources continued to provide a foundation. All of these steps could be completed in a couple of hours and could shave days or weeks off the ramp-up to productivity.

MANAGERS TOOK ACTION

During the discussions about communication in the workshop, the producers and development directors who were the primary managers for the game teams took notes on which of the tools seemed to have the most potential impact for their teams. Over the subsequent weeks and months, they guided their teams toward implementing them. For some teams this meant that everyone started using the Status Report Worksheet from Chapter 2 every single week. Other teams spent 15 minutes talking over the anatomy of a problem-solving question as a way of improving troubleshooting. Many used 10 minutes of each team meeting to have people (especially the experienced people who were feeling the most stress) describe their communication preferences so that the rest of the team could try to respect their wishes. In some instances, the teams created quick web sites to allow employees to post their preferences. This made it easier for new hires to access the silo mentors confidently without inadvertently stepping on toes. Many teams reported a new respect for different learning styles and a willingness to adjust their training approach as necessary.

Each team went after incorporating the ideas in a slightly different way, depending on the managers and the employees themselves. It was exciting for me to receive reports about the immediate effects. One senior producer said, "If you'd told me a month ago that my whole team would be enthusiastically sending and reading status reports every week, I would have told you that you were nuts!"

EXECUTIVES TOOK ACTION

The Peer Mentoring Workshops created a lot of enthusiasm. "When I heard that people were 'line jumping' to get into the class, I knew we were onto something," said Herbert. But, there was still something missing. EAC didn't yet have anyone on-site who was a dedicated training resource. I suggested a role I helped define when I ran the training department at Microsoft. We called the role a "training program manager," wrote a job description, and then helped identify people to fill the position, ultimately bringing five people into the role: one for each job family (engineers, quality, art, development directors, and producers).

We hired current employees who were already experienced and well respected in their fields. We didn't require any training experience, but did look for people who had embraced the peer mentoring tools and were excited to work on the training problem. In addition to ensuring support for knowledge transfer, these program managers would be responsible for supporting their constituencies with whatever training programs were needed (classroom, informal sessions, web-based documentation, brown-bag lunch meetings, cross training, etc.).

The EAC executives made it clear that taking on this role was a great way to get visibility and to show big picture leadership—a nice career stepping stone. The executives understood that some of the program managers would be in their role for less than a year, while others might choose to stay longer. We arranged to have the program managers report into executive producers or senior technical managers, as well as having a dotted line into human resources. In this way, the program managers were very central to the business.

"The existing soft costs far exceeded the cost of the headcount for the program manager position. That was a great investment for us. We also found that it was very important to bring seasoned employees into the position to get the most impact from it," said Herbert.

TRAINING PROGRAM MANAGERS TOOK ACTION

The first training program managers at EAC were Bert Sandie (software engineering) and Matt Manuel (development directors and people and project managers for the game teams). Others filled in for the other job families over time. Both Bert and Matt fit the profile we were looking for right off the bat. They were experienced, well regarded, and had many relationships that they could draw on to help identify silo and primary mentors for the new hires. They were also able to help identify primary mentors who could work at the studio level to help set some standards.

The first thing the training program managers worked on was ensuring that every new hire had the five elements that we identified as defining a consistent onboarding experience. They connected with the Human Resources department to find out who was starting on the coming Monday and checked in with the hiring teams to ensure that a peer mentor had been assigned, a Training Plan had been customized, a First Meeting was scheduled, an Air, Food, and Water list was provided, and a Big Picture conversation was in the works. In some instances this was already happening because the hiring team had taken the workshop and was on top of it. In other cases, some or all of the list was missing and the training program manager needed to step in to facilitate an effective onboarding experience. "We had already been using the peer mentoring tools and bought into the framework ourselves, so it wasn't hard to take that experience into the program manager role," said Sandie.

Within weeks of having the training program managers in their new roles, we were able to say that 100 percent of the new hires coming into the studio could expect a consistent onboarding experience. That was a huge improvement right away!

The next step Bert and Matt took was to get control of the Master Training Plan for their respective job families; Bert took ownership of the Training Plan for all engineers and Matt took ownership of the Training Plan for all development directors. Practically speaking, ownership translated into a combination of gathering and compiling the customized plans that were already in use from the workshop and fleshing the plans out to make them as robust as possible with the help of a few extra meetings with me. "[Having the program managers flesh out the Training Plan] was a big help to the peer mentors and managers who were training new hires because they didn't have to start with a blank Training Plan. They could just customize the Master Training Plan," said Manuel.

Instead of scratching their heads when a new hire came on, the peer mentors and managers could scan the Master Training Plan, as if it were a menu, and make a "wish list" of all of the skills they wanted the new hire to have. They could, then, interview and test the new hire to see what he already knew and check off those skills on the plan. What remained could be put into sequential order, the resources could be adjusted for the circumstances, and a date could be entered to set expectations. I watched Matt customize one of these plans for a new hire (with the Master Plan as his baseline) in less than 10 minutes.

Now, each new hire would be greeted with a plan. That was truly a welcome step forward!

ADDITIONAL PROGRAMS

The Training Plan could also be used as a basis for investing in further programs to develop the skills the studio needed to meet the goals we had set. Bert Sandie recruited more than 40 subject matter experts to develop and deliver content to support the engineers' Training Plan. This is the heart of a 1-week engineering onboarding program that Sandie runs every month. At the beginning of the week, each new hire receives a plan and is told that by the end of the week, he will need to be able to demonstrate competence for the skills on the list. "It really focuses them, to be so clear about what will be expected," said Sandie. Matt Manuel does something similar for the development directors.

EAC doesn't always have enough engineers or development directors starting at the same time to run a formal bootcamp, but regardless of the size of the incoming group, those new engineers still need support to get up to speed. When the number is too low for a bootcamp, the new employees still receive the same Training Plan, but instead of having a formal program all lined up in the "resources" column, they have a different set of resources available. The resources might include online training, documentation, and a series of one-on-one sessions with the silo mentors for each topic. The new hires might also get a little more time than one week to prepare to pass the test. The point is that whether they're part of a bootcamp or are the only new hire that month, they still have a clear path to success.

The results of these efforts were clear to me when I was invited to a presentation that served as a graduation for the first group of development directors who had been through the onboarding program that Matt developed. The presentation team was made up of the five development directors who had been hired six weeks ago. The audience was John Schappert, Brad Herbert, and Jerry Bowerman, three of the four executives running the studio. After six weeks on the job, these new development directors were able to stand and confidently deliver a comprehensive presentation of their own roles, describe the areas in which they knew they'd need to focus using the vernacular of the studio, and take questions as if they were pros. It was such a win! Only a few months earlier, a new development director would have barely been able to find his way around the building in six weeks. Instead, we had leaders who were prepared to take on projects and teams. We had shown good progress on our fourth goal, to identify and support emerging leaders.

BOOK SUMMARY: PUTTING IT INTO PRACTICE

When I think about the most satisfying moments of my work in developing the ideas in this book, it is easy to point to stories, such as the EA story in this chapter, in which I got to be part of something that really changed the work lives of a lot of people. The EAC employees worked from the executive level on down, executed a plan in a disciplined way, and garnered results that were clear and measurable. Of course, that was very exciting for all of us.

Having said that, I'm actually more energized every day by the individuals who have taken my workshop and sent me notes saying that, even though they were alone in the classroom and returned to a work environment that wasn't exactly "progressive," they were able to implement a handful of the ideas and make a difference for themselves and their immediate teams. I love the fact that useful change can happen whether you're the CEO or an employee working on the front line. It really doesn't have to be too complicated. It starts with one person taking steps to improve his or her situation, trying to be clearer, making a bit more of an effort to be disciplined, and then sharing the best ideas with close colleagues. In this way, a culture of communication and knowledge transfer can be built from the bottom up. It can start with you.

With that in mind, there are two messages I want to leave you with at the end of this book. I hope they don't sound too sappy, because I mean them sincerely:

1. **Do something differently today than you did yesterday** to improve your success rate at both transferring knowledge and getting your work done on time. Don't let inertia get in the way! All of these ideas are useful by themselves and take only minutes of investment to get hours of benefits in return.

2. **Bring someone else in on your plan** so that you're not alone. Hand this book to your manager or a co-worker and then have lunch next week to talk about the handful of ideas you'd like to implement together. Then, you'll have a co-conspirator who can both work with you to improve the situation and hold you accountable for doing so as well.

A

Peer Mentoring Tools at a Glance

Table A-1 is a compilation of all the Peer Mentoring tools offered throughout the book. They're shown here in the order in which they appear in the text. For further information on each one, refer to the tool number, title, and chapter listed with each.

Table A-1   Description of Peer Mentoring Tools

Tool Number and Title	Description	Chapter
Tool 1-1: Role Definition Worksheet	Establish the differences between the role of the peer mentor and the manager, and to give the apprentice tips for how to be successful.	1
Tool 1-2: First Meeting Worksheet	Set expectations, clarify roles, and set goals. Sometimes called the "triangle meeting" between the manager, peer mentor, and apprentice.	1
Tool 1-3: Silo Mentor's First Meeting Worksheet	Define the expectations of the subject matter experts who are focused on teaching their specialty.	1

Table A-1   Description of Peer Mentoring Tools (continued)

Tool Number and Title	Description	Chapter
Tool 2-1: Handshake E-Mail Worksheet	Receive e-mails that are easy to read and respond to by using this worksheet to clarify your preferences.	2
Tool 2-2: Telling About Yourself Worksheet	Define your communication preferences, including the best time of day for questions, best way to interrupt, best use of e-mail and voice-mail, etc.	2
Tool 2-3: Status Report Worksheet	Define the best ways to stay in touch, handle interruptions, communicate progress, and still get your day job done.	2
Tool 2-4: Anatomy of a Problem-Solving Question Worksheet	Establish the best way to think through and organize a question before asking it.	2
Tool 3-1: Air, Food, and Water Worksheet	Provide the foundational information needed at the beginning, before diving into content.	3
Tool 3-2: The Big Picture Worksheet	Provide an explanation of how new content fits into the job, the customer relationship, the rest of the organization, etc.	3
Tool 4-1a: Training Plan Template	Outline priority, measures of success, timing, and resources available.	4
Tool 4-1b: Suggested Measures of Understanding Worksheet	Assess whether or not the apprentice really knows the topic using a menu of test questions	4
Tool 5-1: 5-Minute Meeting Plan	Organize a lesson plan before beginning to teach.	5
Tool 5-2 : Demonstration Technique Worksheet	Deliver a demonstration using a six-step process	5
Tool 6-1: Learning Styles Model	Teach in a well-rounded way to ensure that the apprentice learns, regardless of his or her learning style.	7
Tool 7-1: Assessment Questions	Assess what the apprentice has learned before, during, and after the peer mentor delivers content using three questions.	6
Tool 8-1: Feedback Worksheet	Give peer-appropriate feedback.	8
Tool 8-2: Apprentice Feedback Request Template	Ask for feed-back from a manager or a mentor when you're the apprentice.	8

B

Sample Training Plans

Tables B-1 through B-6 illustrate sample training plans from six different jobs. They provide an additional perspective on the ways others have deconstructed a portion of their roles. You may notice that some have more detail in them than others. Regardless of how complete they are here, each would need to be customized for the individual apprentice who is about to use the plan. The sequence, date, and resource columns would be updated each time based on the experiences of the apprentice, the work that needs to be done, and the mentors and other resources that are available when the apprentice starts.

For more information on training plans, see Chapter 4, "Developing a Training Plan."

Table B-1   Software Tester Training Plan

Skill / "Do Statement"	Sequence	Success Measure / "Test" Be able to explain:	Accomplish By (date)	Resources
Design Tests: Functionality (User Interface)		• How quality is measured • What standards exist and how rigorously they are applied • The steps in the process and why each is important • The relevance of this process to my job • The relationship between functionality and structural		Mod 2 in Excellence for New Software Test Engineers
Design Tests: Structural		• How quality is measured • What standards exist and how rigorously they are applied • The steps in the process and why each is important • The relevance of this tool/process to my job		Mod 3 in Excellence for New Software Test Engineers
Design Tests: Write stress/security/reliability/ performance/privacy/regression tests		• How quality is measured • What standards exist and how rigorously they are applied • The steps in the process and why each is important • The relevance of this tool/process to my job • The relationship between stress and regression tests (how it fits in the Product Cycle) • The top 3 things that often go wrong • 3 best practices for this topic		Mod 5 in Excellence for New Software Test Engineers

Skill / "Do Statement"	Sequence	Success Measure / "Test" Be able to explain:	Accomplish By (date)	Resources
Define components of a test plan		• The relevance of this tool/process to my job • The relationship between test plan and test cases (how it fits in the Product Cycle) • How "quality" is measured • Who is/should be involved/affected/consulted and why		Class: Test Documentation
Automate test cases using C#/C++		• The top 3 things that often go wrong • How to troubleshoot the 3 most common problems • 3 best practices for this topic • Define blackbox, whitebox • How to determine when to automate and when not to		• Classes: C++, C# • Introduction to Test Automation—Blackbox Test Design Approach • Introduction to Test Automation—Whitebox Test Design Approach
Manage Bugs: Open, Verify bug fix		• Top vocabulary words: priority, severity • # steps in the process and why each is important • What standards exist and how rigorously they are applied • How "quality" is measured • The relevance of this tool/process to my job		• Online class on http://<proprietary> close using <proprietary tool name> • Examples (good/bad) • Handbook • Team template • SME= _____ for your team • Software Tester Trainee Program Manual
Check in and update files using <proprietary tool name>		• 3 best practices for this topic • Who is/should be involved/affected/consulted and why • The top 3 things that often go wrong • How to troubleshoot the 3 most common problems • The first 4 things to check when troubleshooting anything		• <proprietary tool name> Introduction • Infocenter

Table B-2   Game Producer Training Plan

Skill / "Do Statement"	Sequence	Success Measure / "Test" Be able to explain:	Accomplish By (date)	Resources
Use Photoshop to perform the following tasks: Mock up screens and camera angles		• The relevance of this process to my job • The steps in the process and why each is important • The relationship between mock-ups and X? (how it fits in the Product cycle) • The top 3 best practices for this topic • How quality is measured		http://www.adobe.com/digitalimag/film.html
Do side-by-side comparisons		• The relevance of this tool/process to my job • The steps in the process and why each is important • How to identify and define a problem vs. a crisis in this area • How to troubleshoot the 3 most common problems • Who is/should be involved/affected/consulted and why		
Develop screen flows		• Who is/should be involved/affected/consulted and why • How quality is measured • The relevance of this process to my job • The top 3 best practices for this topic • Where to find resources (docs, people, samples, web sites, etc.)		

Skill / "Do Statement"	Sequence	Success Measure / "Test" Be able to explain:	Accomplish By (date)	Resources
Use Visio to perform the following tasks: Communicate screen and game flow		• Who is/should be involved/affected/consulted and why • The steps in the process and why each is important • The top 3 best practices for this topic • The top 3 things that often go wrong • The relevance of this process to my job		http://msdn.microsoft.com/ office/understanding/visio/
Communicate timelines and deliverables		• The relevance of this process to my job • Who is/should be involved/affected/consulted and why • The relationship between deliverables and meeting the holiday shopping marketing opportunity • The top 3 things that often go wrong • How to identify and define a problem vs. a crisis in this area • How to escalate a problem or a crisis in this area		
Develop a Strategic Design Doc		• The relevance of this tool/process to my job • The steps in the process and why each is important • What standards exist and how rigorously they are applied • How "quality" is measured		
Develop a schematic diagram for components and subcomponents		• Who is/should be involved/affected/consulted and why • The top 3 things that often go wrong • How to troubleshoot the 3 most common problems • 3 best practices for this topic • How to identify and define a problem vs. a crisis in this area		

Table B-3   Interface Designer Training Plan

Skill / "Do Statement"	Sequence	Success Measure / "Test" Be able to explain:	Accomplish By (date)	Resources
Read the creative brief		• The relevance of this process to my job • Where to find resources (docs, people, samples, web sites, etc.) • The relationship between creative brief and X? (how it fits in the Product cycle) • How to identify and define a problem vs. a crisis in this area		
Read the Visual Requirements Doc		• The relevance of this tool/process to my job • Where to find resources (docs, people, samples, web sites, etc.) • The relationship between Visual Requirements and X? (how it fits in the Product cycle) • How to identify and define a problem vs. a crisis in this area • How to troubleshoot the most common problems with this document		
Narrow the concepts down to a short list		• Who is/should be involved/affected/consulted and why • How quality is measured • The relevance of this process to my job • The top 3 best practices for this topic • How to escalate a problem or a crisis in this area • The top 3 things that often go wrong		

Skill / "Do Statement"	Sequence	Success Measure / "Test" Be able to explain:	Accomplish By	Resources
Participate in the Concepts sign-off		• The steps in the process and why each is important • The relevance of this process to my job • Who is/should be involved/affected/consulted and why • The top 3 things that often go wrong • The top 3 best practices for this topic		
Describe the boundaries and creative solutions for the concept phase		• The relevance of this process to my job • Who is/should be involved/affected/consulted and why • The top 3 things that often go wrong • How to escalate a problem or a crisis in this area • 3 best practices for this topic		
Create a Visual Style Guide		• The relevance of this tool/process to my job • The steps in the process and why each is important • What standards exist and how rigorously they are applied • How "quality" is measured		
Prepare for the Core X Presentation		• Who is/should be involved/affected/consulted and why • The top 3 things that often go wrong • How to troubleshoot the 3 most common problems • 3 best practices for this topic • Where to find resources (docs, people, samples, web sites, etc.)		

Table B-4 Manufacturing Training Plan

Skill / "Do Statement"	Sequence	Success Measure / "Test" Be able to explain:	Accomplish By (date)	Resources
Measure Outside Diameters	6	• Steps in the process and why each is important • 3 most common mistakes • Standards to follow		Tech at next measurement workstation
Measure Inside Hole Diameters	7	• Steps in the process and why each is important • 3 most common mistakes • Standards to follow		Tech at next measurement workstation
Select Jigs and Blocks	5	• Steps in the process and why each is important • 3 most common mistakes • Standards to follow		Refer to online QA procedures
Select Measuring Tools	4	• Steps in the process and why each is important • 3 most common mistakes • Standards to follow		Refer to online QA procedures
Read QA Prints and Specs	3	• Steps in the process and why each is important • 3 most common mistakes • Standards to follow		Tech at next measurement workstation
Access QA Prints and Specs	2	• Steps in the process and why each is important • 3 most common mistakes • Standards to follow		Any QA person

Skill / "Do Statement"	Sequence	Success Measure / "Test" Be able to explain:	Accomplish By (date)	Resources
Tag Pickups	8	• Steps in the process and why each is important • 3 most common mistakes • Standards to follow		Refer to online QA procedures
Create an NCR	9	• Steps in the process and why each is important • 3 most common mistakes • Standards to follow		Any QA person
Edit and Attach Documents to an NCR	10	• Steps in the process and why each is important • 3 most common mistakes • Standards to follow		Any QA person
Close and Forward an NCR	11	• Steps in the process and why each is important • 3 most common mistakes • Standards to follow		Any QA person
Look Up "Jobs for Sale" in A&I	1	• Steps in the process and why each is important • 3 most common mistakes • Standards to follow		Online Help in A&I

Table B-5　Wetland Scientist Training Plan

Skill / "Do Statement"	Sequence	Success Measure / "Test" Be able to explain:	Accomplish By	Resources
Describe the parameters that determine a wetland boundary		• What standards exist and how rigorously they are applied • Top vocabulary words: hydric soils, hydrophytes, and their classifications • 3 best practices for this topic		Regional Hydrophytic Plant List at http://www.wetlands.com/coe/87manapc.htm
Obtain soil samples and use the Munsell soil color chart to evaluate soils to determine if soils are hydric		• Top vocabulary words: redoximorphic features, soil hue color and chroma, … • What standards exist and how rigorously they are applied; how "quality" soil samples are measured		http://www.dnr.wa.gov/htdocs/lm/field_guides/recognizing/soils.html
Delineate wetlands		• What standards exist and how rigorously they are applied • The steps in the process and why each is important • The top 3 things that often go wrong in February and August		http://www.epa.gov/owow/wetlands/ http://www.ecy.wa.gov/programs/sea/wetlan.html http://www.wetlandcert.org/
Evaluate the function of wetlands and apply appropriate rating system		• The steps in the process and why each is important • What standards exist and how rigorously they are applied • The relevance of this rating system to my job • The relationship between the rating system and mitigation requirements (how it fits in the permitting process) • 3 best practices for this topic		http://www.ecy.wa.gov/programs/sea/wetlan.html#rating_systems

Skill / "Do Statement"	Sequence	Success Measure / "Test" Be able to explain:	Accomplish By	Resources
Describe how wetlands are regulated		• The steps in the process and why each is important • What standards exist and how rigorously they are applied • How to troubleshoot the 3 most common problems • The relevance of this process to my job		http://www.epa.gov/owow/ wetlands/pdf/reg_authority_pr.pdf http://www.swl.usace.army.mil/ swdweb/civilworks/regulating wetlands/
Determine the feasibility of permitting a project that affects the wetland		• What standards exist and how rigorously they are applied • The relevance of this process to my job • The relationship between the purpose and need for the project and the function and values of the wetland (how it fits in the permitting process) • Who is/should be involved/affected/consulted and why • How to troubleshoot the 3 most common problems		404(b)(1) Guidelines and related COE and EPA Guidance and Case Laws

Table B-6   Sales Professional Training Plan

Skill / "Do Statement"	Sequence	Success Measure / "Test" Be able to explain:	Accomplish By	Resources
Develop Assortment Plans Using Current Consumer Information		The 5 key elements of the best assortment plans, and how to use consumer info to develop these plans		
Merchandise/Display Products in Retail Stores		The 3 most common merchandising mistakes and how to assess a customer's display		
Organize Account Base		How to use booking reports and other internal sources to understand business and how to understand business when there is no reporting		
Accurately forecast and plan business		The 5 steps to scenario planning and forecasting and give top 3 mistakes		
Create quarterly action plans to support customer strategic objectives		How to ensure action plan is cleary defined and hold appropriate parties responsible for deliverables		
Compare Products to Competition		How to compare top 40 products with top 3 competitors		Competitor web sites

INDEX

Q

U-Z